The Ag

The idea of children's agency is central to the growing field of childhood studies. In this book David Oswell argues for new understandings of children's agency. He traces the transformation of children and childhood across the nineteenth, twentieth and early twenty-first centuries, and explores the dramatic changes in recent years to children's everyday lives as a consequence of new networked, mobile technologies and new forms of globalisation. The author reviews existing theories of children's agency as well as providing the theoretical tools for thinking of children's agency as spatially, temporally and materially complex. With this in mind, he surveys the main issues in childhood studies, with chapters covering family, schooling, crime, health, consumer culture, work and human rights. This is a comprehensive text intended for students and academic researchers across the humanities and social sciences interested in the study of children and childhood.

DAVID OSWELL is Reader in Sociology and Director of Postgraduate Research in the Department of Sociology at Goldsmiths, University of London. He is the author of *Television, Childhood and the Home: A History of the Making of the Child Television Audience in Britain* (2002), *Culture and Society* (2006), *Cultural Theory*, volumes I–IV (2010) and various articles in academic journals and edited collections.

The Agency of Children

From Family to Global Human Rights

DAVID OSWELL

CAMBRIDGE UNIVERSITY PRESS
Cambridge, New York, Melbourne, Madrid, Cape Town,
Singapore, São Paulo, Delhi, Mexico City

Cambridge University Press
The Edinburgh Building, Cambridge CB2 8RU, UK

Published in the United States of America by
Cambridge University Press, New York

www.cambridge.org
Information on this title: www.cambridge.org/9780521604703

First published 2013

A catalogue record for this publication is available from the British Library

Library of Congress Cataloging in Publication Data
Oswell, David.
    The agency of children : from family to global human rights / David Oswell.
        p.   cm.
    ISBN 978-0-521-84366-9 (Hardback) – ISBN 978-0-521-60470-3 (Paperback)
    1. Children–Social conditions.   2. Children's rights.   3. Child development.
    I. Title.
    HQ767.9.O78 2013
    305.23–dc23

ISBN 978-0-521-84366-9 Hardback
ISBN 978-0-521-60470-3 Paperback

Contents

Part IV   Conclusions

Figures

Acknowledgements

To my three daughters – Beatrix, Matilda and Amelia – who are always an inspiration; and to my gorgeous Maria.

Thanks to various colleagues and undergraduate and postgraduate students for always keeping me thinking. And thanks also to the production and editorial staff at Cambridge University Press.

PART I

Introduction

1 | *Introduction*

The long twentieth century is, and has been, undoubtedly the age of children's agency. Children are not simply seen to be, but seen, heard and felt to do. Children are not simply beings, they are more significantly doings. They are actors, authors, authorities and agents. They make a difference to the world we live in. Over the period from the late nineteenth century up until now, in the early twenty-first century, children's capacity to do has intensified and the areas in which they are able to do have proliferated. Children have been seen and felt to do in the life of family, the life of society, the life of politics and the life of economy.

It is not simply that the child in the singular has become a focus of huge emotional, social, cultural, technological and economic investment; rather, it is that over the course of the last hundred years or so children as a class or group or collective of people have become more vocal, more visible and more demonstrable in ways that resonate across our contemporary world. Across this period of time it is not only the presence of children as social actors that is of importance; it is also children's presence as biological and non-social or pre-social actors that has intrigued investigators, provoked debate, and led, among other things, to research, surveying, institutionalisation, building, support, sanctions and regulations. And children's presence has been felt by them and by others not simply because somehow children over this period of time have gained a voice which was before hidden, or that they had a strength and political power that has until now not been revealed. No. Rather, children's capacities to speak, act and become disclosed in particular social, natural and technological contexts has been dependent on their being networked, assembled or infrastructured with other persons and things in such ways as to endow them with powers, which they alone could neither hold nor use.

To put this crudely, over much of the twentieth century we have seen the emergence, development and embedding of children as being seen to have a stake in the institutions and processes which govern their lives and others'. Children are increasingly seen and related to as democratic subjects. Nobody is saying, nor have they said, that this is straightforward, nor even that it has been achieved (whatever that might mean), but across the major social institutions of family, school, criminal justice, health and medicine, consumer culture and work, and political structures proper it is impossible now when talking about children not also to talk about their stake in the decision-making process and their role in shaping the institutions and organisations that shape them. What power do children and young people have in modern families? Should children have a say over the school curriculum? Does it make sense to talk about infants and babies as having political rights? Alongside the democratisation of our relations with children, we see a huge investment in children as consumers. Either directly as consumers of toys, television programmes and computer games, or as influencing the purchasing decisions in the household, children are addressed as significant economic agents. As many commentators have shown, the relationship between children as democratic subjects and children as consumers demonstrates often intertwined histories (Cook, 2004; Oswell, 2002). The growth of the modern mass media of novels, magazines, film, radio and television address children as distinct and separate audiences and often narrate their lives in ways that endow them with power over their lives, their environment and the lives of others. Different again, our thinking about crime and illegality frequently involves concern with children's power on the street or in the ghetto, or with children as the vehicles of crime through generations and across time. The sins of the fathers and mothers are seen by some as most visibly present in the infant, whose nakedness is often seen to conceal the wickedness of a changeling. And the health of populations is now often seen to reside in either the neglect or wellbeing of children. Panaceas, for example, directed to the psychiatric disorders of young children playing in the nurseries repeat a long-standing hope that the agency of children will, like a *pharmakon* (both cure and poison), bring about a new Jerusalem.

Of course, the narration of children setting off on adventures and becoming kings and queens in strange lands in worlds of fiction is a long way from children sitting in a council chamber making decisions which affect how we live our lives. The buying of a computer game is similarly very different from being able to determine with whom one lives during the process of family divorce. And the transformative power of an educated child is different from that of a genetic disorder. To suggest otherwise would be ridiculous, but across the different modalities of power and expression, the different apparatuses, institutions and organisations, the different materialities and relations, and the different histories, temporalities and geographies, sociologists of children have provided research and ideas that demonstrate how the capacity for children to determine their and others' lives has emerged and grown, certainly over the long twentieth century, but also slowly and incrementally over the last two to three hundred years.

In sociology, but also in anthropology, psychology, literary theory, art history, media analysis, history and various other disciplines, groups of pioneering scholars began to provide empirical and theoretical understanding for the emerging, developing and extending agency of children. My concern in this book, though, is not to attempt the huge task of surveying and synthesising an interdisciplinary field of childhood studies (as it is now often termed), but the more modest, but equally huge, task of building on the significant research in the sociology of children, which has grown significantly since the late 1980s and 1990s, regarding the emergence and distribution of children's agency. This book is a contribution to the growing field of childhood studies, but is only so from a particular perspective and trajectory. In that sense, this book emerges out of a particular disciplinary formation and it is framed in the context of questions and debates that come from that field of study and research. But more than that, it is a book that hopes to introduce newcomers to the field in a manner that acknowledges the huge debt of much original and significant research from the sociology of children. I should note here that, although there is some discussion over the use of these phrases, I use 'sociology of children' and 'sociology of childhood' interchangeably.

For many people who are studying and researching children, there are four central questions: what is a child?; in what ways is childhood differentiated from adulthood?; how do we understand the growth of a child?; and, what freedoms or controls are appropriate to be placed on the child? For many people, these questions are intimately related. We know what a child is in the context of how that child is different from an adult and how they might be seen to progress from one stage of being to another. And we govern our relations with children according to the age of a child, according to their maturity, and according to their closeness or distance from adulthood. Even those who would baulk at the thought of such thinking are, by and large, caught by the attraction of trying to understand children through the divisions and walls that separate them from adults. We can refer to this as the identity/difference thesis, namely that children (or childhood) have a distinct identity, whether this identity is considered in social or biological terms. Moreover, this identity is understood only inasmuch as it constitutes a difference from adults (or adulthood). Thus, we know children and childhood only by virtue of their difference from adults and adulthood. Equally, though, there are many people for whom such natures and divisions have a lesser importance and for whom living with or as children is a matter of the singularities or particularities of that particular being, doing and becoming. There is a need, it can be argued, to tilt the balance away from questions about identity and difference and towards ones about children's lives and experiences. But, we argue, any tilting needs to be done in such a way to make intelligible how those lives and experiences are entangled in complex webs of bodies, technologies, and associational patterns. Children are certainly subject to difference machines, to scalar devices, and to measuring systems. In some cases these machines, devices, and systems are stacked up and consolidated; in other cases any relation is unclear, imprecise and fuzzy; but in many cases there is no consistency across differentiations, scales and measures. There is no common standard for children; no difference is well-executed. In that respect, this book hopefully touches on the sympathies that have grown up in a relatively young field of knowledge, not to police any line of difference, but simply to observe, to investigate, and to describe.

This book is concerned with a series of questions about children's agency not inasmuch as agency might be paired with social structure (although that certainly is a focus of Chapter 3), but inasmuch as it allows us to think through children's and young people's capacities to make a difference (rather than being constituted as a difference) and inasmuch as it allows us to think through the different ways in which children and young people have been and are actively involved in emergent, innovative, experimental and substantive forms of solidarity and coexistence. But also it allows us to think through how children and young people are, whether in whole or in part, the focus of innovation and investment in the shaping and reshaping of social existence. My concern in this book is to locate in broad terms how the troubled idea of children's agency might be suggestive of novel investigations and pathways rather than a restrictive and limiting notion. For what we see across the broad and growing field of research in childhood studies is, for sure, the repetition of a normative model of social science which endlessly returns to the dichotomy or duality of structure and agency. But we also see a huge array of innovative studies which empirically and descriptively offer novel analytical interpretations of children's active engagement with their everyday lives and with the enduring patterns of social and historical presence. Over the course of this book I intend to survey some of this work in a way that offers a series of sketches of the different, complex and multiscalar articulations of children's agency. In that sense, the book is intended to provide a series of meta-observations on this growing field in order to make visible an array of descriptions of agency in the lives of children.

The design of the book is quite simple. It is shaped by an intention to review some of the existing literature both in the field and in peripheral fields. It is intended as an exploration of children's agency in a way that does not reduce agency to a self-present consciousness or reflexive subjectivity of the unitary child, but which considers agency in all its mobilisation, networking and experimentation. If children's agency is not centred on a point of origin, then the ascription of agency as 'children's agency' becomes less a labelling of possession. Agency is not, then, performed in the manner of He-Man the Master of the Universe, 'I have the power'. If anything, it is 'We have the power', but both the 'power' and the 'we' are supported through human and non-human arrangements and infrastructures. Moreover, agency, since it is not seen to be centred on human reflexivity, is distributed across human and non-human arrangements and infrastructures, but it also rests as much on parts of children as on whole children. Rarely is there concern about children or the child in an holistic sense; it is more likely that government is concerned with 'disruptive behaviour' or medics with a 'viral infection' or psychologists with 'cognitive functions'.

In what follows these issues are considered through a series of key problem spaces, which have attracted concern and investment from a range of different actors, including academics, experts, governmental authorities, children, teachers, parents and various others.

These spaces – concerning the family, schooling, crime, health, play and consumer culture, children's labour and children's rights – can be seen to comprise some of the main concentrations of research in the field of childhood studies. The areas are defined, in part, by the social and historical contexts of children's relation to parents, to the state and to the market, namely to those concentrations of government and economy with respect to their lives as children. By and large the book reflects the limitations of the field of childhood studies inasmuch as it is shaped within the histories, social contexts, economies and govern-mentalities of Europe and North America. The more recent research that has become visible in the field from Latin America, India, China and Africa raises serious questions and points of discussion and dia-logue with much of what I say. But also there are many bridges and continuities across the different national and regional contexts. I have included some of that emerging material, but too little.

The book opens up the problem of children's agency for further investigation and attempts to provide, not any kind of theory of children's agency, but something more in line with what Foucault refers to as an 'analytics' (Dreyfus and Rabinow, 1983). In that sense, its intentions are limited to making more visible a rich analytical and descriptive language for thinking through the complexity of children's agency as a sociological topic.

2 | *Agency after Ariès: sentiments, natures and spaces*

In this chapter I return to a seminal work in the sociology of childhood, written by the historian Philippe Ariès over fifty years ago. The book, *Centuries of Childhood* (1962), was originally published in French as *L'Enfant et la vie familiale sous l'Ancien Régime* (1960). It offered a history of childhood, but also, perhaps more importantly, it provided a way of understanding and perceiving children not only as actual children in the 'here and now', nor even childhood as an image, but as children whose very distinctiveness as children is a consequence of their history. What Ariès gives us is a sense of children as imbued with a historicity. Children are seen as having an historical particularity, as constituting not only a social or psychological, but an historical subjectivity. For the question Ariès asks, 'How did we come from that ignorance of childhood to the centring of the family around the child in the nineteenth century?' (Ariès, 1962: 8), is one which is not only about the status of an idea (despite what Ariès insists), but also one which changes our relationality with and as children. It is only with the work of Ariès and others in the 1960s that this particularity is able to be understood qua historical particularity: namely, as an aspect of historical self-reflection and reflexivity. But also this sense that children have an historical existence implies that the experiences and agencies of children are disclosed within a horizon of historical reflection.

Nevertheless, the sociology of childhood has really only been concerned with three aspects of Ariès' argument: namely, that childhood is an historical invention; that childhood is thus a social institution (not a biological given); and that childhood constitutes a form of division and segregation between children and adults. In the proceeding sections I follow Ariès obliquely in order to provide brief genealogies of three main thematics which undergird much of this book. In doing so, I am sympathetic to, but also highly critical of (a standard sociological reading of) Ariès' argument inasmuch as I argue that children are not reducible to categorical forms of conceptualisation; children as a collectivity are not reducible to a social invention; and children as modern collective subjects are not reducible to their enclosure within purified 'child only' spaces. These three reductions, I argue, have been highly significant in delimiting questions about children's agency within the sociology of childhood.

Sentiments and descriptions

A pivotal idea in the sociology of childhood is that childhood is a social construction. Those beings which we perceive as children are perceived and understood as separate entities with definable attributes and qualities only by virtue of their being socially constructed. Thus when sociologists talk about children's agency, they do so with this in mind inasmuch as children's agency is conditioned in some sense by their being defined as children; inasmuch as they are constrained by the institutions which reproduce this category of childhood; and inasmuch as their agency is directed to either reproducing or contesting this structurally reproduced category of childhood.

Iconographies and the accumulation of description

The sociological argument about childhood as a social construction or a social institution is an argument that, as I have mentioned above, sociologists trace back to Ariès; namely, that childhood is a social and historical invention and that, although children (as those in a state of biological immaturity) have existed for all time, childhood as a 'conception' (Archard, 1993), or as a 'mentality', has had a finite and specific period of existence. Ariès boldly states that

In medieval society the idea of childhood did not exist; this is not to suggest that children were neglected, forsaken or despised. The idea of childhood is not to be confused with affection for children: it corresponds to an awareness of the particular nature of childhood, that particular nature which distinguishes the child from the adult, even the young adult. In medieval society this awareness was lacking. (Ariès, 1962: 128)

Much of Ariès' argument is taken up with a discussion of the history of the school, the centrality of the school in shaping modern ideas of childhood, and the school as constituting a 'disciplinary system' (Ariès, 1962: 397). But in the context of his discussion of the family, he develops an argument about the emergence of an 'original iconography' of the family, and also of the centrality of the child and an image of childhood within that family (340–1). For Ariès, the idea of childhood is an expression of a more general idea of the family. But what is significant is his presentation of an argument about the idea of childhood in terms of the emergence and growth of a particular iconography. For him, an awareness of the existence of children as different and as particular in their own right is made visible, in part, through representational practices and visualising technologies. Thus, he argues: 'Medieval art until about the twelfth century did not know childhood or did not attempt to portray it. It is hard to believe that this neglect was due to incompetence or incapacity; it seems more probable that there was no place for childhood in the medieval world' (31). And he continues:

It was in the seventeenth century that portraits of children on their own became numerous and commonplace. It was in the seventeenth century, too, that the family portrait, a much older genre, tended to plan itself around the child ... In the seventeenth century too, subject painting gave the child a place of honour, with countless childhood scenes of a conventional character ... No doubt the discovery of childhood began in the thirteenth century, and its progress can be traced in the history of art in the fifteenth and sixteenth centuries. But the evidence of its development became more plentiful and significant from the end of the sixteenth century and throughout the seventeenth. (Ariès, 1962: 44–5)

Childhood is made visible literally through a series of descriptions and the development of new iconographies. These iconographies have aesthetic form, but they also have material and cultural durability inasmuch as their effect is able to accumulate over time and inasmuch as a clear concept can be seen only as a consequence of such an accumulation.

What is also interesting about Ariès' argument is that childhood is not seen to emerge in a momentous instance, a single creative event, but through the *longue durée* across historical, social, geographical and economic time. It is the consequence of a number of contingencies that only in their accumulation become visible as a single phenomenon (Bloch, 2006; Braudel, 1980). This sense of the historical duration of the becoming of children as definable beings is something which has been sometimes overlooked by sociologists of childhood, who often focus on social constructions as accomplishments in terms of the conditions of people together in the 'here and now' (or, as sociologist say, in conditions of co-presence). Where Ariès is concerned with agencies which come together over the long temporalities of tens and hundreds of years, sociologists have tended to be microsociological, focussing on small delimited arenas of time and space.

Concept, conception or sentiment?

The philosopher David Archard clarifies Ariès' thesis by making a distinction between a 'concept' and a 'conception' of childhood. Crudely put, all societies have a concept of childhood and yet different societies at different moments in history might have different conceptions of childhood. Whereas the former identifies an object or being which is as yet undefined or which lacks concrete attributes, the latter refers to the actual definitions or attributes of childhood (Archard, 1993: 21–4). Adrian Wilson had stated earlier that although medieval society lacked '*our* awareness' of children, 'this is not the same as saying that it had no such awareness' (Wilson, 1980: 142–3). Archard, and Wilson before, refer to this as 'presentism', namely a Whiggish enterprise of viewing the historical past from the perspective of the present. There is, of course, a secondary aspect to this discussion, concerning whether an awareness of childhood refers to an awareness of children in the singular (i.e. to my child or to this particular child in front of me) or to children with some sense of collective presence (i.e. children as a collectively understood body of people).

Many historians since Ariès have subsequently uncovered a wealth of evidence regarding how past societies imagined and acted in relation to children. But in many ways it was Ariès' bold analysis which helped to open the field, not least because Ariès focusses on the descriptive devices and forms of description through which children could become intelligible to themselves and to others. The focus on portraiture is highly significant in this sense. Children become visible by virtue of the descriptive devices which shape them as beings in the world and beings in relation to others. Although sociologists now talk of descriptive assemblages (Savage, 2009) or inscription devices (Latour and Woolgar, 1979), Ariès talks about a 'sentiment' (i.e. an awareness or feeling) of childhood. The notion of an inscription device is that it is seen to have a direct relationship to that which is recorded, but also that through inscription (i.e. writing and recording) a social order is materially made (Latour and Woolgar, 1979: 51 and 245). In this sense the observations of children by various artists help to establish children within a particular form of social order (i.e. with regard to social class and status, a relation to the household and countryside, a relation to adults and family, and a relation to forms of dress and comportment). But the notion of 'sentiment' (i.e. awareness or feeling) of childhood suggests something slightly different, something more evocative of the senses, and something less cognitively framed or experienced. And yet Ariès frames the pivotal point of his argument through a limited sense of what that sentiment might be, namely a sense dominated by the visual and the image. The original English translation of Ariès leads to an understanding of 'sentiment' as meaning a 'concept' or 'idea', and thus such a translation helps to frame a history of childhood in the context both of a history of visual culture and a history of the relationship between image, concept and ideology (see Mitchell, 1986).

Notwithstanding the visual, we should not forget, nor disavow, the breadth of sentiments, sensations and materialities through which relations are constructed in the world. If we assume such a leading position for the concept or category or image as cognitively defined, then we might justly ask where is the history of children's sounds or their touch or their taste or their smell or even the synaesthetic phenomena of children's collective being. How have children been assembled through those sentiments, sensations and affective relations? Anecdotally, we might note how adults talk, for example, about the smell of a young baby as an index of affection, more so maybe than how a baby looks. Moreover, the smelling of a new baby by a parent is often followed by a closer embrace or kiss: 'They smell so good I could eat them!' It is arguably the combination of senses that facilitates any feeling of intimacy or distance for the child, and any sense of what the child is. A number of historians writing in the 1960s and 1970s – over and above Ariès' comments about 'affection' (see above) – supported a thesis, generally stated, that over the course of the eighteenth and nineteenth centuries there developed a greater intimacy between parent and child (DeMause, 1974; Shorter, 1975; Stone, 1977). Much of this historical research has now been either seriously amended or outright dismissed. But much of the criticism has focussed on the historical accuracy of the findings or corrections inasmuch as intimate relations between parents and children have been discovered, for example, in the medieval period and in the ancient world. What has been forgotten, by and large, is the notion that children might owe their existence as children not solely by virtue of their conceptualisation, but through a whole series of different kinds of affective and sensory relations, or perhaps, to coin a phrase, a whole array of 'sentiment devices' (namely, devices through which feelings are able to be recorded, offered support and given durability).

Collective subjectivity and categorical thinking

There has been a predominant focus on childhood as conceptualised and classified as a discrete identity such that we might divide up human beings of all ages into either those who belong to childhood or those who belong to adulthood. Attributes can similarly be distributed between the two categories. Often books on childhood divide up work and play, school and work, innocence and knowledge, and so on, between the two. In this way, sociologists then tend to talk about discourses or ideologies of childhood as if childhood constituted a particular idea or category or a way of labelling, identifying and defining social structure. This is of course correct in some sense. For example, two leading figures in the field, Allison James and Adrian James, definitively state that '"childhood" is the *structural* site that is occupied by "children", as a *collectivity*. And it is within this collective and institutional space of "childhood", as a member of the category "children", that any *individual* "child" comes to exercise his or her unique agency' (James and James, 2004: 14). But this is in many ways to provide a cognitivist framing of children in such a way that the capturing of the group nature of children as empirical collectively defined subjects implies reducing such collectivity to a concept or category, which then stands in for, but also gains constitutive power, inasmuch as 'childhood' (now defined) has the power to include a multitude of people and things within its remit and moreover includes as its support a form of social structure. Such a reduction to the category of childhood often forgets the accumulation of sentiment, iconographies and description. We caution against an overemphasis on categorical thinking.

The problems are sixfold. Firstly, understandings of childhood as a category (or as a categorical identity) often fixate on the category as having power and agency and less on the assemblage of agencies and processes that do the work of classifying. In this sense, categorical thinking has a tendency to focus on the outcome and not the process. Secondly, categorical thinking often assumes a logic of identification, such that those subsumed within categories are put there as if by a magic which resolutely glues like with like, with no messiness or difficulty or agency. Thirdly, categorical definitions of childhood assume that the category either acts like or names a container or a box. The box has a structure, it has a name and rules of membership (i.e. childhood as a category) and only some individuals can be contained within this category. Often, though, children fail to be boxed into the category of childhood, not because the boxes do not fit, but because the multitude of experiences which we might talk about as being to do with children fail to be explained through a single identity. The singularity of children as a collectivity is such that it is enormously experientially rich, textured and detailed. Fourthly, understandings of childhood as categorical often presume that those who fill the container are individual children, either children constituted as individual subjects through the power of discourse or ideology, or children whose agency is demonstrated only by virtue of their individuality, consciousness, reflexivity, will or intentionality. The sociology of childhood often repeats and reframes such a notion of individual agency, whether in terms of the individual child contesting or affirming ideologies or categories of childhood, or in terms of the interpersonal discursive or conversational relations between two or more individuals. The notion of the 'child-as-agent', as a sacred object of the sociology of childhood, seems unwittingly to have all the hallmarks of a social universal. It is an assumption held prior to any empirical investigation; a stock belief of this relatively new social science. All children are constructed through the figure of the sociological child – such a child is always agentic or has the capacity for agency, a capacity across all historical and social particularity. Fifthly, classifying children within the category or concept of 'childhood' often means prioritising language as discourse or as propositional structure or as cognitive schema to the detriment of a diversity of media, material artefacts, technologies, affective relations, sentiments and cultural forms through which children come together. Moreover, the means, media and points of connection through which children come together have grown and proliferated over the last two to three hundred years. Finally, it is not, then, that 'childhood' as a category is not put to use, but that it is not a rule-defined container for individual agents with respect to social structure. The category 'childhood' does not define, a priori, a set of people who belong to it; rather, it constitutes a point of reference, mobilisation and contestation and is only mobilised in particular social situations.

Paradoxically, despite the constant reference to childhood as a form of social structure, sociologists of childhood are conscious of not seeing children and childhood through the lens of generalising categories. They are critical of claims about 'medieval art' (i.e. in its entirety) or 'the contemporary western concept' of childhood. They argue that just as there is no general and totalising conception of nature, so too is there no general and totalising conception of society. To talk about the 'social construction of childhood' (although prioritising the 'social') is thus to think about particular constructions constructed by particular sets of social agents. For the sociologists of childhood, it has been important to disclose 'children' as social agents and not simply to see 'childhood' as constructed by adults alone (James and Prout, 1990). It is important to recognise the agency of both children and adults in the construction of childhood, but it is equally important to recognise that the accumulation of descriptions and sentiments problematises that construction as occurring in a sociological present and that the positions from which descriptions are produced and valued are themselves problematised as a consequence of such accumulation. For us, to ask about 'agency' is not to restrict the range of responses to the question but rather to attempt to grasp the complex processes, patterning, stability and consistency, yet also the contingency and particularity, sometimes over short periods, sometimes glacial, sometimes local and sometimes global. The issue, for us, is to locate agency throughout what others might term structure and not to bifurcate the two in terms of a totalising or individualising polarity; to understand the extension of agency along different temporalities and spatialities, not always returned to the individual child, categorically defined, as a point of origin or end point.

Natures

Ariès starts his work on the family by dismissing two stock beliefs at the time of his writing, namely that modern industrialisation has led to a weakening of the family, and that, since the eighteenth century, core family values have been under attack from liberal individualism. On the contrary, Ariès argues, over this period of time the family has had a much stronger hold on – and increasingly marked out a space of privacy separate from – 'society'. Importantly, he suggests that the growth of the idea of the family as 'a value, a theme of expression, an occasion of emotion' is linked to its having 'freed itself from both biology and law' (Ariès, 1962: 8). The role of the idea of childhood, for Ariès, is to bring about the emergence of the modern family around a moralistic set of ideas about immodesty, and it brings into play an idea of the centrality of childhood innocence. For Ariès, the disclosure of childhood as an idea is similarly a freeing of children from biology; historical analysis provides the means through which the biological can be shed and the idea freed in order to for it to take on value and affect and to be communicated beyond its natural habitat. It is interesting to note that, for Ariès, an understanding of the family and of childhood as an idea does not mean that such an idea (or sentiment) is 'social'. On the contrary, for Ariès, the emergence of the modern family implies a separation of the private from a public, social world.

In my discussion I try to hold a line which does not assume, but questions, any simple division or determinacy of the biological and the social. Moreover, any discussion of the nature of children cannot assume that our knowledge of that nature is one written solely by adults and from the perspective of adults. Any history of children's agency (as informed by the sociology of childhood) must also seek to find a way of thinking (evidence permitting) of that agency as an influence.

Either society or biology?

The sociology of childhood most often draws from Ariès the idea that childhood is a social and historical construction. It is precisely this understanding of childhood and the family as historical that is read in terms of the determining influence of society rather than biology. It is seen to constitute a bifurcation, or a splitting, of children into an idea, or social construction, on the one hand, and a biological and natural entity, on the other, in such a way that the latter is discarded but also that the agency of children might be disclosed as a purely social (and hence not biological) agency. Allison James and Alan Prout, in their programmatic statement for a 'new sociology of childhood', claim that '[t]he immaturity of children is a biological fact of life but the ways in which this immaturity is understood and made meaningful is a fact of culture' (James and Prout, 1990: 7). In that sense, any sociological study of children needs to understand that over and above any natural growth and change (that is ontologically existent but epistemologically indeterminate), the social shaping, construction and constitution of childhood as an identity and differentiated state of being is one formed through social institutions, discourses and agencies. On the one hand, the 'being' outside the social is epistemologically discounted in order to study what is knowable and visible to the social scientist, namely social being; but, on the other, in practice social scientists have honed in on the 'natural' and the 'biological' as fresh territories ripe for exploitation, in order to reveal their underlying social constructedness.

A number of historians have been critical of the basic assumptions of social constructionism, however. The criticisms have largely been on the grounds that childhood is predicated on child development, that the latter is seen as fundamentally biological, and that childcare is predicated on an equally biologically determined relation between parent and offspring. Thus the medieval historian Shulamith Shahar has stated:

the central thesis ... is that a concept of childhood existed in the Central and late Middle Ages, that scholarly acknowledgement of the existence of several stages of childhood was not merely theoretical, and that parents invested both material and emotional resources in their offspring ... although it cannot be valid to discuss childraising and parent–child relations purely in terms of instinct and natural conduct, there are certainly immutable factors involved. A considerable part of the developmental process is biologically determined. (Shahar, 1990: 1)

Similarly, Linda Pollock has argued, on the basis of parental diaries, that the eighteenth century does not bring about a sea change in relations between parents and children inasmuch as parents might be seen to begin to demonstrate an affection and intimacy towards their offspring. For her, there was no incremental increase in emotional investment by parents to their children from the thirteenth to the sixteenth century. On the contrary, she argues that children have always been seen as special and that parents have always shown affection to them. She argues that

Many historians have subscribed to the mistaken belief that, if a past society did not possess the contemporary Western concept of childhood, then the society had no such concept. This is a totally indefensible point of view – why should past societies have regarded children in the same way as Western society today? Moreover, even if children were regarded differently in the past, this does not mean that they were not regarded as children. (Pollock, 1983: 263)

For many historians, then, the argument over social construction is one that is confirmed or refuted in the context of historical time. Arguments for a social constructionism, and the criticisms against it, can be understood in the context of a zero sum game: either a concept of childhood has always been present throughout history, and it has been so because childhood is fundamentally biological and a universal feature of human society; or childhood is fundamentally social in origin and has been absent for much of human history, and it only emerges at a particular moment in space and time.

There are two issues to consider. Firstly, there is often an assumption that while biology endures through historical time, the sociality is only revealed through the differentiation of historical periods or is marked by its fleeting particularity. But it is Ariès' argument, and one drawn from the Annales School of history, that historical change is geological. Childhood as a 'mental framework' constitutes a 'prison' of the *longue durée*, such that it forms limits 'beyond which man and his experiences cannot go' (Braudel, 1980: 31). Childhood is seen as social structure, a form of stability and security over history and across generations. The shedding of the biological, as it were, is not at the expense of an understanding of an enduring quality of childhood. Childhood is understood as a particularity, but not one swayed by the capricious and the 'breathless rush' of the event (Braudel, 1980: 27). Some have criticised Ariès for his indefiniteness with regard to the actual date for the invention of childhood. When is the birth of the concept of childhood? Is it at the end of the eighteenth century or in the Renaissance or the Middle Ages (Flandrin, 1964; Becchi and Julia, 1998a)? But such criticism ignores the nature of Ariès' argument, whatever its faults and inaccuracies. For Ariès, the particularity of childhood is not understood in the context of the historical moment, but across the long movement of historical time. Of course, on this point, it is also important to note that some sociologists of childhood, in a somewhat contradictory manner, have stressed the particularities of social constructions of childhood (i.e. with respect to the primacy of the social as against the biological) and have also reproduced the idea of childhood as a universal (i.e. across all history and geography) – this time, though, as a social structural, not a biological, universal. In this sense, there is an element of the sociology of childhood which, while criticising naturalistic accounts of children and childhood, simply repeats the form of that construction.

Secondly, many historical studies since Ariès show how different periods of history reveal different forms and aspects of children's lives and different notions of childhood. But these studies do not make any simplistic arguments which favour either 'the social' or 'the biological'. There is caution about any simple social or biological reductionism. French medieval historians have argued and demonstrated how concern for the child was clearly evident in Europe from the fifth to the early sixteenth centuries (Alexandre-Bidon and Lett, 1999; Fossier, 1997; Riché and Alexandre-Bidon, 1994: see also Orme, 2001). Children are documented in their everyday lives in the context of the church, in places of education and learning, in the family, at work, in the castle and on the streets (Alexandre-Bidon and Lett, 1999; Riché and Alexandre-Bidon, 1994). There is no doubt that there were understandings in the medieval period of what a child was and how to care for it. The 'raising' (*tollere*, to take up) of the child by the father in order to hold off the threat of abandonment was more than a literal act at the birth of an infant; it was also a metaphor for the growth of the child (Boswell, 1988). Even further back in time, historians of the ancient Greeks and Romans have similarly shown how a conceptualisation of the child is not peculiar to the modern period (Dixon, 2001; Becchi and Julia, 1998a and 1998b). Throughout recorded history it is clearly evident that there has existed some understanding of the child as different in nature to the adult, and that there has also existed a demonstrable concern and affection for the child as addressed in various writings and representations. Children have long been seen as objects of affect and affection. Even if we take the cases of child abandonment (Boswell, 1988) or the sending of babies for wet-nursing (Shahar, 1990), there is no evidence to suggest that this constitutes a lack of affection or care. On the contrary, over and above the difficulties of historically accounting for 'affection', there are clearly different distributions of care at different historical moments and across social class, but also different conceptions and social organisations of such 'care' (Hendrick, 1997). That the infant and the child were the object of experience, attention and adult discourse is not at issue. It is also worth noting that historical evidence of children often points to them being addressed by and large (although not exclusively) in the singular (i.e. as a son or daughter, or as a child learning). Children's horizontal affections or experiences with other children are not by and large the focus of attention (i.e. children may have reciprocal affections toward adult teachers or parents, but not toward other children). Moreover, the documenting of children has been by adults and children, by and large, have not, until relatively recently, been active and agentic subjects of those documented accounts.

Biopower and writing on the life of the child

In a twist to the standard reading, we should understand Ariès' classic account of the diaries of the physician Héroard regarding the infant dauphin Louis XIII not (as Ariès has been understood by sociologists as saying) in the context that poses a social constructionist argument against a biologistic one, but in the context of an emerging focus on the body of the child, in such a way that that focus is provided by a circulation of signs and interests. For Ariès, Héroard's writings indicate a complete lack of modesty toward the infant Louis XIII. He states: 'No other document can give us a better idea of the non-existence of the modern idea of childhood at the beginning of the seventeenth century' (Ariès, 1962: 98). On the contrary, though, such a document indicates a significant piece of evidence for the argument that the child is a fundamentally biopolitical entity. Héroard's diaries constitute a natural history of the child. Héroard documents the life of Louis XIII in astonishing detail. He follows him everywhere. He asks him about all aspects of his life. All areas from sexual activity to defecation to eating to social behaviour are documented. In this sense, contra Ariès, the sexualisation of the young dauphin as recounted by this physician does not point to an exemplary difference between seventeenth-century and

present-day conceptions of childhood (i.e. with regard to sexual innocence), but rather that Héroard's account is a vivid demonstration of
the relationship of the sovereign palace household to the body of the
young, naked and bare child. Héroard's account marks the beginning
of a relationship to the child, one that describes and catalogues and
visualises their body along a scale from sexualised fantasies to medical
definition (Foucault, 1979). Before this time there were certainly child
prostitutes and adults who preyed on young children's vulnerability.
Girls in domestic servitude were often open to abuse, and, once 'dis-
honoured', many found their way on to the streets and the brothels
(Alexandre-Bidon and Lett, 1999). But Héroard's diaries demonstrate
a relation between biography and medical case history. They demonstrate a relation between writing, observation, and the life of the child.
As one historian has noted:

In his manuscript it becomes clear that Louis's physical and mental processes
were manipulated and controlled by the doctor, to the extent of his powers,
from the child's very first day. Héroard appears to have sought complete
control of the intake and output of his infant charge, intervening continually
and disruptively. (Marvick, 1993: 289)

There is a definite continuity with the present inasmuch as the child
constitutes a privileged focus for the proliferation of writing and
concerns about sexuality, but also a privileged focus with regard
to a correlation between child observation, descriptive devices, biographical existence, biosocial history and governmental intervention.
   Cultural historians, such as Ludmilla Jordanova, have talked
about the growth of the natural and moral sciences, and also about
the popularisation of medicine in the eighteenth century, in such a
way that does not simply repress the child's body under the weight
of discourse, but demonstrates how that body, in all its complexity,
is articulated and rearticulated (Jordanova, 1989 and 1999).
Jordanova argues that in the eighteenth century the family 'is at
once natural and social' (Jordanova, 1999: 164). The life of the
family revolved around not only the emerging natural sciences but
also the emerging social sciences, and was concerned with the habits,
sensibilities and relationships between men and women and parents
and children. In her research, Jordanova makes it clear that social
relationships were integral to understandings of the natural. She
argues that

In the late eighteenth century, life was commonly associated with activity and plasticity, with the adaptive powers of organisms to respond to the environment, and with organization, that is, the structural complexity of a living being, a concept used to explain the special properties of animals and plants. Life was a notion of synthesis, system and fusion ... A rigid demarcation between mind and body thus made no sense, since the organism was one integrated whole. Hence, clearly, the moral and the social emerged out of the natural organization of living matter. Life, then, was a fertile concept. (Jordanova, 1999: 175)

Moreover, the particular descriptions of children were mapped out in terms of their similarities, closeness, differences and distance from the natural world. Thus, children were talked about in relation to their animality or their plantlike nature, or in terms of their instinctual or bestial conduct (Jordanova, 1989). The enduring nature of these descriptions is still hugely resonant now.

In a different vein, Carolyn Steedman argues that our modern understandings of childhood find their history in the natural sciences, such as physiology and medicine. Understandings from these expert knowledges were disseminated (for example, through childcare manuals) across the body politic, and especially to parents and those who had a duty of care to children; they provided 'a means of aligning and amalgamating a phenomenon and a name for the phenomenon, of eliding growth and childhood and childhood and death' (Steedman, 1994: 76). For Steedman, childhood itself is a phenomenon that helps to locate a series of problems and questions about the 'inside' and the 'outside' of the body and the self: 'by embodying the problem of growth and disintegration in children, children become the problem they represented: they become the question of interiority' (76). Steedman's historical analysis of the interiority of the child and the problem of growth is central to our understanding of children as a collective experiential subject, but also to a more general sense of experience as growth. A notion of growth as interior to the body of the child is to be distinguished from earlier ecclesiastical writings on original sin and infancy (i.e. what has wrongly been seen as a problem of innocence and experience) and natural philosophical work on predetermination (i.e. the problem of the homunculus). For example, in relation to the former, recent work on St Augustine (whose writings initiate the medieval discussion of original sin) shows how he constructs the infant not as one who commits actual sinful acts (i.e. not guilty of specific sins), but as a 'non-innocent' (i.e. one whose soul is informed by the sin of Eve) whose baptism brings entry into the community of the Christian church (Stortz, 2001; Traina, 2001). It is only as the infant develops speech that it becomes accountable for its actions and is thus capable of actual sin. And in relation to the latter, preformationism holds that the embryo is not a moment of creativity and growth, but a point of sameness with the soul of the parent. The embryo, and later the infant and the child, are merely larger versions of the same soul that is enclosed in the forebears, and their forebears, and so on.

In contrast, the growing child (the generationality of interiorised life) becomes a condition of the experiential relations of children in the nineteenth century. The nineteenth-century physiological writings on development and interiority fold growth into the body of the child. Moreover, as others have argued, in the problematic of growth and interiority (i.e. of the development of living organisms) the 'child' has a privileged place in offering its body (as a supposed site of universality) for the narration of the story of life. The temporality of the growth of the child (as a linear development) is one that is seen to mirror the development of the human species. Hence the development of any individual child is seen to re-present the story of the human species, and importantly of 'racial' differentiation (Castañeda, 2002). Thus, for example, in the 'biographical sketch' by Charles Darwin of his children or in Spencerian sociology or in Charles Fourier's utopian social thought, the writing of and about the child's body articulates that individual body with the body of a collective population or species, and does so in a way that figures the temporarily of both as a linear progression. In contrast to any suggestion that the child is either social or biological, recent historical and social research would argue that the child is disclosed as a phenomenon within a field of problematisation concerning the biopolitical and biopolitical production (i.e. about the politics and labour of life) (Foucault, 1979 and 2004).

The lives of children and literary culture

It is easy with talk of science (whether natural or social) to exclude children, by default almost, from having any role, subjectivity or agency. But what is clear is that the making of science from the eighteenth century onwards also rested on the mobilisation of children and the enlisting of their agency. A key factor in this was the development of a literary culture for children. Thus, the discussions of John Locke and Jean-Jacques Rousseau on children's learning, language and entry into civilisation are, in their different ways, not only philosophical treatises on education and the child but also texts which reveal particular notions of middle-class civilisation and particular artefacts and tools for becoming civilised. The use, for example, of ABC books to images of nature was not generalised at the time of their writing. These tools for reading and writing, and for learning about the world, were not widely distributed; they were rarefied technologies. It was only later that they were generalised through the standardisation of education from the late nineteenth century onwards. The circulation of these tools goes hand in hand with the growth of children's publishing and of a literary culture for children. In the late eighteenth century, alongside the growth in children's fiction, encyclopaedias and taxonomic collections for children emerged as new cultural forms. In 1770, Francis Newbery published *The Natural History of Birds by T. Teltruth*, which contained appropriated passages from Thomas Boreman's *Description of Three Hundred Animals* (1730). *The Good Child's Cabinet of Natural History* (published in 1801 by John Wallis of London) contains chapters on beasts, birds, fish, insects and flowers, and within each chapter there is a series of images and descriptions of particular species. Darton, in his five-century survey of children's literature in England, tells us that natural histories for children would bear the generic traces of a wide range of literary forms, such as the fable, the 'decayed history', the fabulous monster and the fairy tale. This genre of writing for children might be described as 'legend' (Foucault, 1970), but it also demonstrates an understanding of children in the context of scientific enquiry and construes children as subjects of scientific experiment and investigation. The child is constituted with the authority of the scientific gaze. They are able to bear witness to nature. They are authorised to give testimony to the empirical before them and to have credibility conferred to their experience. But equally this is a science of the marvellous real, both fact and spectacle. Although the children's encyclopaedia takes the form of tabular expression, its nomenclature and the ordering of its signified are 'non-scientific'. Its content, in this sense, is mythic and popular. It is a *marvellous* natural history.

The deployment of literary signification for the child provides a medium that both marks a transition from infancy to childhood (i.e. in terms of literacy as an acquisition) and is also a necessary perversion of the primary experiential relation between infant and world (i.e. inasmuch as the relation between child and world is now seen to be mediated through literary language). In this respect both Rousseau and Locke agree on the 'imperfection' of words (Rose, 1984: 46). Jacqueline Rose, in her work on children's fiction, notes the importance of Locke in the innovation in pedagogic publishing for children; she refers to the publication, in 1756, of *A Little Lottery Book for Children, containing a new method for playing them into a knowledge of the letters* as a demonstration of Locke's idea of pictorial language. But she states that Locke's proposal for an intimacy between word and image (that is now so typical of young children's books) 'was inseparable from a deep suspicion of written language, and a desire to hold the written word as closely as possible to the immediacy of the visual image' (Rose, 1984: 46). We might add that Locke, in *Some Thoughts Concerning Education*, talks about an immediacy not simply to the image but also to the thing and to play (Locke, 1996). Rose also notes that in Rousseau's *Emile*,

the child is being asked not only to retrieve a lost state of nature, but also to take language back to its pure and uncontaminated source in the objects of the immediate world ... [T]he constant stress throughout [is] on the purity of the visual sign ...Whether it is a case of physical gesture and expression, or of pointing out objects in the real world, what matters is that signs should immediately *speak*. (Rose, 1984: 47–8)

For Locke, infants are experiential subjects (i.e. they have the capacity for experience and to be experienced) and it is only by virtue of their being so that 'human understanding' is possible. For him, but also for Rousseau, our relation to the empirical is necessarily mediated by the condition of maturity. Although Montaigne may have posed experience in the context of maturity and death, it is Rousseau and Locke who frame experience in the context of infancy and signification.

The early nineteenth century witnessed an increase in the rates of literacy in the British population, and also an increase in religious revivalism. In the 1830s three-quarters of working-class homes possessed books, mainly religious. In 1801 less than 15 per cent of all working-class children between the ages of 5 and 15 attended Sunday schools, but by 1851 the figure was 75 per cent. Although illiteracy was not a 'primary obstacle' to children's engagement with a children's literary culture (Drotner, 1988: 31), it – alongside 'a taste for debased, sensational fiction' – was identified as a social pathology (Donald, 1992: 53). Such concerns only intensified as the century progressed and the new one began. As James Donald has argued, '[T]he illiterate became the target of the "administered" forms in which the standard language and the national literature were taught in the elementary schools set up after Forster's Education Act in 1870' (Donald, 1992: 53). The governmentalisation of education (i.e. the bringing of education within the authorities of the state) and the standardisation of pedagogy were firmly established by the early twentieth century (Hendrick, 1997: 63). From this point on, all children within particular national territories were brought within the purview of a universal set of measures. Compulsory schooling for sections of the population between particular ages constructed childhood as a national standardised entity (Sommerville, 1982), but also extended the domain of the social across that particular national territorialised body of people and across forms of conduct (Rose, 1989). In this sense, 'society' is not seen to pre-exist children and childhood; it is not seen to be that into which children are socialised. On the contrary, the social is, adjectivally, that which describes a set of processes through which a population is disclosed, through the emergence of particular problems (e.g. literacy, poverty and so on) and through the development of particular technologies (e.g. schooling). Society is a consequence of, in part, the institutionalisation and governmentalisation of children's schooling. Schooling has been one site in which this process can be seen to have occurred. But equally, we could consider the emergence of standardised forms of health and measurement for children or the standardisation of welfare generally. Accordingly, in this context too, the social is defined within the purview of the national.

Rose also argues that

Language for children – how it is spoken both by and to the child – is subject to strictures, and characterised by differences, which need first to be located inside the institution where language is systematically taught. This is an issue which bears on our relationship, not only to children's writing, but to literature as a whole – the fact that language has an institutional history which determines how it is written, spoken, and understood. (Rose, 1984: 89)

My concern here is not with the institutionalisation of a dominant literacy or the shaping of an English literature, but with the configuration of a medium (literary culture) as a medium of children's experience in the context of 'nationalisation', 'standardisation' and agencies of the state. Certainly the school was important, but so were other institutions of welfarist state policy (Sommerville, 1982; Hendrick, 1997). In this sense, through the historic capacities and capabilities of the nation-state (Sassen, 2006), a collective experiential subjectivity for children was able to be formed. Moreover, it was precisely through the development of those capacities that children have been able to contribute to their own description and to the knowledge of their own nature in a manner certainly novel and innovative.

Spaces

Much of the argument about spaces has been made in the preceding sections, so I will not labour the point. In the closing chapter of *Centuries of Childhood*, Ariès quotes a passage from *The Little Prince* by Antoine de Saint-Exupéry:

He was free, infinitely free, so free that he was no longer conscious of pressing on the ground. He was free of that weight of human relationships which impedes movement, those tears, those farewells, those reproaches, those joys, all that a man caresses or tears every time he sketches out a gesture, those countless bonds which tie him to others and make him heavy. (Ariès, 1962: 395)

For Ariès, the history of childhood and its place within the development of the school is a history of imprisonment. He states that

The school shut up a childhood which had hitherto been free within an increasingly severe disciplinary system, which culminated in the eighteenth and nineteenth centuries in the total claustration of the boarding-school. The solicitude of family, Church, moralists and administrators deprived the child of the freedom he had hitherto enjoyed among adults. It inflicted on him the birch, the prison cell – in a word, the punishments usually reserved for convicts from the lowest strata of society. (Ariès, 1962: 397)

This was not the mark of indifference, but of an 'obsessive love which was to dominate society', a love which helped construct 'the wall of private life between the family and society' (Ariès, 1962: 397). In many ways, Michel Foucault's discussion of discipline and governmentality (which we will discuss in Chapter 6) rests on this earlier analysis, but what is distinctive about Ariès' discussion is that he constructs, firstly, a notion of childhood, which is institutionalised and which, in doing so, curtails the agency of the child; secondly, a history of the transition from the medieval period to the modern period in terms of a history of the reduction and curtailment of that freedom; and, finally, an analysis of that transition in terms of the passage from heterodox to homogenous, purified and enclosed space.

This story of the tabulation of knowledge, of confinement and of modern civilisation is one that certainly finds its grounding in that earlier period. For example, in the late eighteenth century there were stories of a strange creature, boy-like but also animal-like, running across the fields and hills of southern France and scavenging for food in the local villages. The 'savage' who, naked, ran on all fours, had escaped capture twice, but was finally brought to heel in January 1800. Abbé Pierre-Joseph Bonnaterre, Professor of Natural History at the Central School for Aveyron, was able to make some initial observations of the savage before the boy was taken to Paris. There was an intention to make the child a property of the new French republic, under the supervision of the Society of Observers of Man. By July of that year, after some irritation, the savage boy was finally taken to Paris, to the Institute for Deaf Mutes, in the care of Jean-Marc Itard and his housekeeper, Madame Guérin. The boy, now renamed as Victor, was of great interest to the newly emerging moral sciences. The story of Victor is also the story of a child's relation to society. But it was not yet 'Society' as named by the great social scientists of the nineteenth century; it was a society that carried the connotations of noble association. It was a society synonymous with civilisation. In contrast to Ariès, the becoming social of the child was not in opposition to its education. Nevertheless, society was a rare phenomenon, too precious to be distributed evenly across the whole population. In Itard's discussion of the boy, he talks of places of social gathering – such as particular houses, a village and the city – and he talks of particular manners, tastes and forms of conduct (i.e. certain senses, sensibility, gentlemanliness, gesture and posture). Victor's entry into society was an entry into Parisian bourgeois society, into a particular European 'civilisation'. Moreover, it was through learning how to speak, how to listen and how to write that Victor, it was hoped, would be introduced into French middle-class society. Victor learned to adopt some of the manners and modes of conduct of French society, but in a highly idiosyncratic way. For all their (Victor, Itard and Madame Guérin) collective efforts, the boy, although he enjoyed the warmth of affection and the heat of a good bath, and could use letters to request a glass of milk at restaurants in Paris, could never speak and he never fully progressed out of his wild nature. Toward the end of the period that Foucault calls the Classical Age and a period of the Great Confinement, the wild boy of Aveyron was figured as a life unconfined, on the edge of 'society'. It is particularly apposite, then, that the discovery and education of Victor at the beginning of the nineteenth century should be marked by such an ambivalence concerning his nature and socialisation, his wildness and learning, his discipline and freedom. The agency of Victor is of a person forever in exile from – on the cusp of belonging to – civilisation and society, the French Republic, and the birth of a new nation. The attempts to normalise Victor constitute an exemplary moment in the formation of modern power, but also in the history of modern childhood (Foucault, 2004).

But Ariès sees things slightly differently. For him, childhood is the result of a process of quarantining children, keeping them separate until they are sufficiently mature to live with adults. The school (as initially a means of guardianship of the soul and then a site of training) and the family (as a blanketing of children within the comforts of a private life separated from 'society') both constitute a way of thinking about the institutionalisation of childhood alongside a geometric division of space. Thus, for example, in the closing page of his book, Ariès argues that

The old society concentrated the maximum number of ways of life into the minimum of space and accepted, if it did not impose, the bizarre juxtaposition of the most widely different classes. The new society, on the contrary, provided each way of life with a confined space in which it was understood that the dominant features should be respected, and that each person had to resemble a conventional model, an ideal type, and never depart from it under pain of excommunication. (Ariès, 1962: 399)

The heterodoxy of the Middle Ages – a diversity and mixing of classes and ages – is contrasted with the modern, clean, spatial and conceptual division between generations.

On reflection, the clean differentiation of adults and children just doesn't seem to hold, but generational distribution seems equally obvious. The question for us, then, is not so much the division of children from adults, but, contra Ariès, how children's agency (their capacity to act and be acted upon) is less geometrically and more topologically dispersed, but also less captured by a single perspective and more constituted through multiple planes and multiple scales. It is interesting in this respect that Ariès does not take the lesson from Saint-Exupéry that children and adults are both drawers of worlds and themselves drawn into those worlds. The Little Prince is nothing if not drawn and described by an artist and aviator whose work is misrecognised by the grown-ups and hence, as a consequence, aligns him more with children than adults, and whose work carries him into other worlds, fantastic and mysterious. It would be foolish to think that a return to an equally drafted world of the medieval period, a world with less modesty, would somehow deliver a world of greater freedom and less discipline. Of course, all worlds are heavy in their connections. But then we are never free from the equipment and devices, forms and descriptions which make us who we are.

The cultural analyst Mieke Bal, in an introduction to narratology, talks about the relation between modes of description and types of novelistic form. She says:

Whereas Cervantes' anti-hero is declared 'mad' for seeing what is not there – for seeing an army in a cloud of dust produced by a herd of sheep – and Zola and Co. boasted the referential existence of their described objects, modernism, with its dual philosophy of subjectivity and chance, is well placed to demonstrate an altogether different status for description. (Bal, 2009: 40)

Modernist forms of writing play with the framing of description and place the frame as an element within the complexity of description (cf. Smith, 1981). Ariès' understanding of the clean spaces of modernity, then, owe a debt to naturalistic forms of writing and thinking about space as external to the act and process of inscription, but also to Euclidean ideas about geometric space (Law and Benschop, 1997).

Ariès positions himself outside of those spaces of confinement in such a way that he can survey those spaces, document their existence and account for their emergence. Of course, the luxury of that position – the position of the professional academic historian – is dependent on the passage through the education system so described. But also Ariès' clean spaces of modernity are only possible if he forgets to include or ignores those others who people, build, support, organise, discipline, punish and care for those children who are aggregated in the schools or families. Are those who build and manage the boundaries inside or outside those spaces of confinement? If those people, for example parents and teachers, have been party to the removal of children from 'adult society' (Ariès, 1962: 397), are those people then not part of 'children's society'? If, in Ariès' terms, family and school have 'advanced in proportion as sociability has retreated' (393), then how might we understand the social relations (friendships, habits, play, love, teaching and so on) 'inside' those spaces? It is also striking that those spaces which appear most oriented to children are also those spaces around which we find a huge aggregation of adults, as if the confinement of children involved not a removal of adults but, on the contrary, their concentration. Equally, what we find is that, as a consequence of that intensity of attachment and investment, new forms of social relationality are incubated and distributed outside those nests. The classroom is less a space in which children are locked, than it is a shaper of teacherly relations, pupil interactions, cognitive measures and pedagogic technologies. On their journey to their local school now, children walk with friends or parents or guardians or grandparents or older or young siblings or parents of friends; some may take the bus, others a train, yet others drive. Along the way they mix with conductors, drivers, commuters and other children. Some children may even board at school and wake to matrons and prefects and housemasters, and breakfast in a school canteen peopled by cooks and other staff. When lessons begin, another entourage of people and things are assembled. Moreover, the lessons learned in the classroom may form the basis of learning at home with a parent; but equally, a pedagogic style might find its way on to a television programme or a computer game. What seems clear, as will be demonstrated in the body of this book, is that the descriptive devices through which children's and adults' spaces have and might further be defined and detailed have been dispersed across the social. And in doing so, the framing of spaces as 'for children' or 'not for children' cannot simply be seen in terms of a clean differentiation and positioning of adulthood and childhood. What is important, then, is not to look at the division of labour between children and adults, but rather to investigate the labour of division (Law and Benschop, 1997).

Conclusion

It will have been clear that my argument with and against Ariès has been based on a sociological fiction. The Ariès I have interpreted, argued against and talked alongside has been a mythical figure, one that resonates across and often implicit within much of the sociology of childhood. My intention, then, in this chapter, has been to talk through that mythical construction in the context of the rich and detailed sociological and historical research on children, which presents a genealogy of modern children in a different vein. Instead of repeating the three reductions of concept, society and space, I have presented a sense of the historical disclosure of children as experiential and collective subjects in terms of the accumulation of descriptive and sentiment devices; in terms of the complex entangled histories of the social and the natural; and in terms of an understanding of the institutional stamp of modernity not simply in terms of the enclosure of children within the sanctified spaces of discipline and care, but rather their aggregation alongside and their necessary mingling with adults in spaces certainly more heterodox and topological than many seem to want to acknowledge. Important in that history is the need to reveal where and to what extent children have been seen to have an influence.

Social theories of children and childhood

In Part II I look at theories of children and childhood initially in the context of modern or classical social and sociological theories and then in terms of (what some may term as) postmodern social and cultural theories.

In Chapter 3 I review debates on social structure and agency. These debates have been central to the recent (from the later 1980s onwards) development of the sociology of childhood. In part, the sociology of childhood has provided analytical and empirical descriptions of childhood as a social structural phenomenon in the sense that all societies, both past and present, might be said to encode a division between adulthood and childhood, such that a division also implies inequalities regarding power and the distribution of capital (of one form or another) and that a relationship of learning or socialisation is needed for the transition of people from one category of personhood to the other. On the other hand, a wealth of empirical studies have considered children as agentic beings, namely as social beings who make a difference to the social worlds around them, whether in terms of their capacity to interpret and make meaning or in terms of their capacity to materially manipulate their environment. Also, research into the sociology of childhood has sought to understand structure and agency, not as mutually exclusive devices for understanding and describing the experiences of children but as two sides of the same coin.

Nevertheless, structure and agency are sociological abstractions and emerging out of this central problematic have been different kinds of research and analysis guided more by attempts to understand children and their social worlds as more partial and negotiated. This diverse body of research, broadly conceived, has endeavoured to understand children's agency as situated and emergent from particular social and cultural contexts. I consider different theoretical perspectives on children's situated, negotiated and interstitial agency in Chapter 4.

In the third chapter of this part of the book, I look at post-structural and post-social understandings of the social. Some of this work comes from cultural studies or associated disciplines, some from science and technology studies and some from material cultural studies. In Chapter 5 I talk about the importance of language in problematising any notion of agency which is simply centred on an individual and unitary subject. Language, and the dialogic textual nature of it, forces us to think of agency as dispersed and fragmented. Children's agency is understood as being akin to a text or a performance in which different characters or actors are orchestrated through plot, voice and staging. But, of course, such a model of children's agency fails to account properly for the materiality of agency, and it is at this point that I turn to studies of agency which see it as distributed across the human and the non-human, the social and technological, and the cultural and natural. In this material turn, various ideas concerning the arrangement of different elements are considered. I review work on the assemblage, network, apparatus and infrastructure. In doing so, I try to get a sense of the complex arrangements through which children's agency is figured, the mixing of various part-objects, the variety of scale, but also without losing sense of children as people.

My intention in framing this part of the book in this way is to return to some of the debates within post-structuralism which emerged in the 1980s in a concerted way across the social and cultural sciences, but which were largely dismissed by the reimagining of the sociology of childhood in the late 1980s. In doing so, I want to hold on to some of the strengths which were initially mapped out by the 'new sociology of childhood', but to rearticulate them within a series of discussions and ideas which problematise a rather prosaic and individualised understanding of structure and agency which is normalised in the work of Anthony Giddens (which in many ways provides an anchor point for much of the 'new sociology of childhood'). In making this move, my turn to work within actor-network theory and assemblage theory does so with that post-structural terrain as its horizon. In doing so, hopefully a material semiotics emerges (admittedly in very partial form) which makes intelligible the complex terrains across which different types of agency are framed and entangled.

3 | Modern social theories: agency and structure

By and large, sociologists of childhood have, whether explicitly or implicitly, held the focus of their study on children with speech and from school years and above. The questions of agency and power, culture and interpretation, politics and rights have largely, but not exclusively, been oriented to those children in their mid to late years, rather than to infants (in the literal sense of those with no speech). Many sociologists of childhood take Durkheim's lead and discuss what he refers to as 'childhood in the usual sense of the word' (Durkheim, 1979: 149). And yet some sociologists, notably Priscilla Alderson, have argued that any sociology of childhood needs to include those younger children, infants and babies, as well as the older ones (Alderson, 2000). Indeed, the question of infancy has been at the heart of the issue, and to circumscribe a priori what constitutes the domain of study would certainly seem to jump the gun. In many ways, there is an acceptance that children are individuals and have various abilities and competencies. But it is also accepted that such individuation is a facet of development and that prior to individuation is a state of preformed human-beingness inasmuch as individuation is *social* individuation. A central problem, then, for sociologists of children has been not simply the question of agency, but the problem of agency as both individuated and predicated on human growth inasmuch as growth is defined as the propensity to sociality. Much of the recent sociology of childhood, certainly since the late 1980s, has sought not only to construe children (often in some indeterminate sense) as having agency (as making some impact on the world), but also to reconfigure our understanding of social structure as more open to the dynamic interactions and influences of children as agentic beings. Whereas the presumption of the immaturity of infancy has often led to a fixing of the social or 'society' as something imposed on those new to the social world (i.e. as socialisation), or as an inherent schema through which a propensity to normality is defined (i.e. as

normal development), sociologists of childhood, in their explorations of
social agency, often refuse at first base such a fixity. The intention of the
sociology of childhood in the late 1980s was, in part, to find a place for
children without returning to such a fixity. This chapter will provide a
detailed account of some of the issues concerning structure and agency
within the sociology of childhood; it will also make evident some of
the substantial problems with such a formulation. That said, it also
needs to be said that much of the writing on children's agency draws
on a particular rendition of the relation between agency and structure,
which largely ignores the huge wealth of writing more broadly within
sociology on this topic. The initial turn to children's agency in the late
1980s centred on the work of Anthony Giddens, and to a large extent
that focus has remained as part of the common sense of the field. In part,
that focus might be seen to be motivated less by a concern to theorise
children and childhood, than by a concern to frame the issues in political
terms. The original interest in children's agency was less an exercise in
theory than in politics. Its purpose was, in many ways, to rebalance the
perceived inequalities of power or to find ways of researching children
that did not reproduce the prejudices of power.

In this chapter, then, I consider briefly the lineage of modern social
theories of agency and structure with respect to children. I do so via
foregrounding the correlation of agency and individuation, the dominance of the social and the ascription of structure as a unitary totality.

Social being and becoming

The late nineteenth- and early twentieth-century French sociologist
Emile Durkheim understood childhood as essentially a problem of
growth: 'a period in which the individual, in both the physical and
moral sense, does not yet exist, the period in which he is made, develops
and is formed' (Durkheim, 1979: 150). The growth of the child is not
open and indeterminate; rather, it has a clear teleology and objective.
For Durkheim, childhood growth is understood only in the context of
individuation. Moreover, the state of growth is typified by Durkheim in
terms of both weakness and mobility: 'the person who grows finds
himself in a sort of unstable and constantly changing equilibrium; he
grows because he is incomplete, because he is weak, because there is
still something he lacks' (150). Adulthood is constituted as a comple-
tion, a fullness, a 'full development'. For Durkheim, this growth and

incompleteness are understood as 'becoming' (150). Such becoming from weakness to strength requires, Durkheim states, 'a wonderful environment of careful attention, of consideration, of favourable circumstances and protective influences'. This becoming is both generational and generative, and it is always moving, ceaseless: 'it is capable of everything except rest and inertia' (150). Such 'ceaseless progress, intensity and inexhaustible exuberance baffle the imagination' (151). Physically, intellectually and morally the child is transformed from weak to strong. Body, mind and will are slowly formed and their excitement stabilised in the movement to adulthood. The child's becoming adult is understood by Durkheim in terms of an increasing regularisation. Instability is overcome through the acquisition of habit. The child's life becomes 'regularized and thoroughly ordered' (153). In doing so, Durkheim declares, 'nature does in fact place in our hands the means necessary for transcending it' (153).

Durkheim's discussion of the becoming of the child is a way of imagining the wonder of growth, of generationality, and of the transformation of the child from a state of nature to one of society. Durkheim's sociology was predicated on the analytical and methodological priority of the social institution; social existence was defined according to the 'beliefs and modes of behaviour instituted by the collectivity' (Durkheim, 1982: 45). And yet, his discussion of becoming is one that bears some similarities to those taking place in other disciplines of the social sciences, notably a little later in the developmental psychology of Jean Piaget. It was this understanding of childhood as development, as the transition from asocial to social individual, that is common to much subsequent sociological thought. Sociological thought, though, in contrast to the psychology of Piaget and others, clearly places the outcome of childhood growth (i.e. the normative *telos* of adulthood) as a social institution, as a form of being defined by the collectivity (and not by the maturity of the mind – both cognition and emotion – alone).

Many recent sociologists of childhood have been critical of any conceptualisation of childhood as a becoming from nature to society. Thus the British sociologist Chris Jenks comments on the problem of reading social definition from physical growth:

The social transformation from child to adult does not follow directly from physical growth and the recognition of children by adults, and vice versa, is not singularly contingent upon physical difference. Childhood is to be understood as a social construct, it makes reference to a social status delineated by boundaries that vary through time and from society to society but which are incorporated within the social structure and thus manifested through and formative of certain typical forms of conduct. Childhood, then, always relates to a particular cultural setting. (Jenks, 1996: 7)

We might add that Jenks' comments can equally be applied to psychological and emotional, as much as physical, becoming. For Jenks, but also for other sociologists of childhood, notions of the child as progressing from stage to stage along a normatively defined line of development are understood as social constructions that are situated within particular social contexts, particular discourses and knowledges, and particular social institutions. In such developmental perspectives, children are viewed only inasmuch as they are moving toward a normatively defined notion of what is an adult and, in that sense, sociologists of childhood have been critical on the grounds that children are only ever known, assessed, measured and normalised according to the criterion of adulthood.

In contrast, sociologists of childhood from the late 1980s onwards have argued that children should be understood and researched as social 'beings', not becomings. According to the main protagonists of this perspective – sociologists Chris Jenks and Alan Prout and the anthropologist Allison James – the notion of social being implies that

The child is conceived of as a person, a status, a course of action, a set of needs, rights or differences – in sum, as a social actor ... [T]he 'being' child can be understood in its own right. It does not have to be approached from an assumed shortfall of competence, reason or significance. The 'being' child is not, however, static, for it too is in time. Like all social actors, it populates history. (James, Jenks and Prout, 1998: 207)

The notion of the child as a social being, then, implies that we research children without prejudice. It implies that we hold off any hierarchically ordered normative judgement as to how we imagine or desire them to turn out. It implies that we understand them, not in terms of any imperative as to what they must become, but in terms of what they are, in terms of how they act themselves in social worlds, and how they interrelate with others.

There has been a clear shift from the late 1980s onwards that foregrounds the study of 'actual' children as opposed to children seen simply as caricatures predicated on adult fantasies and projections. This argument construes children as people, ones valued in their own right, not as adjuncts to adults, family or school, and not measured according to normative adult views and structures. The focus is, in the first instance, on children in the positive sense of their action and being in the world. Children are conceptualised as active in their own construction. Thus, it is not simply that childhood is a social, as opposed to biological, entity, but that its construction is a consequence of both adults' and children's agency: 'childhood is both constructed and reconstructed both for and by children' (James and Prout, 1990: 7). Prout argues that children should be seen and studied as the 'participants shaping, as well as being shaped by, society' and 'that this possibility has been muted in sociological engagements with childhood for so long is testimony to how strongly adult-centric a discipline it has been' (Prout, 2000: 2). In this argument, children are not to be seen as 'incomplete adults'. Moreover, Prout argues in the context of questions about the child body that 'children understand and perform their bodies in ways often different from adults; entering into their world is thus an essential step in an adequate sociology of childhood bodies' (2).

There are questions, though, as to how we make sense of the proposition that children are agentic social beings. What do we mean by agency? Is it individual or collective? Is it only social or is their agency hybridly formed across the social, psychological and biological? Is it purely human or does it rely on non-human (i.e. technological and natural) resources? Do all children, across age differences, have agency? Do some have more agency than others? Does agency always rely on others to mediate and translate one's actions? If the agentic child is 'in time' and populates 'history', does it also change within itself, or become different, as a consequence of its actions? Does the child have proprietorial rights, as it were, over its own agency? Is the individual 'child' the site of a single agency or of many? Or do many agencies work through that site? These questions will be addressed in the ensuing pages, but one thing is clear: children cannot simply be assumed to fit within a normative teleological structure, and any understanding of contemporary children must take seriously the fact that childhood is negotiated through competing generationally located agencies. And agency, at some basic level, refers to the capacity to do things. Thus, children are conceptualised as beings who have the capacity to do things in the world, where that doing may be physical, cognitive, emotional or other, but such that that 'being able to do' implies that children are not passive 'blank slates'. In this respect, the sociology of childhood is able to learn from earlier philosophies of childhood and psychologies of children that construe them as active. Nevertheless, the main focus of a sociology of childhood has been to consider agency in the context of a series of broader questions about power, structure and culture.

The duality of structure and agency

Contemporary sociologies of childhood have largely been concerned with the question of power and social order and much recent theoretical and empirical work in the field has focussed on children's agency in the context of childhood as a structural form. Traditionally, structure and agency have been seen in terms of two opposing traditions or approaches to the question of society and social association. Marx, Durkheim, functionalists such as Parsons and structural anthropologists such as Levi-Strauss might be taken as examples of approaches that prioritise 'structure', whereas Weber, phenomenologists such as Schutz or ethnomethodologists such as Garfinkel might be seen to prioritise agency or social action. On one side of the equation the emphasis is seen to be on determining structures, on the other, creative and interpretative action. Such a dichotomy is far from adequate for explaining the lengthy discussions in sociology concerning the nature of social order and the question of agency.

Parsons, systems and roles

A significant voice in the argument concerning social structure is Talcott Parsons. His functionalist analysis of social systems has helped to shape a dominant strand of thinking about childhood socialisation, the internalisation of social order. He argued over fifty years ago that

The acquisition of the requisite orientations for satisfactory functioning in a role is a learning process, but it is not learning in general, but a particular part of learning. This process will be called the process of *socialization*, and the motivational processes by which it takes place, seen in terms of their functional significance to the interaction system, the *mechanisms of socialization*. These are the mechanisms involved in the processes of 'normal' functioning of the social system. (Parsons, 1951: 205)

For Parsons, the social is understood in systemic terms. Society is a social system that functions organically and that can be understood according to the functional and the dysfunctional, namely those personalities and those forms of conduct that can or cannot be successfully socialised. Children are socialised, Parsons believes, primarily through the institutions of schooling and the family. But, at the time of Parsons' writing, other academics from sociology and social psychology were conducting research and considering the influence of mass media on children's socialisation (e.g. Bandura, Ross and Ross, 1961). For Parsons, the notion of the 'role' is conceptualised as that which accords with the positioning and identification of the individual within and with a particular functionality within the system. The difficulties of socialisation into any particular role may derive from the exigencies of the natural drives of the child toward resistance, and thus don't allow an articulation of individual personality with the structure of the social system. Jenks notes: 'Personalities are, of course, significant [in Parsons' work] but their embodiment, namely social actors, come to be constructed in terms of the features they display that are pertinent to their functioning in the wider context, not those relevant to their difference and individuality' (Jenks, 1996: 19). He talks about the identification and isomorphism that is central to the elision of the growing child to the social system in the process of successful socialisation. This problematic is one that has concerned a number of social scientists in the 1960s and 1970s (Giddens, 1979). For the sociology of childhood, it presents a clear problem with regard to the reduction of children to an abstraction and to a theoretical model that fails to provide an understanding of the everyday lives of actual children (James, Jenks and Prout, 1998: 25). In contrast, then, the sociology of childhood has made an attempt to understand a more dialectical relation between social structure and social agency. The work of Anthony Giddens on structure and agency has been central to this attempt.

The turn to Giddens

Giddens did not work directly within the discipline of the sociology of childhood, and yet it is his work in particular that has helped to frame much contemporary debate in the area. James and Prout state that '[a]lthough Giddens's attempt to resolve this debate has been criticized, some such view of how structure and agency complement each other seems to be an essential component in any sociology of childhood' (James and Prout, 1990: 28). The sociology of childhood as enunciated by James and Prout thus construes, on the one hand, children as social actors (interpreting and acting upon their world), and on the other, childhood as a social institution, objectivised as social structure. In their programmatic statement for a paradigmatic shift in the study of childhood, they quote Giddens: 'Every act which contributes to the reproduction of a structure is also an act of production, and as such may initiate change by altering the structure at the same time as it reproduces it' (Giddens, 1979: 69, quoted in James and Prout, 1990: 28). The understanding of structure, though, is one that is also understood through the work of the Danish sociologist of childhood Jens Qvortrup. Qvortrup's empirically focussed work has considered childhood as a structural constant across all human societies. He argues that within any given society (and here Qvortrup tends to conflate 'society' with 'nation') children 'have a number of characteristics in common' (Qvortrup et al., 1994: 5) and that those children can be compared to other structural collectives within that society (e.g. the elderly). For Qvortrup, 'childhood is perceived as a structural form or category to be compared with other structural forms or categories in society' (6). The separation of children from adults is, it is argued, common to all societies; it is a structural universal. This basic tenet is taken up by many sociologists of childhood. Thus, William Corsaro states clearly that 'For children themselves, childhood is a temporary period. For society, on the other hand, childhood is a permanent structural form or category that never disappears even though its members change continuously and its nature and conception vary historically' (Corsaro, 2005: 3). All children, except fictional ones, either die or grow up. They are all born, and they are all born into structural relations not of their choosing. In that sense, the sociologists of childhood argue that children are necessarily born into the structural relations of childhood, into childhood as a structural form. The exact nature of that structural

form, it is argued, may vary from society to society and across historical time, but the form itself is a constant. In that sense, such an
argument would be at odds with any understanding of childhood as
simply a social construction that was completely contingent and had
no relation to social structure; it is also one that seems to be at odds
with a notion of childhood as a social and historical invention. Nevertheless, this idea of social structure is one which constitutes a structural
totality that is not fixed because childhood is a fixed biological or
psychological essence, but because it is a social universal. That said,
as with adults, children, it is argued, have agency with regard to social
structure. They are not simply and passively fitted into pre-existing
social roles. Rather, children are seen both to affect and be affected by
social structure and by the constructions and institutions of childhood
therein.

Giddens talks about the dialectical relation between structure and
agency in terms of a 'duality of structure'. He does so with reference
to distinctions between structure, system and structuration. He
states that

> Structure, as recursively organized sets of rules and resources, is out of time
> and space, save in its instantiations and co-ordination as memory traces, and
> is marked by an 'absence of the subject'. The social system in which structure
> is recursively implicated, on the contrary, comprises the situated activities of
> human agents, reproduced across time and space. Analyzing the structura-
> tion of social systems means studying the modes in which such systems,
> grounded in the knowledgeable activities of situated actors who draw upon
> rules and resources in the diversity of action contexts, are produced and
> reproduced in interaction. (Giddens, 1984: 25; see also Giddens, 1979: 66)

It is not, then, that 'structure is external to individuals', but that
structure and agency are two sides of the same coin. The 'structural
properties of social systems are both medium and outcome of the
practices they recursively organize' (Giddens, 1984: 25). Giddens
argues that '[t]he concept of social system, understood in its broadest
sense, refers to reproduced *interdependence of action*', and he defines
that further, with reference to Etzioni's work on 'the active society',
as 'a relationship in which changes in one or more component parts
initiate changes in other component parts, and these changes, in turn,
produce changes in the parts in which the original changes occurred'
(Etzioni, 1968 quoted in Giddens, 1979: 73). This idea of social system,

as defined through its reciprocal and recursive relationality, is one that finds its recent history in cybernetic thought from the 1940s.

The Giddensian notion of the duality of structure is not accepted uncritically by some scholars. Berry Mayall has turned to the work of 'critical realists', such as Roy Bhaskar and Margaret Archer, to make an argument that people and society are very different sociological entities and that they are not part of a single process. She provides an argument that questions the degree of creativity and agency that social actors have with regard to social structuration, and makes a distinction between 'creative agency' and 'transformative agency'. She says that '[s]ociety has no ontological depth; it would not exist without human activity, but people do not now in the present create it; they reproduce and transform it' (Mayall, 2002: 33). Social actors transform with the resources to hand; they do not create anew. In this sense, she argues that any understanding of structure and agency needs to take account of history and material continuity. Social structure pre-exists the individuals who make use of its resources; it provides 'a necessary condition for their activity' (Bhaskar, 1979: 46, quoted Mayall, 2002: 34).

The issue is not that Giddens pays no account of history, but that he perhaps overemphasises the creative capacity of individual agents. Individual agents are not tasked with (re)producing the totality of social structure; rather, other and different agencies produce environments, built and peopled at different moments, historically and geographically, which may then be occupied by others at other moments, in the inventive process of occupation. The creative capacity of agents is certainly a significant issue with regard to the sociology of childhood. What is the extent of children's agency? Is the agency of children to be understood in the same terms as the agency of adults? Does the notion of 'agency' refer to a capability that is evenly distributed across all children of all ages everywhere? Is agency a social universal? Or is agency differentiated, between some children of different ages and in some circumstances rather than in others? Is agency accumulated? Is its power or extension dependent on the mobilisation of others (both human and non-human)?

For Giddens, the question of agency is fundamentally one about power. Agents have a capacity and capability to make things happen, to have an influence and to have some sort of control. He argues that agency is not simply about being able to act, but about being able to make a difference. He says:

To be able to 'act otherwise' means being able to intervene in the world, or to refrain from such intervention, with the effect of influencing a specific process or state of affairs. This presumes that to be an agent is to be able to deploy (chronically, in the flow of daily life) a range of causal powers, including that of influencing those deployed by others. Action depends upon the capability of the individual to 'make a difference' to a pre-existing state of affairs or course of events. An agent ceases to be such if he or she loses the capability to 'make a difference', that is, to exercise some sort of power. (Giddens, 1984: 14)

In Giddens' account, social actors have agency with respect to geographical space, the day-to-day and the *longue durée* of institutions. The space and time of the locale, but also the historical structure of institutions, are seen to be 'reversible'. In contrast, he talks about the passage of a person through the life cycle in terms of 'irreversible time' and about the *longue durée* of institutions in terms of the repetition of the life cycle. The matter warrants little discussion from Giddens, but it is of considerable importance to sociologists of childhood. It matters because if the *longue durée* of institutions is reversible and if children are agentic social actors, then the institutionalisation of childhood as a structural form (and a significant categorisation of the life cycle) would itself be reversible and open to social and historical change. However, if the structural form of childhood is not reversible, then we would need an account of its irreversibility. Moreover, such an account may need to include discussion of the limitations of children's agency and may need to have recourse to the ideas developed by Mayall. Research within the sociology of childhood has tended, by degree, to favour one or other position with respect to the reversibility or not of social structure and the capabilities of agency with regard to structure.

Giddens lays great stress on an understanding of agency in terms of knowledge and reflexivity (i.e. the ability to know the world, but also to change the world as a result of that knowing). He states that '*every social actor knows a great deal about the conditions of reproduction of the society of which he or she is a member*', and continues: 'The proposition that all social agents are knowledgeable about the social systems which they constitute and reproduce is a logically necessary feature of the conception of the duality of structure' (Giddens, 1979: 5). For Giddens, human agency concerns the reflexive monitoring or rationalisation of action. He talks about discursive and practical consciousness and also about unconscious motivation. The question for any sociology of childhood is the extent to which these distinctions might be applied to the investigation of children's agency. As children represent the very problem of 'rationalisation' as a matter of maturity, it would certainly not be sufficient simply to ascribe 'reflexive rationality' to children of all ages. We should note that when Giddens is talking about agency in this way, he is referring to 'competent members of society' (Giddens, 1984: 26). The production of action and the repro-duction of the conditions of that action in the everyday is thus the privilege of those with the requisite competency. Giddens draws on the work Erik Erikson (but also Sigmund Freud) to talk about 'the formation of capabilities of autonomous action' and about diffe-rent stages of development of agency, from simple agency concerning the ability 'to causally intervene in a sequence of events to [sic] as to change them' to the development of emotional competency and trust and the recognition of a distinct and generalised human agency (i.e. over and above the human agency of parental figures) (Giddens, 1984: 58). Certainly, the research on very young children, for example by Alderson (2000) and Urwin (1984), would provide a significant contrast to any model of the development of agentic capacities and capabilities in the manner Giddens outlines.

Elaborations on Giddens: structural dichotomies

James, Jenks and Prout, in *Theorizing Childhood* (1998) and James and James in *Constructing Childhood* (2004) offer much food for thought in their elaboration and complexification of the structure and agency model. They provide a framework for the sociology of childhood that figures what they see as 'four dominant discourses of childhood' (James, Jenks and Prout, 1998: 199): the socially constructed child; the social structural child; the minority group child; and the tribal child. These discourses or positions are structured in relation to a vertical axis which bundles structure with identity and determinism against agency, volun-tarism and difference. But also along a horizontal axis which bundles particularism, local and change against universalism, global and con-tinuity. The model is intended to map social research on children and childhood in such a way that takes into account the main sociological dynamics. These dynamics (e.g. between the particular and the univer-sal, or structure and agency) are talked about in terms of key

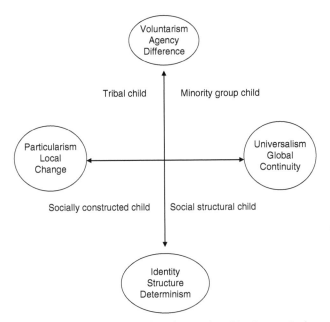

Figure 3.1 Modelling childhood as outlined by James, Jenks and Prout, 1998.

sociological dichotomies. The model, then, is intended to do more than simply map the sociological life of children; it is intended as both an analytical and a hermeneutic aid, but also a model of children's generative sociological existence. As a hermeneutic model, it has its virtues, but it tends to militate against the Giddensian focus on the duality of structure and agency in such a way that hypostatises the poles rather than seeing them as reflexively intertwined, and that hypostatises the four positions of 'the child' (tribal, minority, socially constructed and social structural) in such a way that individualises children as sociological types. The danger, then, is that the model, instead of taking a Giddensian model forward, takes it back to a Parsonian-like model of system and social role. There is a question as to whether more recent versions of this model also repeat this problem of hypostatisation (James and James, 2004).

Conclusion

In this chapter we have considered long-standing discussion in the sociology of childhood on structure and agency, and we have done so using Giddens' analysis as a way of framing the main contours of the debate. For sure, this framing device corsets some writers and some aspects of the debate and some writers thus corseted may not welcome the fact nor recognise such dressing. Nevertheless, the recourse to Giddens helps to typify debates within the sociology of childhood in terms of a fundamental social relation between an individuated agency and a structural totality, both of which are sociological abstractions. The overarching problem with the Giddensian model (and of those inspired by his writing) is that the constitutive and contingent patterning of system (as 'the situated activities of human agents, reproduced across time and space'; Giddens, 1979: 66) is often disavowed in favour of either structure or agency, and in such ways that either totalise, globalise and universalise structure or individualise, localise and particularise agency. A complex, recursive, multilayered and topological sense of system, which may include different forms of materialities, cultural form and social technology, is often foregone in favour of agency in the form of the isolated human individual. The child as social agent is also the reflexive and originary centre of social action. As an atomistic origin of human action, agency itself is never explained. Moreover, the question of the circulation, investment and accumulation of capacity (or power) in the context of system (or infrastructural patterning) is equally foregone in favour of children's agency presented as a social universal. There are clearly problems with an ascription of agency to children as if 'agency' were a social universal, as if the questions of its distribution, accumulation and unevenness were not central questions for empirical investigation, and as if agency simply fell on the shoulders of individuals and not children as collectively defined. In his later writing, Prout acknowledges that '[t]he agency of children as actors is often glossed over, taken to be an essential, virtually unmediated characteristic of humans that does not require much explanation' (Prout, 2005: 65). Of course, the task is to begin to provide an analytics which is able to explain agency in the context of contingent empirical realities.

4 | *Partial and situated agency*

In the context of this broad framing of structure and agency, sociologies of children and childhood have also looked to different ways of understanding agency in terms of social interaction. Social interaction is understood within empirical contexts and inasmuch as the features of that interaction emerge only within that empirical context. Social interaction is broadly conceived as situational. In this chapter I discuss four analytical models concerned with peer cultures, social competence, hegemonic negotiation and tactical agency. All the writers I consider focus on social interaction; but social interaction is framed, whether explicitly or implicitly, within a broader, more fixed and less dynamic sense of children's position and relation to social structure.

Peer cultures

Research which has paid attention to children's cultural interactions has, in many ways, been more attentive to the patterning of children's collective associations. Ethnography, but also conversation analysis, discourse analysis and other forms of qualitative method, it has been argued, allow children's social experience to be made visible and 'allows children a more direct voice and participation in the production of sociological data' (James and Prout, 1990: 8–9). These spaces of association, these collective worlds of children (worlds produced by children, through their social agency), are, to use the terms of Habermas, more akin to 'lifeworld' than 'system'. But they are also cultures inasmuch as these worlds are ways of life.

The work of the sociologist of childhood William Corsaro is illuminating. Corsaro's research on preschool children in Italy and the United States has focussed on children's peer group cultures. For him, what is important is how children of particular age groups interact with each other. These lifeworlds are distinct from those of adults.

As an ethnographer of children's lives, Corsaro 'goes native', tries to get 'inside' the cultural worlds of children, and then to report back to adult experts about those 'exotic' everyday interactions of children. For example, he considers the work involved in maintaining these cultural spaces:

Establishing and maintaining peer interaction are challenging tasks for kids who are in the process of developing the linguistic and cognitive skills necessary for communication and social interaction ... Kids know from experience that at any moment a dispute might arise over the nature of play ('Who should be the mother and who the baby?' 'Should the block go this way or that?'), other kids might want to play or take needed materials, or a teacher might announce 'clean-up time.' Kids work hard to get things going and then, just like that, someone always messes things up. (Corsaro, 2003: 40)

For Corsaro, children's collective social interactions are rule-bound. He talks about 'access strategies' that are used to gain entry to particular forms of social interaction. For example, children wanting to play with another group of children might walk around the group playing ('encircling') and thus not make explicit verbal demands to be allowed to play (see Corsaro, 2003: 42). He argues that children 'collectively teach each other' the rules of participation. The cultural worlds that Corsaro investigates comprise mainly highly localised and face-to-face interaction, namely interaction within conditions of co-presence.

Corsaro talks about peer groups as a 'cohort or group of children who spend time together on an everyday basis' (Corsaro, 2005: 109) and peer culture as 'a stable set of activities or routines, artefacts, values, and concerns that children produce and share in interaction with peers' (131). Peer culture is both symbolic and material. Although Corsaro doesn't say it explicitly, his understanding of 'peer group' is one that is shaped also by a notion of generation, and he conceptualises a clear difference between adult culture and children's culture. Nevertheless, children's peer cultures are not formed in spaces that are exclusively made up of children. Children's peer cultures are formed in families, schools, and also in relation to the media and to toys. Corsaro says:

Families play a key role in the development of peer culture in interpretive reproduction. Children do not individually experience input from the adult world; rather, they participate in cultural routines in which information is first mediated by adults. However, once children begin to move outside the family, their activities with peers and their collective production of a series of peer cultures become just as important as their interactions with adults. (Corsaro, 2005: 131)

Thus, although adults may be absent from some of the peer cultures of older children, for younger children parents, legal guardians, teachers and others play a significant role in arranging and structuring the symbolic and material resources for those younger children. Corsaro has referred to children's relationality between their culture and adults' culture in terms similar to that of the sociologist of 'race', W. E. B. Du Bois. Corsaro talks about children 'creatively tak[ing] information from the adult world to produce their own unique childhood cultures'; 'children are always participating in and are part of two cultures – adults' and kids' – and these cultures are intricately inter-woven' (Corsaro, 2003: 4). The question for us, though, is the extent to which Corsaro's understanding of culture is one essentialised according to a prior structural generational difference. For Corsaro, the term 'culture' allows him to foreground the collectivity and in some sense the solidarity across children (or people within a generational cohort or peer group). But, if children's peer cultures are to some extent mediated and shaped by adults, and if children live across two different cultural spaces of adulthood and childhood, then we might wonder to what extent children have distinct cultures that can be inhabited by either children themselves or by childhood ethnographers, such as Corsaro himself.

Social competence

Ian Hutchby and Jo Moran-Ellis situate their research in the context of 'the present, lived and collective experiences of children' (Hutchby and Moran-Ellis, 1998: 9). Their work stresses an understanding of com-petence not as an a priori of human subjectivity (whether adult or child), but as an accomplishment produced within 'arenas of action'. I should note that, although there is debate about the different mean-ings of 'competence' and 'competency', I use the two interchangeably in this book. Hutchby and Moran-Ellis argue that

The social competence of children is to be seen as a *practical achievement*: that is, it is not something which is accorded to children by adults, like a right, and can thus be redefined or removed. Rather, social competence is seen as something children work at possessing in their own right, the display of which is an active, agentic achievement. (Hutchby and Moran-Ellis, 1998: 14)

Aware of the need to move beyond any moral or political imperative to accord children social agency and competence (as evidenced in much research in the sociology of childhood from the late 1980s to the 1990s), Hutchby and Moran-Ellis frame the issue primarily in empirical terms:

What children's competence actually consists of, the forms that it takes and the relational parameters within which it is enabled or constrained, still need to be ascertained on an empirical level. What research at that empirical level shows is that children's social competence is a constantly negotiated dynamic, a phenomenon which is stabilised, to greater or lesser degrees, in and through the interactions between human actors and the material and cultural resources which are available, and which can be recruited to play a part in the constitution of specific, situated activities. In short, empirical work needs not only to conceptualise children as competent but to establish the *ways* in which children display, can be required to display, and are policed in their displays of social competence. (Hutchby and Moran-Ellis, 1998: 15)

For Hutchby and Moran-Ellis, social competence is not a unitary phenomenon, nor is it something that can be simply possessed (although it might be something that is worked at). Competence can only be demonstrated *in situ*. They argue that social competence cannot be seen 'simply as a property of individuals' and that 'whether it is with other children or with adults, in everyday situations of peer group play or in more formal, adult-framed settings, children's manipulation of culturally available resources to manage the trajectories of interaction, as well as the social impact of others' actions in the setting, represents the true grounding for claims about children's social competence' (Hutchby and Moran-Ellis, 1998: 16). Such situated renderings of children's competence 'reveals a picture of childhood as a dynamic arena of social activity involving struggles for power, contested meanings and negotiated relationships' (16).

Hutchby and Moran-Ellis argue against the ideas that children's competence is a form of 'autonomy from adult-controlled culture' and that 'dependency equals non-competence' is simplistic (Hutchby and Moran-Ellis, 1998: 21). Again, they turn not to a priori models of power and competence, but to empirical investigation. Any differentiation and distribution of competence with regard to children and adults, they argue, can only be settled in particular situated arenas of action. But, if children's competence is to be understood as situated and collective, then there are questions as to how we understand that collectivity. If competence is distributed across the arena of action, across material and cultural resources and across both adults and children, in what sense is the social competence about *children's* social competence? If social competence is understood in the context of children's collective experiential being, then there are further questions as to how that collectivity might be understood. Does Hutchby and Moran-Ellis' model, although focussing on competence as a situated interaction demonstrated empirically, rest on a prior conceptualisation of children as a category of person defined through social structure?

Hegemonic negotiation

Research within cultural studies offers a different way of framing the negotiated collective settlement across adults and young people. Reference is made less to arenas of action than to the institutions, discourses and technologies of power, and in such a way that presents children's and young people's lives as constructed in the context of adult hegemony. Whereas Hutchby and Moran-Ellis are concerned with conversational resources largely in contexts of interpersonal relations, a hegemonic approach has recourse to a larger array and scale of resources. Language, or discourse, is still a focus, but it is framed within a broader political context. James and James draw on this approach and argue that

The overarching reach of such institutional processes to define and separate children as a group apart emphasises the hegemonic control that concepts of 'childhood' – what is thought right and proper for children – exercise over children's experiences at any point in time. These processes are therefore also some of the cultural determinants that are central to a cultural politics of childhood, processes which largely work to oppose childhood to that more powerful and relational concept of 'adulthood' – in other words, children are what adults are not. (James and James, 2004: 21)

In this sense, we might understand children's cultures in terms that are comparable to the way in which cultural studies (e.g. Hall and Jefferson, 1976; Hebdige, 1979) has understood subcultures as being structurally related to (and not disconnected from) the parents' cultures of particular class formations. For example, it may be possible to talk of particular youth cultures, such as those based around music and style (e.g. classically in the work of subcultural theory of the 1970s, the mods, punks, skinheads and Rastafarians), not as essentially generational cultural formations but as cultures shaped only in the context of cultural struggle. In some of this research, generational subculture is certainly understood in the double structuration of class and generation, such that cultural meaning is ideological and analysed as the structural expression of symbolic resistance (Hall and Jefferson, 1976). This work within neo-Gramscian cultural theory was caught between forms of structuralism and culturalism (Hall, 1980). It typified an approach and an engagement with the politics of youth that stretched beyond the analysis of subcultures per se. Paul Willis' account in *Learning to Labour* suggests that the peer group culture of the boys is both a product of the social structure of the school (and hence a product of oppositional power relations, not least between adult and child, but also between middle-class education and working-class manual labour) and also a negotiated space in which the boys (although stereotyped as thick and lazy) are able to construct their own forms of 'learning' (Willis, 1977). Other (later, but still neo-Gramscian) research, though, has understood youth subculture as itself constitutive of popular figurations of young people (Hebdige, 1979 and 1988). Much of the latter research (influenced by the reading of the Italian political theorist Antonio Gramsci by Ernesto Laclau [1977], Stuart Hall [1981] and Tony Bennett [1986]) was much more constructivist. As Hebdige states:

In Gramsci, of course the 'we' is neither 'fatal' … nor given, pre-existent, 'out there' … Instead it is itself the site of struggle. The 'we' in Gramsci has to be *made* and re-made, actively articulated in the double sense, both spoken, uttered and linked with, combined. (It has to be at once positioned *and* brought into being.) (Hebdige, 1988: 205)

In this sense, any cultural construction of children as a collective subjectivity is understood in anti-essentialist terms. There is no prior, fixed or essential being of children. Similarly, there is no prior, fixed or authentic children's culture (i.e. as defined, for example, by play or innocence). Rather, children's being, their positionality and their cultural form are consequences and effects of institutional power, discourse and cultural negotiation and contestation. Instead of prioritising conditions of co-presence, this research has an understanding of the cultural formation of collectivities in the context of media and cultural technologies in late modernity. Any sociology of children needs to understand how children's cultural collectivity is mediated not only through face-to-face encounters, but also through a whole array of media and cultural technologies (Buckingham, 2000; Livingstone, 2002). Research in media, communication and cultural studies has developed this understanding (not only, or always, with direct reference to neo-Gramscian theory) not only with reference to 'youth' but also to children (Kinder, 1999). A central aspect of this research is also one of understanding the agency of young people in contesting the media texts and interpretations of the very category of 'childhood' and the terms of their collective belonging (Bazalgette and Buckingham, 1995; Buckingham, 2000).

[C]hildren may resist, or refuse to recognize themselves, in adult definitions – and in this respect, adult power is very far from absolute or uncontested. Nevertheless, their space for resistance is largely that of interpersonal relationships, amid the 'micro-politics' of the family or the classroom. Furthermore, children may be actively complicit in sustaining these definitions of what is 'adult' or 'child-like', if only by default: age differences, and the meanings that are attached to them, are a primary means through which power relationships are enacted, not only between adults and children, but also between children themselves. (Buckingham, 2000: 13)

These cultures are not only for children, they are of children; they are made by both children and adults and the terms of participation are defined in the context of these cultural struggles, negotiations and structures of consent. Nevertheless, however much this theoretical perspective pushes an idea of the 'we', of 'children' and of 'young people' as a consequence of discursive negotiation, there is still on the receding horizon a structural form within which generational difference and positionality is marked. Certainly for some of the earlier cultural studies writers, this dichotomy comes from the Gramscian engagement with the long-standing Marxist problem of the relation between economic structure and cultural form.

Tactical agency

Alcinda Honwana, in her research on young combatants in Mozam-
bique, draws attention to what she refers to as 'tactical agency'. These
young people, she observes, do not have access to the resources to
construct and build space, to control the resources of the built and
governmentalised environment; their agency, by contrast, is 'devised to
cope with the concrete, immediate conditions of their lives in order to
maximize the circumstances created by their military and violent environment' (Honwana, 2005: 49). Honwana finds this notion of tactical
agency in part from Michel de Certeau, who contrasts Foucault's
disciplinary society, a society in which space is strategically controlled
and regulated, with the power of the weak, who occupy space only
through their mobility and their ability to turn it through their movement. Where strategy and strength are conceived in spatial terms,
tactics and weakness are seen as more temporal; the only space the
weak occupy is the space of the other, from which they emerge and
return. Although Honwana does not discuss this, the idea of resistance
that comes from de Certeau also finds its genealogy in theorisations of
urban guerrilla warfare from the 1950s, 1960s and 1970s (Guevara,
Marighella, Red Army Faction and others) that see it as a form of
struggle which is hidden, dissimulated, swift, and which draws on
the resources of the powerful, urban and incisive. For de Certeau, space
and strategy are Cartesian and geometric, such that space contains
and encloses people and objects; in contrast, tactics and time are topological inasmuch as they are defined in terms of vectors and trajectories
(De Certeau, 1984). For de Certeau, strategy concerns 'the calculus
(or the manipulation) of relations of force which becomes possible
whenever a subject of will and power (a business enterprise, an army,
a city, a scientific institution) can be isolated' (De Certeau, 1984: 5).
It is the 'victory of place over time', the mastery of place by vision and
the power of knowing (typified by the ordering of legible spaces) (5).
In contrast, tactics concern the absence of a proper place, movement,
non-totalising, blow-by-blow, poaching and surprises. De Certeau talks
about tactics in terms of memory. He says, in a move reminiscent of
Derrida's interpretation of Freud's mystic writing pad (1968):

memory does its work in a locus which is not its own. It receives its form and
its implantation from external circumstances ... Its mobilization is inseparable

from *alteration*; indeed, memory draws its very capacity to intervene from its alterability – mobile, adaptable, without a fixed locus. It has this permanent feature: it forms itself (and its 'capital') by *emerging from the other* (from circumstance), which it now *loses* (this being no more than a memory): whence a twofold change, both in itself (since its modification is the condition of its own exercise) and of its object, retained only when it is lost. (De Certeau, 1984: 40)

For de Certeau, strategy and tactics are two logics of action. But whereas strategy names action linked to power, tactics names action linked to its reversal, its alteration. For Honwana, tactical agency is also defined as 'interstitial agency'. This is an agency that is not defined through a logic of identity but through a logic of the hybrid, of the in-between. She states that 'By virtue of this borderland condition, they are able to be mobile and grab opportunities the moment they arise' (Honwana, 2005: 50).

Tactical interstitial agency, then, has a more creative, experimental relation to the structures and resources to hand. Children and young people, who so often are denied access to resources and to the means of accumulating resources, find strength through their creative *bricolage*, through their makeshift mash-ups and their making do. Adults, in contrast, so often control the resources, the means of reproduction; they control the space; they make the environment; they build the schools, the homes, the television sets and the computer networks; they people the police, the teachers, the parents and the social workers. This is a schema which sites two camps, the strong and the weak, and the structural form of the one is the inversion of the other. And yet, what are the consequences of this de Certeauan schema? A generational division is mapped on to a division between space and time, strategy and tactics, power and resistance, Foucault and de Certeau. Does not the schema itself replay a spatial geometric separation of generational difference? Is not, then, the nomination of 'strong' and 'weak' the naming of power? Inasmuch as it endures (or, rather, inasmuch as it makes a change that remains), does not the nomination of 'weak' constitute an articulation of power? For de Certeau, the weak comes from the Other (as the condition of its action and its voice): 'The place from which one speaks is outside the scriptural enterprise' (De Certeau, 1984: 158). Of course, Foucault's retort is that power is a site of productivity, precisely at the level of enunciation.

But more than this, enunciation from the site of the Other relies on the resources that are to hand. As Valerian Voloshinov argued some years ago, there is no inner voice, pure and of itself. All enunciation is oriented to another. But more than that, all enunciation and all action relies on its externalisation through material resources in such a way that the force of the enunciation, or the action, is mediated by virtue of that externalisation, by virtue of those resources that are to hand. Tactical interstitial agency is thus, perhaps, lacking a place, a secure and permanent site from which to build a fortress. And yet it finds itself some place. In the gathering of resources, some environment is built, however provisional. Of course, once we consider the process of externalisation and the accumulation of the resources that are to hand, we necessarily involve others who have a stake in the use and utility of those resources. These others may be other people, but equally they may be simply the recalcitrance of objects themselves, or the objectity (to use Latour's terms [2000]) of things, such that this 'public' place is not simply owned nor disowned by tactical agents. Moreover, the building of agency with others (people, animals and things) relies not only on things which are fleeting, insecure and impermanent, but also on things which are more enduring, and yet other things which seem permanent, unmoveable, resilient. The demonstration of agency (to use the term which Andrew Barry has explored [2001]) is across various forms of duration and materiality. To act is to act in an environment which is not static, not a structure, but which is constituted through different and uneven securities and insecurities, permanence and impermanence, swiftness and sluggishness. The earth is not made up of a single substance, and agency resonates through different substances and is demonstrated (or performed) through that variation. In addition, we need to grasp that the things and people through which agency resonates are not all the same size; they are not all of the same scale. Some are large and some are small; some are buildings and some are teeth; some are states and some are clothes. Agency is interstitial, but it is also infrastructured.

Conclusion

In this chapter we have considered analytical models which stress the partial, conditional, situated, empirical and collective disclosure of children within social settings. It is through these writings that we also begin to see how children's agency is far from residing within the individual child as an originary point of origin. That said, although there is an emphasis on the contingent nature of agency as performed in particular empirical contexts, the setting for these localised negotiations has the stamp (however residual) of social structure. Moreover, whereas, on the one hand, microsociological work on conversational and linguistic social interaction stresses conditions of co-presence, interpersonal relationality (if not intersubjectivity) and the delimitation of resources within the spatial and temporal present and, on the other hand, a cultural studies approach looks to institutions and discourses and the relation between subject and institution, there is in both approaches an overemphasis on children's talk and on children's collective presence as defined through linguistic or discursive resources. Although there are different models of discourse deployed (from models of conversation to those of Foucauldian discursive formation), discourse is seen as the medium through which children's experience and collective agency is demonstrated. Some sociologists of children have been critical of reducing agency to discursive agency and instead have turned to research on agency as material, heterogeneous and distributed across social, technological and natural resources and media. It is to these discussions that we turn next.

5 | Subjectivity, experience and post-social assemblages

The sociology of childhood in the early 1990s was often too quick to conflate children's experience with social agency and too quick to dismiss some contemporary theoretical approaches which seemed to deny children experiential authenticity and agency. But it is precisely in such approaches (which some have called 'postmodern' and others 'post-structuralist') that we find a sense of agency which is both dispersed, or distributed, but also fractured, or disarticulated. Post-structuralist approaches, broadly conceived, have been concerned with the unsettling and decentring of the subject (in terms of their originary cognitive individuality, experience, authenticity and authority) by virtue of the fact of language as a symbolic system and of the unconscious. Through a focus on language, discourse and narrative, any notion of agency as centred on the individual child is criticised on the bases of the fracturing of subjectivity and its constructed and performative nature. Dramatic languages of actor, staging, performance and *mise en scène* (stage setting) are often deployed in critical accounts to emphasise the constructed and decentred nature of subjectivity. But the post-structuralist turn has itself been criticised and problematised through a thoroughgoing anti-humanist set of approaches which intend to analyse social relations in terms of objects, material culture, technologies and devices. In this materialist turn there is a sense in which agency is now understood in terms of its being both human and non-human, both social and technological, and both cultural and natural. It is in the context of both these turns (post-structuralist and materialist) that a descriptive detailing is made available which has both problematised any notion of children's agency and made its observation deeper and richer.

Subjectivity and experience

For the sociology of childhood in the 1990s, the Foucauldian discourse analytic and post-structuralist approaches seemed to offer the child only from an adult perspective, seemed to deny any agency to children, and seemed to construct children's experience only as an effect of discourse and power. Some of these accusations are certainly correct. The largely historical and literary methodological focus considered mainly texts and documents written by adults about children. The focus on constructions seemed to take away precisely what the sociology of childhood seemed to offer, namely an agency for children. That said, it is nevertheless worthwhile returning to that earlier work, which considers the child as a discursive construction and as instituted within fields of regulation, in order to tease out an understanding of agency that is predicated on a notion of the subject as non-unitary and distributed across language and the unconscious, not least because it allows us to move beyond any simplistic analysis that assumes a fit between the individual, agency and experience.

In writing on the social production of childhood, influenced by thinkers as diverse as the historian of ideas Michel Foucault, the French psychoanalyst Jacques Lacan, and the linguist Emile Benveniste, the 'child' is seen not as something that has a distinct and separate ontology, or form of existence, from the 'adult', but rather as something that is constructed only as a discursive position, or more broadly, as a position within regimes of power and knowledge. Foucauldian accounts of the discursive positioning of the child subject (at least those ones developed within the context of the social sciences) have talked not just of discourse but also of the relations across discourses, practices and social institutions. The early work of the social psychologist Valerie Walkerdine is notable in this respect. Walkerdine's work on the regulation of the child subject within early years schooling is primarily sociological in tone. Walkerdine, in her work on primary school learning in the UK, looks at the intersection of the discourse of developmental psychology, the practices of child-centred classroom teaching and the institution of the primary school (1984). These practices intersect to produce and regulate the child as a developmental learning subject. Thus she argues: 'What I aim to demonstrate is that the very lynchpin of developmental psychology, the "developing child", is an object premised on the location of certain capacities within "the child" and therefore within the domain of psychology' (Walkerdine, 1984: 154). The 'developing child', as a particular subject position, is one produced and regulated within specific discursive and institutional arrangements that can be conceptualised as 'regimes of truth', to borrow from Foucault's terminology. Walkerdine states:

Particular disciplines, regimes of truth, bodies of knowledge, make possible both *what can be said* and *what can be done*: both the object of science and the object of pedagogic practices. Pedagogic practices then are totally saturated with the notion of a normalized sequence of child development, so that those practices help produce children as the objects of their gaze. The apparatuses and mechanisms of schooling which do this range from the architecture of the school and the seating arrangements of the classroom to the curriculum materials and techniques of assessment. (Walkerdine, 1984: 155)

She is not saying, however, that these apparatuses are uniform in their make-up or their effects, nor that they are the same wherever they are to be found (from one school to another), but that they constitute a form of diagram of power, knowledge and subjectivity.

Although its use of a Foucauldian analysis of discourse and power allows a focus on discursive practice rather than social structure, such an account does seem to present the child only as a construct of the agency of others. In order to deconstruct the allocation of 'psychological capacity' in the child, it foregoes understanding of *any* capacities in the child. However, in her later work on media and culture, Walkerdine draws equally on a post-structural psychoanalytic understanding of subjectivity to frame the complex tensions concerning the positioning of the child and the fantasy relations of children. Here there is talk of structure; not social structure as such, but the structure of the subject (unconscious and conscious) and the structure of desire with respect to language as the structure of the symbolic order. The relation between the structure of the subject (and the mechanism of identification) and particular discursive formations has been the focus of much discussion within post-structural theory. Nevertheless, Walkerdine writes: 'structures are activated in specific ways according to what happens to and the fantasies held by any particular person. This brings the theory much closer to one which allows any subject their own specific history and not a subjectivity determined by the content of media representations' (Walkerdine, 1997: 177).

Central to Walkerdine's analysis is the attempt to understand not only the power of discourse to position and regulate subjects, but also to recognise the investments that subjects have in particular fantasies (e.g. regarding control or seduction) and hence to understand the processes whereby subjects get hooked into certain discourses. However, for Walkerdine any interpellation of a subject by discourse is always mediated by the structures of fantasy that underpin the subject. Moreover, the structure of any particular fantasy cannot be seen to determine the positionality within that fantasy structure. Freud's interpretation of dreams and the unconscious (1991) is instructive here. Freud's analysis of one particular dream concerns a fantasy structure that can be repeated as 'A child is being beaten.' For the subject of this fantasy, there is not one positionality but rather there are many. The subject could identify with the child, with the one who beats, with the act of beating or with the *mise en scène* of the dream itself. At root in this analysis is the notion that agency cannot be located in a particular acting individual. Instead, agency must be seen to be distributed across the unconscious, the conscious and language. Agency must be seen, in this approach, across the discursive or narrative positionalities within the fantasy.

The work of the French psychoanalyst Jacques Lacan is significant here, inasmuch as he provides an account of the entry of the infant into language and of the formation of the subject, and he explicitly talks about agency in terms of the letter in the unconscious, an agency that is nevertheless dispersed throughout the symbolic. In an early essay, he talks about the infant as a mass of drives, a form of being closely tied to the mother. In this state of being the infant knows no other. The infant and the mother constitute a dyadic pair. The infant only becomes a subject as such – namely, as one who has a sense of self that is distinct from others – with its entry into the symbolic order of language. The entry into language is seen, by Lacan, as a form of alienation from an imaginary wholeness with the mother. The unitary individual is seen as a myth of wholeness, an imaginary fixation. For Lacan, then, subjectivity is constituted in the complex that is the alienation of desire, in the distribution of the self in language as a collective phenomenon, and in the division between conscious and unconscious. What is said and known by the subject can never be transparent, the basis of reflexive knowledge and the means of control. On the contrary, in this model, such knowledge is itself open to the disturbance of the unconscious and to the processes of language. In this sense, children in their entry into the symbolic, in their creation as subjects with language, are alienated from any control over their subjectivity and any transparent knowledge of self or world. Children have agency only inasmuch as they are alienated from that agency (which is dispersed through language and the unconscious). Children, as it were, are given the driving seat of a car with no controls, but with the illusion of a steering wheel that works, and a whole lot of baggage that keeps popping up from the back seat, distracting the driving.

Whereas in the Giddensian account of agency the individual social actor has recourse to experience (or the reflexive relationality to time and space) as the condition of social action, for post-structural accounts of subjectivity experience is decentred and held to account only inasmuch as it is constructed within language. As I said above, post-structural understandings of the subject have been articulated by different writers from different traditions. Giorgio Agamben, in *Infancy and History: The Destruction of Experience* (2006), provides an authoritative account of the philosophical reasoning of experience, the subject and maturity running from the sixteenth century to the twentieth century. He discusses the separation of experience and science in Montaigne and focusses on how death is conceived as the limit of experience; experience is conceived in the context of the movement toward death, namely in the context of maturity. Then, through a discussion from Descartes to Kant to Husserl and Heidegger on the relation between the transcendental and the empirical, he comes to the twentieth-century concern with language and subjectivity. In Freud, Agamben sees a reversal of the relationship between experience and maturity, such that the limit of experience is now turned backwards toward infancy; a passage that he also sees in grammatical terms as a turn from the first to the third person inasmuch as the primary site of experience is now seen as the unconscious. In Benveniste and others, Agamben understands the 'I' as a textual position and infancy as providing that 'moat' between language as a system and discourse as utterance. He provocatively states that

The constitution of the subject in and through language is precisely the expropriation of this 'wordless' experience; from the outset, it is always 'speech'. A primary experience, far from being subjective, could then only be what in human beings comes before the subject – that is, before language: a 'wordless' experience in the literal sense of the term, a human *infancy*, whose boundary would be marked by language. (Agamben, 2006: 54)

There is no pure experience from which either voice or agency emerges. What we get from Agamben, but also from many others, is that the splitting of the subject into conscious and unconscious, but also the 'I' of the statement (the subject of the enounced) and the subject speaking the statement (the subject of the enunciation), places a big question mark over the authority of any statement and any subject. Cultural critic Homi Bhabha, for example, states that

> The concept of cultural difference focuses on the problem of the ambivalence of cultural authority; the attempt to dominate in the *name* of a cultural supremacy which is itself produced only in the moment of differentiation. And it is the very authority of culture as a knowledge of referential truth which is at issue in the concept and moment of *enunciation*. The enunciative process introduces a split in the performative present, of cultural identification; a split between the traditional culturalist demand for a model, a tradition, a community, a stable system of reference – and the necessary negation of the certitude in the articulation of new cultural demands, meanings, strategies in the political present, as a practice of domination, or resistance. (Bhabha, 1988: 19)

There is no simple certainty regarding such authority because there is no simple authorisation of meaning. In this argument, meaning and the identity of the subject (i.e. as if it were a discrete unitary individual) are only fixed as an imaginary relation, as a mythical or ideological certainty, or as cemented within a regime of knowledge and power.

The impact of this post-structural turn and the focus on subjectivity as both split and dispersed through the symbolic order of language is radical in terms of how we understand children's agency. On the one hand, it means that we must be sceptical of claims which simply collapse experience and agency into an individual child. But on the other, more positively it means that

(a) we are able to investigate the dispersion of discourses on and about children and childhood
(b) we are able to consider the positionalities of 'the child', 'children' and 'childhood' within those discourses
(c) we are able, as with Walkerdine, to investigate how those discourses and positions are also correlated with relations of power
(d) we are also able *not* to assume that those who identify with those discourses on children and childhood are themselves 'empirical children' (i.e. they could be adults), but also that those discourses

may in fact be, even in the first instance, primarily addressed not to children but to others (e.g. adults)

(e) we are able to differentiate between the spoken child (the subject of the statement, of the enounced), who is spoken about in discourses, and the speaking child (the subject of enunciation), who is positioned through the act of speaking (or reading or receiving)

(f) we are able, moreover, to understand that such a differentiation between speaking and spoken subject is not rooted in a unitary individual speaker, but is a relational (or textual) construction, such that we may see relations of speaking within relations of speaking (i.e. as a layering over layers, a palimpsest)

(g) we are able to understand how the relations of speaking, of the voices and the genres through which voice is spoken, are dependent on a genealogical field of other voices, texts and speaking relations

(h) and, finally, we are able to understand that our capacity to speak as children with experience and with respect to our claims about those experiences does not imply that our utterances are able to secure those claims, to control their meaning or to authenticate them.

Thus the impact of the post-structural turn on the social study of children has been to frame questions of agency as questions located within the domain of language and the symbolic inasmuch as that domain is a complex of voices, agency, speaking relations and forms of power. Neither child nor adult can speak in a manner which draws on their experience as a source of either power or truth. Any authorial or authoritative voice is always differentiated and dispersed through other voices and texts. Social relations in this sense are akin to a novelistic text, in which the author writing may adopt a particular position and voice as a narrator; in turn the narrator may tell a story in the context of other characters and plot, such that the characters have voices; but also such that, in turn, those characters may narrate stories with characters and plot; and in turn this textuality of the novel problematises the notion of the author as him or herself standing outside the text as their position is similarly told within another text (or series of texts). Social relations, in this sense, are understood as dialogical and intertextual.

That said, there are certainly problems with understanding the constitution of the subject in the context of language, as if the experiential were primarily or only mediated through the symbolic. The writing of Karin Knorr-Cetina has helped to reframe Lacanian models of subjectivity in the context not only of a symbolic order, but also of a post-social order that is littered with both words and things (Knorr-Cetina, 2001). In late modernity, she argues, the subject recognises and misrecognises itself across material worlds. The subject has agency in a world of objects, but such that its agency is decentred and distributed across those objects. For Knorr-Cetina, any understanding of the constitution of the subject must take account not only of the human, but of the non-human as well. She argues that 'the self need not be seen as frozen into a lacking subjectivity for life at the mirror stage. It is at least as plausible to conceive of lacks in a more sociological idiom as permanently recreated by relevant institutional processes in a post-industrial society' (Knorr-Cetina and Bruegger, 2002: 173). For Knorr-Cetina, the attempt to recognise oneself in the mirror is no longer framed within the imaginary pre-Oedipal stage of the mother–infant dyad, but across the various media and forms of consumer culture. It is this sense of the distribution of subjectivity, not only or primarily through language but through a material post-social world (including images, media, languages and objects), which helps to frame our understanding of children's agency as infrastructured or as constructed within and across infrastructural cultures.

Material, heterogeneous and distributed agency

There has been an interest in the research of Michel Callon, Bruno Latour and others associated with what has been called actor-network theory or the sociology of translation. This line of thought has been especially useful in helping scholars understand children as both natural and cultural; it is also significant in providing intellectual resources for thinking about agency, not as located within the individual child faced against social structure, but as itself distributed across a network of agents or actors, both human and non-human. The term Callon and Latour use is neither agent nor actor, but 'actant'. This is a term that derives from the structural semantics of A. J. Greimas in his analysis of the structural and generative elements of narrative. For Greimas, the notion of an actant defines a narrative device above and below the level of character, inasmuch as it defines a narrative function which may be adopted by a single character or by a group of characters, but equally a single character may embody more than one actantial function (Oswell, 2006). Thus, in the story of the Wizard of Oz, Glinda the good witch of the north constitutes a single actant (the helper, who helps Dorothy). But equally, that actantial function of helping may be seen to be distributed across other characters as well, such as the Scarecrow, the Tin Man and the Lion. For actor-network theory, though, the notion of actant is used to foreground the fact that the characters or agents of a network may be both human and non-human.

Across sociology and cultural theory from the 1990s there has been a material turn which has sought to understand more concertedly relations across the human and the non-human. For example, the work of Donna Haraway has been centrally important in figuring subjectivity as fundamentally 'cyborg' (i.e. human and machine) in late modernity (Haraway, 1991). Some of this work within the sociology of childhood has been explored in the context of the body (Prout, 2000) and some more generally in relation to social theories of childhood (Castañeda, 2002; Prout, 2005). For us here, these resources help to provide an understanding of and to initiate a discussion about association, materiality and the distribution of agency in order to think about children's agency as assembled or infrastructured across the human and the non-human. Prout, drawing on this kind of approach, argues that 'Using the metaphor of "network" it suggests that childhood could be seen as a collection of different, sometimes competing and sometimes conflicting, heterogeneous orderings. These can be fragile but they can also be stabilized, become widespread and, therefore, found on a large scale' (Prout, 2005: 71). He goes on to discuss how actor-network theory provides a way of avoiding any opposition between structure and agency by recognising, in the first instance, that actors are hybrid entities (both human and non-human, natural and social), but also that stabilised entities, such as 'structures', are consequences of the process of the stabilisation of a network of actors. Structures, in this sense, Prout argues, do not pre-exist their mobilisation as such. Networks can stabilise, but equally fail. Prout argues that 'new forms of childhood arise when new sets of network connections, for example between children and technologies such as TV and the internet, are made'. He continues: 'A key question, therefore, is what makes up the network that produces a particular form of childhood?' (71–2).

We should perhaps note here that Giddens' whole theoretical project concerned the overcoming of the dualism of structure and agency and his understanding of the duality of structuration are attempts to envisage structure as a contingent outcome of agency. Moreover, his understanding of system as the practical domain of interaction, understood as it was through ethnomethodology and symbolic interactionism, appears very similar (albeit stripped of the human–non-human hybridity) to the notion of an actor-network as described by Prout (and also to how Prout develops the ideas of actor-network theory in subsequent sections). The significant difference between the concept of system, as discussed by Giddens, and actor-network, as discussed by Callon and Latour but also by Prout, is that the former is often conceived as an organic totality that is able to reproduce itself, but also change according to systems of information and feedback, whereas the latter is one that is conceived in terms of the openness of the network with regard to the mobilisation of new actors. Whereas systems theory presupposes the givenness of the system prior to its instantiation and hence is able to analyse the development and change within any given system or systems, actor-network theory promises to only consider the actor-network as a consequence or outcome of mobilisation. Theoretically (although rarely in empirical investigation), it is also able to consider the falling apart of any actor-network.

Actor-network theory talks about the mobilisation of different actors to form particular actor-networks, such that actors become spokespersons for other actors mobilised within the network (see Callon, 1986; Callon and Latour, 1981). Such an understanding might construe the process of representation in any network as itself a form of repression, of speaking for another in the other's absence. Such an understanding would certainly be useful for the sociology of childhood in terms of its offering the possibility of thinking about children as so frequently constructed in the representations and knowledges of adults. Actor-network theory is thoroughly anti-humanist. It offers a methodology which doesn't rest on the consciousness or reflexivity of the human individual. We might imagine not children as whole individuals, but as part objects. For example, ophthalmology considers the child's eye (or even bits of the eye) in relation to particular technologies of measurement and particular technologies of vision in order to construct a notion of 'normal sight'. Or, the dental surgeon is not interested in the development of the whole child, but primarily with the teeth (or rather with the whole child only inasmuch as that entity might have an impact on the health of the mouth) and with the relationality of teeth and the mouth to decay, hygiene and daily conduct (e.g. brushing of teeth). In this sense, actor-network theory has opened the way to investigation of particular configurations of bodies of different kinds.

Actor-network theory is fundamentally interested in thinking about the association between things and the organisation of those things, such that the association and organisation have no form or substance prior to their collective actualisation. It is as a result of that radical understanding of contingency that actor-network theory has in many ways also moved beyond any simple logic of representation. If, during a regular sight test, the ophthalmologist speaks for the child's eye and for the child's vision, it is not because the child's eye has been *spoken over*, as it were, by the ophthalmologist, but because the materiality of the eye (and its ability to see in certain ways rather than others) affords certain things that can be said about it, and it does so in the context of the voice of the child in recounting what the eye sees on the wall chart. The expertise of the ophthalmologist needs these others in order to speak authoritatively. The expert does not speak alone, but only collectively with others. In that sense, there is a process of translation across these material entities and actor-network theory, as a sociology of translation, is able to investigate this translation as it is fundamentally about sociality as an association and a relationality between things, *in media res* (see Oswell, 2006). But although actor-network theory provides a model of thinking agency and networks as necessarily connected, and although when Latour says 'follow the actors' he means any actors – from viruses to motor cars – the analytical framing of actor-networks means that all actors become both reduced to atomistic entities and conceived with respect to a single scale or plane. The fact that Callon and Latour (as with systems theory) state that if one actor changes in the network then all the elements change doesn't mean that the interdependent relationality is multiscalar. And that is perhaps a problem.

Post-social assemblages and collectivities

Other writers have also considered the question of solidarity across different heterogeneous materialities. Thus, Gilles Deleuze and Felix Guattari talk about the 'rhizome' as the abstract form of particular organisations of different materialities (Deleuze and Guattari, 1983) and about 'assemblages' or arrangements as particular formations across materialities that have recourse to an ideal-typical generative and formative source, or in their terms, an 'abstract machine' (Deleuze and Guattari, 1988; see also, for a discussion regarding childhood, Lee, 2001 and 2005). But the use of the term 'assemblage' or 'arrangement' in this chapter owes as much to its use by those working within actor-network theory, and is to be seen as part of a broader 'semiotics of materiality' (Law, 1999: 4). Assemblage is the translation of the French word *agencement*, which ordinarily would be translated as arrangement. The sense it is given here is that of the overriding primacy of the eventfulness of connections with and between 'stuff' (both things and people). An arrangement carries with it the connotations not only of network, which may appear sometimes static and flat, but of an assemblage which is a composition of dynamic, generative and agentic parts, such that those parts have temporality, movement and capacity only by virtue of their being composed or arranged. In the discussion that follows we get a sense also of how the notion of assemblage borrows from broader discussions about power, infrastructure and collectivity.

Foucault's apparatus

In some ways, the notion of the assemblage is similar to Foucault's notion of the apparatus (*dispositif*) as a 'heterogeneous ensemble'. But perhaps more so for Foucault, the organisation of materialities is intimately tied to the actualisation of power, inasmuch as power relations have no prior form and are only made visible in particular relations across institutions, practices and discourses. He defines 'apparatus' accordingly: firstly, it is 'a thoroughly heterogeneous ensemble', including in some instances 'discourses, institutions, architectural forms, regulatory decisions, laws, administrative measures, scientific statements, philosophical, moral and philanthropic propositions – in short, the said as much as the unsaid'; secondly, any element is not fixed and can change its function, meaning and position, in the sense that 'a discourse can figure at one time as the programme of an institution, and at another it can function as a means of justifying or masking a practice which itself remains silent'; thirdly, it is 'the system of relations that can be established between these elements'; fourthly, it is defined in terms of its relation within a field of force relations; fifthly, within these force relations the apparatus takes on a strategic function, for example, in the control of an unruly population and the socialisation of that population into a functioning economy; and sixthly, its formation is always premised on an experimentation and innovation, it is never a repetition of the same (Foucault, 1979: 92–3; 1980: 194–5; Deleuze, 1992). The apparatus is not defined by something external to it; it is not made intelligible with reference to one particular logic or model. Rather, the organisation of the apparatus is immanent to itself; it is 'the multiplicity of force relations immanent in the sphere in which they operate and which constitute their own organization' (Foucault, 1979: 92). The apparatus is not external to power; it is the shape and organisation of power; it is the singularity, or specificity, of power.

We can certainly draw on a Foucauldian analysis of the *dispositif* to understand how a relation across particular discourses of childhood is mobilised across particular institutions and practices and in the context of particular populations. Nikolas Rose, for example, has explored in detail how 'the child' has been discursively figured within the discipline of psychology in terms of 'adjustment' and 'maladjustment', how these discursive figurations are mapped across institutional practices such as the school and the family, and how knowledge of the child in these terms constitutes forms of normalisation and pathologisation (Rose, 1985 and 1989). The arrangement of power and knowledge is directed toward the child, but in doing so others (parents, teachers and so on) are caught within its operations. In that sense, power is not understood in binary terms (i.e. there are those who do have it and those who don't); rather, its workings are more insidious and fluid. Moreover, in Rose's analysis, but also in that of Foucault himself (Foucault, 1979) or his followers such as Jacques Donzelot (Donzelot, 1979), there is no simple contest of power between social structure and agency or between the state (as a unitary entity) and the individual. In this sense, power is not located as a possession in the hands of the adult, the parent, the expert or the state. On the contrary, power is inventive, creative and contingent. Power is disaggregated across different forms of organisation. Power is relational with respect to resistance and freedom. Resistance is not the unitary domain that opposes power, but rather it is its support and is itself the emergent field of counter-powers (Foucault, 1979). Freedom again is not the limit of power; it is not that which power seeks to control and repress. Freedom, in the context of modern advanced liberal regimes of authority, is that which constitutes a pivotal relay in the extension of power. Power works, not against, but through freedom. The agencies of power are collective, decentred and disaggregated in particular contingent associations and *dispositifs*, but also that agency is itself the outcome of power. Such that what is seen as having agency within particular situations – from a dental surgery to an opticians to a school classroom or a family sitting room – is constituted as an effect of the particularities of the arrangement and the visibility of a particular problem or set of problems. A Foucauldian understanding of *dispositif* provides an understanding of the relationality across disaggregated complex materialities and of their relationality to relations of power. An understanding of the effectivity of the *dispositif* also allows us to investigate its capacity to endow capacity upon elements. Subjects are constructed with capacities inasmuch as those subjects are understood in the context of relations across individual, population and government.

People as infrastructure

The analytical models of the network and the *dispositif* provide important resources for any sociology of childhood. They raise significant questions regarding power, agency, materiality and solidarity. They do so in a manner that questions the spatiality of organisation and the geography of power. And they do so in a manner that allows us to consider 'childhood' as a circulated, contested image, 'the child' as constructed through particular regimes of power and knowledge, 'child parts' as constituent elements which have an effect on the regulation and lives of children, and children as a collectivity endowed with capacity. Moreover, the formation of these 'objects' may be considered in such a way that the necessary distributiveness of agency and power means that all those agents in the configuration of either alliances or networks are affected. Thus, experts, parents, schools, homes and so on are all affected in the particular agentic configurations through which the child or childhood or child parts or children are the primary object of concern. In such a mix, it would be easy to lose sight of people, of children as people. Abdoumaliq Simone, in his ethnography of Johannesburg, provides an analytical tone which holds the significance of an analysis of the material sociological assemblage without losing the fragility, resourcefulness and inventiveness and the blood, sweat and toil of people. The term he uses is 'infrastructure', and he defines it as follows.

Infrastructure is commonly understood in physical terms, as reticulated systems of highways, pipes, wires, or cables. These modes of provisioning and articulation are viewed as making the city productive, reproducing it, and positioning its residents, territories, and resources in specific ensembles where the energies of individuals can be most efficiently deployed and accounted for. By contrast, I wish to extend the notion of infrastructure directly to people's activities in the city. African cities are characterized by incessantly flexible, mobile, and provisional intersections of residents that operate without clearly delineated notions of how the city is to be inhabited and used. These intersections, particularly in the last two decades, have depended on the ability of residents to engage complex combinations of objects, spaces, persons, and practices. These conjunctions become an infrastructure – a platform providing for and reproducing life in the city. Indeed, as I illustrate through a range of ethnographic materials on inner-city Johannesburg, an experience of regularity capable of anchoring the livelihoods of residents and their transactions with one another is consolidated precisely because the outcomes of residents' reciprocal efforts are radically open, flexible, and provisional. In other words, a specific economy of perception and collaborative practice is constituted through the capacity of individual actors to circulate across and become familiar with a broad range of spatial, residential, economic, and transactional positions. Even when actors do different things with one another in differ-ent places, each carries traces of past collaboration and an implicit willingness to interact with one another in ways that draw on multiple social positions. (Simone, 2004: 407–8)

Such an approach suggests that there is no prior structure or even structure as an ideal-type (i.e. as a consequence of the systemic patternings in the time-space). It offers a way of thinking about the dynamic and complex topologies of organising. But importantly it does so without losing sight of people. For example, the HIV virus that is passed on at birth, the anti-retroviral drugs taken at regular intervals throughout the day, the silence and secrecy of the condition, the fear regarding school mates and the routine visits to the hospital: these constitute a collection of partial objects connected to other arrange-ments, but also connected to each other in the context of a very singular case of a 16-year-old girl living in north London. These are 'collectively shared experiences, dispersed across different arrangements. But where is the centre to this? And what holds them together? To talk of children as people does not imply that people are the glue which does the binding together; it is simply to stress that they are a significant part of this assemblage.

Children as a collectivity

But what kind of collectivity might 'children' be and how might that collectivity be reconsidered in the context of the complex topologies of ideas, power and materiality discussed above? Over and above any questions about the extent to which 'children' constitutes a class in itself (as structure) or a class for itself (collective self-consciousness), there is a major question as to whether it makes sense to construe children as a collectivity. Allison James and Adrian James make this problem very clear when they say: 'it is ... the case that even within one generation of children, in any one society, each child's experiences of "childhood" will nonetheless be tempered by the particularities of their social circumstances' (James and James, 2004: 22). Children are centrally constituted through differences of age, sexuality, gender, class, disability, geographical location and various other particularities of upbringing. Children as a collectivity comprise a multitude of experiences and positionalities.

If children are constituted as a collectivity, it is not because all children within that class of persons are the same. Such an understanding of class (i.e. in the sense of class and classification, and not simply social class) would be one that reduced a class of things to a single sign or measure, one that disavowed the possibility of difference within a single class, and one that conceived of difference only in terms of identity (Deleuze, 1994). Already in the discussion above we have seen that contemporary thinking on the matter of collective agency conceptualises collectivity as a multiplicity, such that each singular item within a class is not reducible to any single measure. Not all classes, as with milk, have to be homogenised. The notion of multiplicity means that we can think of a singularity, such as children, as plural. Moreover, it might also be the case that plurality and difference (not reducible to identity) enriches the collectivity, deepens its collectivity, through intensifying the questions of what it is, its singularity. Let us return to the example of paediatric ophthalmology. As we've already stated, various elements are constituted as having agency within particular infrastructured settings. But across the infrastructures at different moments children are constituted as collective subjects. In order to ascertain appropriate measures and protocols for treating children in eye clinics, surgeries, at home or in school, tests need to be completed and children divided and assessed. Children with no knowledge of each other, with no shared experiences, are brought into experimental settings and aggregated. Moreover, as a consequence of these tests, particular eye defects are identified and procedures, exercises and technologies developed for their rectification. At another moment children are sitting, waiting for a regular eye examination (a Snellen test) in their eye clinic, and in the meantime other children are being examined, for others the prescription written, and yet other children are being fitted with spectacles. The capacity to see is enhanced through the spectacles; their capacity to act in the world is enhanced through the facilitatory technology of lens and metal frame. Of course, less than a hundred years ago, having the correct prescription glasses meant the difference between being labelled educationally dull and being normal. At another moment in the school playground, a small boy is being teased about his spectacles by some older children; two older girls, also wearing glasses, step in and threaten to wallop anyone who issues another insult; the small boy and the bigger girls exchange smiles.

If children's collectivity does take the form of a multiplicity, then it is one that is arguably in some instances and perhaps increasingly transnational and global. Although there is significant evidence – historical, sociological, psychological and anthropological – to suggest that there are connections (albeit complex and non-unitary) to be made across children of similar and different age groups in many individual nation-states and across geographical locales that are connected through historic migration and family ties, exchanges of social and public policy, connections through international media and communications, and so on, there is a risk that our understanding of such complex and uneven networks across the global might be flattened and made static. Some might argue that across such complex topologies we understand children as a multiplicity in terms of a latent humanism, such that underpinning the collective connections of children is the fact that they share the same universal biological determinations. But as we have already seen, there are many who have investigated the interface between the social and the natural and discovered that certainly biology (in its crudest sense) plays a significant role in our understanding of children. However, the biological cannot be simply seen in opposition to the social or the cultural; rather, both are hybridly constituted within a rapidly developing sphere of biosocial and biopolitical production. If the collective subjectivity of children appears 'human', it is only inasmuch as that biopolitical humanity is on the horizon of complex hybridly formed connections across the social, the technological and the natural. In that sense, children – as a multiplicity and as a collection of singularities – are, as we all are, constantly on life-support on interconnected machines. No body lives or acts alone. That said, the intention is not to reduce these substantive hybridities to a flattened ontology. What we get from Simone is that people are the locus of a knotted and knotting arrangement, such that although 'people' signify a point of importance (ethical, political, economic, social, technological, biological and cultural), they cannot be cut from the arrangement without destroying the umbilical knot.

A return to generation

Before concluding, I want to return to the question of children's collectivity as defined through generational difference. For whatever reason, what has distinguished children for certainly the last century and before is that they represent growth. The Finnish sociologist Leena Alanen has argued that instead of providing a sociology of childhood, we should be thinking of a sociology of generation or generationing. Her discussion draws upon, but is different from, the discussion of childhood as a structural phenomenon and generation in the work of Qvortrup and colleagues (1994). In a move similar to the argument against women's studies and in favour of gender studies, Alanen argues that '"[g]eneration", in the end, constitutes the social phenomenon of "childhood" itself, and the fact that in our kind of societies there exists the practically effective category of "children" is to admit that the social is generationally structured' (Alanen, 2000: 3). She draws on Karl Mannheim's analysis of generation. Mannheim argued that members of a single cohort (defined by age) undergo similar historical and social experiences, they develop certain commonalities across their group or generation. In Mannheim's analysis, the notion of generation provides a link between the linear process of a group of people getting older and the longer process of history as a linear movement. Alanen discusses this in the context of an analysis of class formation and of the relational positionality of 'adult' and 'child'. In her terms, each position implies the other. For Alanen, then, the question of children's agency is fundamentally connected to children's positioning as children and not adults, and such a positioning implies a relation of power between the two: 'being a child (or an adult) does make a huge difference (or differences) in terms of one's activities, opportunities, experiences and identities' (10). There is clearly a question concerning the role of children's agency in contesting one's positioning within such a relational process of generationing. It is significant that Mayall, who also talks of this process of generationing, also talks of the role of children as agents in contesting the positioning by adults and of the different context in which such interaction might occur (Mayall, 2002).

This is not the place to review the research on generation, cohort or life stage (see Närvänen and Näsman, 2004). But let us consider the idea that generationing constitutes, as it were, a dividing practice through which children as a collectivity are differentiated from and subordinated to adults. In the context of schooling and the forming of cohorts, individuals are aligned under a single measure; they are constituted as a class of individuals of the same age (where age is a measure or unit of unification). Certainly the making of classes, for example, in schools helps to constitute shared experiences based on similar ages (where similarity is understood within the measure of an age range between set dates, such as 1 September to 31 August over the period of a year), a common history inasmuch as those shared experiences are predicated on shared habits within a common institution and a common identity insofar as the class is constituted as a definite bounded group of individuals. But away from that institution, whether after the end of the school day or in the school holidays or after leaving school, one's constitution within a generational cohort is dependent on other factors. At home one has a generational relation to other family members; on the football pitch one's generational cohort may change dependent on one's skill and on the organisation of the under 12s, under 15s and under 18s teams, but not according to the school class cohort; on leaving school and taking up employment, one's relation to a generational cohort will also depend on one's identification with school age as a form of classification (e.g. one's nostalgia for school, one's sense of age hierarchy, etc.). All of these are contingencies and need empirical investigation. They cannot be assumed a priori. The relationality across the school, family and football pitch is uneven and constituted in terms of different measures and scales. But also, what about the teachers, the classroom assistants, helpers and others, all of whom are consistent features of a year group? The stability of the year group is defined in terms of those aspects that are seen to 'progress' through the school. The cohort, in this sense, is also defined against those elements (such as whiteboards, physical classrooms, but also teachers) that are seen as fixed and as part of the institution. The 'cohort' alone (circumscribed through various devices) is seen to embody 'progression'. The approaches to the study of assemblages, networks, apparatuses and infrastructures discussed in the sections above lead us to different ways of understanding generational difference. They might stress that

(a) it is important to investigate particular assemblages with respect to the question of generation, such that any distribution of the connotations of 'static' and 'dynamic' are seen as internal to the apparatus and not defined a priori with respect to prior concepts of the ontology of 'a child' as against 'a teacher' or 'a physical classroom'

(b) similarly, temporality or becoming or progression, cannot be assigned a priori to some actors rather than others

(c) generational progression needs to be investigated in terms of its foregrounding within particular assemblages, through, for example, particular measurement and standardisation devices (such as progression from one level to the next on the basis of examination or age at a particular point in the annual calendar)

(d) instead of seeing generation in terms of children pushed through a pipe (Qvortrup) or as a performative dividing practice (Alanen), it is important to investigate children as productive beings within an assemblage, such that their agency is relative to other agencies within the assemblage, but also such that those other agencies are themselves generative

(e) and, although elements within an assemblage may have productive and generational capacity, there are unequal relations with regard to the capacity to accumulate value as a consequence of productive agency (or labour).

Children have historically been unable to accumulate capital of different forms. Their love for their parents or those who look after them may be traded for shelter and protection and education, but children are not able to profit from their emotional labour. Their work at school is returned in the form of certificates and diplomas, but not in terms of control within the institution of schooling itself. Their consumption of popular culture and their exchange of artefacts and communications has, historically, little value except as trinkets and memories. Children have historically lacked the means, not of forming and belonging to networks, but of maintaining them, building them up over time and providing the material means of their support and of their reproduction. In that sense, children are often thought to have the means of association, but no means of institutionalisation. They can certainly be creative, but they are thought fundamentally to lack the means to distribute and reproduce that creativity. The issue of accumulation that we begin to discuss here is one that is intimately tied to the biopolitical nature of children as collective beings, but also to the different temporalities or rhythms within which they might find themselves located. This is never simply about the accumulation of resources over historical time or the distribution of those resources in geographical space. In the context of children, it is also a question of their accumulation and distribution with respect to biographical time and the infrastructuring of generational differences across different organisational spaces (such as school, family, social media, the street, and so on).

Ricardo Paz left school at 11 years of age. He started out as a foot soldier of a gang in Guatemala City. He killed ruthlessly. His murders were public spectacles and public threats, and they marked his reputation. He rose quickly through the ranks of the gang to become the leader of a city zone by the age of 20. He had killed over twenty people: bus drivers, gang members, shop owners and various others. He was in control of 200 gang members and was earning over £3,000 a week (*Guardian*, 29 June 2011: 23). The trajectory of Paz from age 11 to age 20 is generational only inasmuch as it traverses people, rituals, weapons, know-how, courage, psychopathology and the partitioning of territories, and inasmuch as elements from this trajectory are able to be accumulated with respect to his value within such an infrastructure. To measure the difference between Paz at the two ages without any understanding of the complex paths in between would be a facile exercise. The lack of the means to accumulate may be a consequence of the relatively short-lived nature of the life of a child. As childhood is a passing phase, children soon grow up and once adult are able to accumulate capital and to individually profit from that accumulation. It may be, though, that the appearance of the short-lived nature of childhood is a consequence of children's lack of the means to accumulate. It is important, then, to avoid a notion of generation which simply presumes an interiorisation of growth within the human body, such that temporality is seen to reside within, according to an interiorised logic, and that external to that body is an environment or context which is largely seen as static. Conceptualising generation in the context of the assemblage implies considering the different temporalities and lines of growth and generation distributed across the network.

Conclusion

This chapter, then, has considered children and childhood in terms of post-structural analyses of subjectivity. These forms of analysis problematise subjectivity inasmuch as subjectivity is understood in terms of its fundamental insecurity, which is brought about by its entry into language, its alienation from an originary claim to experience and its agency decentred through relations across texts and performances. Forms of analysis and interpretation, which emerge from literary and cultural studies, inform an understanding of children's agency and experience in terms of their complex performative fabrication. But although such interpretative methods enrich the sociological study of children and deepen our descriptive languages, the chapter has argued that we also need to understand children's experiences and experimentations in the context of material arrangements. Moreover, we have investigated the ideas of network, assemblage, apparatus and infrastructure in order to foreground and facilitate an understanding of the experiences of children as thoroughly material and distributed through a material world. It is only in this context that we can properly begin to understand generational relationality, namely as a complex distributed effect and generative cause of particular arrangements.

Spaces of experience, experimentation and power

In Part III I look at some of the major sites within which and through which children and young people live, experience, experiment and are constructed. My intention is to understand how particular significant problem spaces have been formed, but to do so in the context of understanding the assemblage of languages, practices, technologies and objects through which children's agency is constructed, mobilised and dispersed. I consider, in particular, the spaces that have, in the present but also historically, attracted intellectual ideas, governmental strategy and economic capital. These spaces are key focal points for sociological writing. In particular, I consider ideas about family, school, crime, health, consumer culture and play, children's work and children's human rights. These seem to me to be key sites for thinking through what the sociology of children and childhood (but also surrounding disciplines and sociological fields) has to offer an understanding of children's agency inasmuch as that agency is understood as a complex arrangement.

The spaces I consider are, firstly, problem spaces. The anthropologist Paul Rabinow defines these problem spaces (although he uses the term 'problematisation') through a discussion of the pragmatist philosopher John Dewey's essay on experimental logic and experience. To think of problem spaces is to think of how thought emerges from both experience and experimentation, but also importantly emerges between places (literally, in milieu). Thinking is an action which comes into being through discordances, tensions and unevenness, that is, as an attempt to put things straight, to realign things (Rabinow, 2003: 16). These discordances bring about a richness of thought and add detail to thinking. Rabinow further defines problem spaces with reference to Foucault's notion of 'problematisation', inasmuch as problem spaces are those spaces in which thought does not simply represent a given thing, nor does it bring into being a thing previously non-existent. These spaces are both discursive and non-discursive. For

Foucault, they are spaces which bring something into the light with regard to its truth or falsity, but for us problem spaces have a character closer to that which Dewey poses with regard to experience and experimentation. Problem spaces are spaces of thought, experience, experimentation, but also of power inasmuch as they constitute a way of thinking about the lines of force which are part of, or bring into being, particular assemblages. Thinking about children's agency, then, in the context of the school cannot be divorced from the lines of force and the genealogical site of power through which the architectures and pedagogies of the school are brought into being.

Secondly, these spaces are spaces of description. Health, for example, is at once a definition of a state of being, in our case with regard to a child. But it provides a resource for talking and describing children's bodies, their relation to other people, but also their relation to things. Health also provides a productive site of metaphors and analogies, for talking about children's hygiene, about their cleanliness, about their infectiveness or about their purity. Descriptions of children, though, are often aligned with assessments, measurements, standard-isations, normalisations and judgements. The designation of a child as unfit or unwell also brings into play a series of potential actions, for example, the child needs either more exercise (if the former) or diagno-sis and therapy (if the latter). Such simple judgements and actions are dependent on forms of measurement and the standardisation across populations with regard to understandings of fit and healthy children. Observation and the language of description, but also the devices which facilitate description, are crucial.

Thirdly, these spaces are not uniform, either in the accounts we may give of them or in their material composition. With respect to the latter, they are materially heterogeneous. They are not made up of one thing. In fact, their consistency and extension are dependent on their being com-posed of different kinds of things, different kinds of people, and different forms of mediation and translation between these. We argue that it is redundant to reduce, for example, the problem of consumption and consumer culture to a question of the interpretative agency of children in the context of overarching corporate power. For us, to think about children's agency means understanding assemblages in such ways as not to reduce them to flat ontologies and flat knowledges.

Fourthly, these spaces of experience, experimentation and power are sites of investment, innovation and the accumulation of capital.

Children's agency does not rest within a political space that simply distributes resources in terms of those who have them and those who do not. On the contrary, the question of the value of resources, and the dynamic movement of value, is crucial to understanding children's agency and the capacity for leverage within an assemblage. Children's voices in the family, for example, have weight nowadays by virtue of long historic alignments of forces, some political, some social, some cultural and some economic.

In this part of the book I survey some key problem spaces in order to provide a sense of how children's agency is observed, formed, arranged, experienced and described.

6 | *Family and household*

The family and household from the late nineteenth century, if not earlier, have been seen as incubators of children's agency. The family and household were seen as coextensive and as locations for children's passive socialisation, but they are now recognised as often being disarticulated and as major sites of democratisation. Family and household are now seen to be generators of emotional economy and labour, saturated by media and communications, and often as spaces of talk, fun, love and laughter, but also of anxiety, fear, abuse and violence. But what do we mean by 'family' and 'household'? Sonia Livingstone, in her research on young people and new media, rightly points to the distinctions between, yet often overlapping histories of, the categories of 'family', 'household' and 'home' (Livingstone, 2002: 166). 'Household' more often refers to the dwelling of people in a particular place. It refers to the living of people together and the doing of things together (i.e. 'social groupings which typically share a range of domestic activities in common' [Allan and Crow, 2001: 5]). It often gets discussed in terms of people's 'co-residence' (Gittins, 1993; Morgan, 1985 and 1996). In all these definitions there is a tendency to prioritise social relations predicated on conditions of 'co-presence' (i.e. the 'being there together' of a social group), but it is not simply the co-presence of individuals anywhere; it is the co-presence of individuals within a house or a flat; within a particular kind of built place. Ownership or rental of that built environment may be an important element in understanding co-residence; but it would equally disqualify any kinship group that had a nomadic existence. If the dwelling constitutes the concretisation and infrastructuring of living in a place, then 'household' designates a fixed dwelling, to the exclusion of other forms of non-fixed itinerant dwelling. There are certainly problems with a definition of household, but it serves the purpose of foregrounding a notion of the 'family' as one that is not necessarily articulated with living in the same house or sharing the same activities. Households do not necessarily contain individuals related as kin. We may talk about student households or about friends living together as a household or about single-person households. In contrast to household, 'family' constitutes a particular series of social relationships predicated on kinship and life-cycle relations (brothers, sisters, fathers, mothers, grandparents, granddaughters, aunts and uncles), and it may also refer to particular ideologies which foreground particular relations of kin as social ideals (Barrett and McIntosh, 1991). Although 'family' might have suggested social relations based on heterosexual reproduction, such that families may get defined through 'bloodline', 'family' (as a series of social relationships) defines a series of relational positions for those not related by 'blood' to adopt. In this sense, 'fatherhood' may be defined through a particular positionality and practice that may be taken up by a person not related to the child through an act of sexual reproduction. 'Brother', 'sister', 'father' and 'mother' define familial positions that may or may not contain the prefix 'step', if referring to a relation not of 'bloodline'. Similarly, lesbian and gay couples with children, or adoptive families, may rightly refer to themselves as 'families'. 'Family' may be used to designate emotional closeness and distance. Thus, a single mother with children may refer to their household unit as a 'single parent family' in order to present a distance between that unit and the physically and emotionally distant 'biological father' living in a separate household. Equally, 'family' may be used to refer to family members separated across different households in order to foreground a close social relationality not predicated on conditions of co-residence. 'Home' frequently refers to the condensation of the family within the household; it names a physical as well as an emotional and ideological sense of belonging. The trope of nostalgia (literally homesickness) is a recurrent theme in modernity.

   In the late twentieth and early twenty-first centuries many commentators have talked about the privatisation of social life in terms of both the physical enclosing of social relations within the household and the social extension of family relations outside of a single household. In doing so, any notion of a naturalised family as 'co-residing close kin' is deeply problematised. As Michele Barrett and Mary McIntosh argue, '[t]he meaning of family life extends far beyond the walls of concrete households' (Barrett and McIntosh, 1991: 31). Parents may live in different households; siblings may live in different households and may be both 'biological' and 'social'; children may be adopted or fostered or live with familial guardians other than their 'natural parents'; older children may move in with friends or boyfriends or girlfriends; parents may need to live apart for some of the time due to pressures of work or for other reasons; grandparents may remarry and grandchildren may find themselves with new family members, new cousins, new nieces and nephews. Movement, relocation and communication technology constitute significant forces in the changing social relations of family and household and in foregrounding understandings of social life that do not prioritise conditions of co-presence (Giddens, 1991). In this chapter I consider the changing contours of children's agency in the context of this changing landscape of family and household. I do so by considering, initially, some historical and sociological research on the emergence of the modern family and its relation to modern forms of power. I then discuss more recent research on the family as a space of democracy and changing forms of intimacy.

Socialisation and social system

As was noted in Chapter 3, Parsonian social theory, but also much work in sociology and social psychology, developed and deployed a model of 'socialisation' such that to become 'social' implied the adoption of a social role, becoming 'individual', and having a defined functionality within the social system. The family and the school have often been seen as the two main institutions through which children become socialised. With increases in the reach and growth of television from the 1950s and 1960s, mass media was often noted as the third key institution of socialisation in modernity. Whatever the problems may be with this historically dated model, many have declared the family as the quintessential unit of social reproduction. Thus, Christopher Lasch wrote in the late 1970s:

If the reproduction of culture were simply a matter of formal instruction and discipline, it could be left to the schools. But it also requires that culture be embedded in personality. Socialization makes the individual want to do what he has to do; the family is the agency to which society entrusts this complex and delicate task. (Lasch, 1979: 4)

Such a model, in its very general form, often conflates 'family' and 'household' and assumes households 'to be organized, by and large, on the basis of a division of labour between a primary breadwinner (male) and a primary childrearer (female)' (Barrett and McIntosh, 1991: 7; Morgan, 1996). In its crude form, the family is understood in terms of social reproduction and the passage of ideological meaning from parent to child. For example, Louis Althusser, the French Marxist philosopher, conceived of the family as a central 'ideological state apparatus', such that the dominant ideologies of a social formation could be transposed from one generation to the next, but also such that the divisions of labour in society (between men and women and between manual and mental) could be ideologically reproduced (Althusser, 1971). In its more sophisticated form, the family has been seen to comprise not simply a means of ideological reproduction, but also a discrete social unit, or system, in itself, such that any understanding of that unit must pay attention to its internal dynamics and economy. Thus, power relations and dysfunctions are not the property of individual family members, but of the sociality and psychological dynamics of the family itself. For example, one version of this model, family systems theory, understands the family in terms of the emotional flows between family members. The misbehaviour of a child, for example, may equally be a consequence of a lack of communication and emotional antipathy between the husband and the wife or may be a consequence of the over-investment by the parents in another sibling, hence producing sibling rivalry (Goodman, 1983). In this sense, socialisation is understood in the context of social interaction, inasmuch as social interaction is bounded within the familial and emotional relations of a particular household.

Thus, in either its crude or more sophisticated form, a socialisation model – as presented across a range of theoretical and methodological paradigms and perspectives – construes the family as the relay, or mediator, between society and the pre-individual, pre-social child. The proper functioning of the family is understood in terms of the clarity of communication across generations and across the natural and the social. Such a model provided the broad rationale for a number of critiques of the family in the 1960s and 1970s, from socialists to feminists to anti-psychiatrists (Firestone, 1979; Laing and Esterson, 1970; Poster, 1978).

Socialisation as the government of the 'social'

Emerging from the context of a generalised critique of the family in the 1960s and 1970s (often in the context of broader arguments about patriarchal power, liberal government and modern capitalism), a number of writers talk about historical invention and development of the modern family in the eighteenth and nineteenth centuries. Many discuss the changing nature of intimacy (primarily in relation to children) within the family from this period, but different writers provide different accounts as to the significance of 'the family form' within contemporary society (Ariès, 1962; DeMause, 1976; Donzelot, 1979; Foucault, 1979; Lasch, 1979; Shorter, 1975; Stone, 1977). These writers offer different theoretical and political understandings of the family (e.g. regarding whether the family is in crisis, in need of support, whether it needs to be radically reinvented, or regarding it as a political technology). Lasch, for example, locates a crisis in the family, not in the 1970s, but a hundred years earlier. He talks about a breakdown of 'the traditional family' and does so with reference to the social forces of 'the divorce crisis, feminism, and the revolt of youth'. But instead of locating these forces in the 1970s, he sees their origins in the late nineteenth century. It is at this historical moment that the family begins to be massively reorganised and its relations of authority and expertise are reconfigured. Lasch argued that the family was primarily a means to socialise children and for children to internalise parental authority. For him, 'the father's absence allows early fantasies to persist unmodified by later experience, the child fears the terrible vengeance that his father can inflict even while he scorns the everyday father who never inflicts it' (Lasch, 1979: 188–9). The refusal of the father to enforce his patriarchal authority, and the lack of possibility for the child to stage a confrontation with that authority, for Lasch, was seen to have consequences not only for the developing child but also for society. The consequence of children not contesting the authority of the father was that they were never able to take up a position of responsibility themselves. The child, now grown up, is never able to surpass their fantasies of retribution. They are forever destined to remain within a narcissistic personality structure, forever to remain childish.

Furthermore, Lasch argued that a whole army of experts emerges and develops to support this new constitution of the self. He refers to 'the socialisation of reproduction'. An array of therapeutic experts assemble around the family to support its emotional instability, to offer knowledge and diagnosis, and to advise on what to do. Lasch says:

The history of modern society, from one point of view, is the assertion of social control over activities once left to individuals and families. During the first stage of the industrial revolution, capitalists took production out of the household and collectivized it, under their own supervision, in the factory. Then they proceeded to appropriate the workers' skills and technical knowledge, by means of 'scientific management', and to bring these skills together under managerial direction. Finally they extended their control over the worker's private life as well, as doctors, psychiatrists, teachers, child guidance experts, officers of the juvenile courts, and other specialists began to supervise child-rearing, formerly the business of the family. (Lasch, 1979: xiv–xv)

Lasch talks about the family as 'besieged' by these forms of expertise. They intrude upon the preserve of the family, 'the haven in a heartless world'. Those duties and activities once housed within the family have been usurped by 'society': 'Society itself has taken over socialization or subjected family socialization to increasingly effective control' (189). His argument encountered a lot of criticism, not least from feminist writers. Barrett and McIntosh provided a detailed critique of it in terms of Lasch's implicit privileging of 'family' as middle class and his ignorance with regard to different contemporary and historical family forms and practices. But also they expose Lasch's argument as a profound form of social conservatism with regard to patriarchal power (Barrett and McIntosh, 1991). Not least, there are problems with his analysis of feminism as itself seemingly a product of the socialisation of production and reproduction. For Lasch, the feminist critique of women's role in the home as the carer of children, the politics of allowing women into the public sphere of paid work and their subsequent recognition therein, and also the anti-feminist argument concerning the professionalisation of childcare and housework are different sides of a single societal shift toward a rationalisation of the family, a devaluation of its traditional authorities and its subordination to the authority of external experts, such as teachers, social workers, doctors, psychologists and others (Lasch, 1979: 10–14).

Michel Foucault and those sympathetic to his genealogical under-standing of power, such as Jacques Donzelot, make a series of arguments that are both very similar to but also very different from Lasch's. Although Foucault talks about the changing intimacies of the family, he does so in the context of broader shifts in social organisation. In volume I of his *History of Sexuality*, Foucault states that the system of noble estates and family alliances of the eighteenth century 'lost some of its importance as economic processes and political structures could no longer rely on it as an adequate instrument or sufficient support' (Foucault, 1979: 106), and he talks of the family, from this time on, as being located at the 'interchange' between a system of alliance and a new regime of power and knowledge (in part based on new discourses of sexuality). A system of family alliances constituted a system of exchange of women as wives. This was both a social and a political system. Moreover, such noble families (which, it is argued, formed the basis upon which a definition of 'family' rested) included not only kin but also servants and others within the extended household and estate. Foucault's argument is that the shift from this model of government to modern forms of power can be seen in the major shift in thinking and conduct. As a medium of power, it is argued by Foucault, the discourses of sexuality allow for a productivity and an extension that is far greater than that of the system of alliances alone. To talk of sexuality in the context of the family, he argues, allows experts, but also family members themselves, to interrogate their lives in terms of their fertility, their psychobiography, their development, their normality, their perversions. For Foucault, greater intimacy within the family is a consequence of a sexualisation of the social. Hence the opposition between incest taboo and infant care (that can be seen in DeMause's argument regarding the progressively better treatment of children by their parents) is deconstructed such that sexual abuse may be seen alongside parental care and within a broader investment in the family as a site of sexualisation and hence a central site, for Foucault, of modern power and knowledge. But Foucault's work on sexuality is just one area in which he works through an argument about modern governmentality.

The governmentality that emerges in the eighteenth century moves away from an historic form of the noble family and the power (*potestas*) of the *pater familias* and towards the 'normal family' as an element within the population. Foucault argues that in the eighteenth century, partly as a result of demographic expansion, government based on the model of the ancient family became seen as limited and problematic.

The model of the ancient family constituted a patriarchal system of powers and a system of alliance: namely, 'a system of marriage, of fixation and development of kinship ties, of transmission of names and possessions' (Foucault, 1979: 106; see also Flandrin, 1964; Minson, 1985). In Donzelot's supporting discussion of the family under the *Ancien Régime,* the system of alliances constitutes not the private realm of the family (separate from, impinged upon or supported by the state) but the domain of the public and the political. In this sense, political power was formed through the ability of a patriarch to mobilise support within and across the system of alliances, across kin, generations, patrons and servants. In this context, the economy, Foucault argues, was not an entity distinct from the family; rather, it referred to the organisation of people and things within the household and the estate: in this sense, 'oeconomie' referred to the domestic economy, the management of property and people (i.e. the estate) through the capacity of the father. But we need to be cautious about this argument, not least because some historians argue that there is little reliable evidence for a shift from the extended family to the nuclear family at the time of industrialisation (Cunningham, 2005: 88). That said, such criticism is argued on the basis of family size rather than in relation to the broader Foucauldian argument about the nature of political rule and government. In the context of children's experience, abilities and capacities and the development of infrastructures which support such agency, the issue is not simply the size or composition of units of care, but the relation between family members and others and the mobilisation of capacities by virtue of those connections.

In his work on governmentality, Foucault gives weight to the authority of statistical knowledge in its ability to provide an understanding of the totality of the population (i.e. to figure it as a measure of quantity). In the eighteenth century we see the emergence of statistics (as a science of the state), which is deployed in relation to the 'population', such that the population is seen to have its own regularities (e.g. rates of birth and death, distribution of disease, and cycles of growth [Hacking, 1991]). At this time, statistics (as a description of the state) is combined with the art of government; it becomes used as both a means of analysing the habits and forms of conduct, laws and regularities of a population living within a territory, and as a means of government (Foucault, 1991: 252). Importantly, the population is now seen as being directly related to the economic (in terms of the generation of wealth, spirals of labour, cycles of growth). The economic is now seen as a distinct entity, separate from the family and closely aligned to the population. It, too, is seen to have its own laws and forms of management. Foucault states that 'from the moment when ... population appears absolutely irreducible to the family, the latter becomes of secondary importance compared to population, as an element internal to population: no longer, that is to say, a model, but a segment', but, he continues, 'it remains a privileged segment, because whatever information is required concerning the population (sexual behaviour, demography, consumption, etc.), it has to be obtained through the family' (100). The family now emerges not as a model of government but as an object and instrument of government: 'the family considered as an element internal to population, and as a fundamental instrument in its government' (99).

For Donzelot, the emergence of the modern family is linked to the redefinitions of 'public' and 'private' and the emergence of liberal governance. He doesn't see the 'private' and 'public' as two distinct reified domains, but rather as plural, sometimes overlapping, categories, fields and forms of government. Liberalism as a form of government is predicated on the distinction between public and private, such that the latter is a domain not to be ordinarily trespassed by political powers (i.e. the state). The 'family', as problem, forms a solution, Donzelot argues, to the liberal definition of the state (Donzelot, 1979: 53). In its now limited and modern definition, the family is seen as that which primarily supports the socialisation and upbringing of children. Thus, the 'child' becomes a central means through which individuals and populations can be governed. While domestic privacies are protected through legal practices, families are normalised and regulated through public concerns about delinquency, child abuse, neglect, family disharmony and so on. Families are construed through the lens not only of the moral binaries of good and bad, but also the disciplinary binaries of normal and pathological. Donzelot talks of the establishment of 'psy' experts (such as those practising psychiatry, paediatrics, psychology, psychotherapy and psychoanalysis) whose knowledge maps out the mental spaces and times of the domestic. But others, such as Nikolas Rose and Valerie Walkerdine, have analysed the role of the social sciences (with particular reference to psychology) in the governance of the child, family and home

(Rose, 1989; Walkerdine, 1984 and 1997). Although the child is constructed as the object of disciplinary knowledge and power, and is divided from the 'adult', the 'rational' and so on, such knowledge is deployed in relation to those who are not children as well. The family is not seen in realist terms (i.e. as a form of social structure) but as an instrument and object of power and knowledge. It facilitates particular forms of regulation and governance and it has no 'reality' outside of this nexus. Donzelot talks about alliances formed between the medical profession (i.e. the family doctor) and the mother of the bourgeois family in the nineteenth century. Through a discourse of family medicine and family hygiene, and through an address in popular medical and hygienic literature, the bourgeois mother becomes allied to particular forms of medical and hygienic expertise. She is made responsible, in these discourses and through these interlocking agencies, for the wellbeing of her family. She both educates her family and others through a mix of moralising philanthropy and promotional feminism. The children of these middle-class homes grow up within a 'supervised freedom'. Moreover, in taking up this responsibility, the Victorian middle-class mother was able seemingly to contain the limits of her familial world within the limits of her domestic supervisory gaze. In contrast, the working-class family was open to more direct and authoritarian forms of intervention from outside. The pathologised working-class family, now set against and compared to the middle-class norm, could be constructed as a site of constant surveillance and reform, initially by an army of philanthropists and latterly by those working for the welfare state. In both cases, we see a relation developing between forms of familial government, forms of mothering and alliances with particular experts and forms of expertise. These forms of government have grown and developed over the twentieth century in response to therapeutic expertise and medical knowledge and their circulation in the media (Furedi, 2002). Similar to Lasch's understanding of the extension of 'socialisation' as social control, a Foucauldian analysis construes 'the family' as the means through which the 'social' is both constructed and governed and through which a whole series of social sciences and social experts can emerge and take hold. There are feminist critiques of this approach. Significantly, Barrett and McIntosh (1991) take to task Donzelot's argument about the alignment of women-as-mothers with the development of the liberal state apparatus.

Transforming intimacy and democratising the family

Research, in the late 1990s, by Carol Smart and colleagues at the Centre for Research on Family, Kinship and Childhood, University of Leeds, paved the way for a substantial rethinking of academic conceptualisation of the family, of family policy, and of the agency of children in families. At a time when in the UK there was much discussion about the responsibilities and rights of fathers with regard to their children after separation or divorce from the mother, Smart looked not only to the adults for an understanding of parental separation, but importantly to the children as well, and in so doing helped to put flesh on the legal skeleton set in place by the Children's Act of 1989, which legally provided for children to have some kind of voice in matters that affected their lives. Smart talked to children and young people and in doing so was able to begin to frame an understanding of their experiences of contemporary family life. Her research took as one of its guiding frames the recent sociology of childhood articulated by James, Jenks and Prout and others. But, as Smart and her colleagues say, 'Treating children as reflexive social actors is more than a theoretical perspective, for it raises questions about the whole tenor of child–adult relationships' (Smart et al., 2001: 14). Drawing on qualitative research methodologies, they argued that they were able to see how family relationships 'are negotiated over time rather than fixed by duty, law or the positional status of family members' (17). Importantly, the shift in conceptual and methodological thinking that they invoke is such that it is no longer presumed that family members 'think or feel the same way, or that their interests and identities are merged within an inseparable or tightly integrated unit' (18). They continue:

In other words, this approach eschews the tendency towards children's familialization … for it grants conceptual autonomy to individual family members. Within this formulation, then, children need no longer be invisible; they emerge as fully-fledged family members, actively engaged in negotiating their own family practices and relationships. They no longer just belong to families; as reflexive agents of their own lives they are part of the creation of families. (Smart et al., 2001: 18)

This perspective inevitably tends to focus on the significance of the child's voice, and in this way the research of Smart and colleagues may be seen to fit alongside other research on contemporary family life that pays attention to children, not only as agents but as speaking subjects. Thus, for example, Jan Pryor and Robert E. Emery, in their research on children's understandings of divorce in the US, declare: 'Children are encouraged to be articulate, to express opinions on everything from bedroom decor to world events, and to be independent' (Pryor and Emery, 2004: 171). Although Smart and colleagues are more cautious about the relation between children's voices and a political transformation of the family, Pryor and Emery state clearly what may be underlying much of this discourse on our attention to children's voices, namely that 'Families have become, by and large, democratic units allowing considerable participation by all members' (171).

A key reference in some of these debates is the social theory of Giddens. For the sociology of children, two aspects of his work are important: that which concerns the transformation of intimacy and the growth of new family forms, and that which concerns the individualisation and democratisation of the family in late modernity. In the first instance, drawing upon the work of Lasch on the narcissistic self, but also upon Richard Sennett's work on the decline of 'public man', Giddens talks about the changing contours of intimacy in late modern society. As with Lasch (1979: 19), so Giddens also argues that there has been a sociohistorical movement from romantic love (and marriage as a facet of that enduring love) to more serialised relationships (inasmuch as marriage and cohabitation are now seen as transitory and non-binding commitments). He states that

The inability to take a serious interest in anything other than shoring up the self makes the pursuit of intimacy a futile endeavour. Individuals demand from intimate connections with others much greater emotional satisfaction and security than they ever did before; on the other hand, they cultivate a detachment necessary to the maintenance of narcissistic ego defences. The narcissist is led to make inordinate demands on lovers and friends; at the same time, he or she rejects the 'giving to others' that this implies. (Giddens, 1991: 173)

As with Lasch, Giddens relates this phenomenon to the decline of the patriarchal family, 'indeed the family in general'. Instead of traditional authorities, the culture of narcissism thrives in a relation with new experts, a new breed of therapeutic experts who help to support the intimate self. Moreover, as narcissism is seen to be a consequence of 'infantile dependency', the new reliance on these new forms of expertise intensifies a sense of powerlessness and thus increases the reliance and the narcissism. But for Giddens such reliance is predicated on a self-reflexivity. Thus in relation to forms of modern marriage – that are seen to rely more on voluntary commitment than compulsion, that include fewer children and that involve a division of gender that is less clear cut – 'individuals are actively restructuring new forms of gender and kinship relation out of the detritus of pre-established forms of family life' (Giddens, 1991: 177). These shifts, documented twenty or more years ago, are now sociologically well entrenched. In the 1990s Giddens argued that (based on the empirical research of Judith Stacey on familial relations in California) we were witnessing a 'massive process of institutional reconstitution'. He states:

'Recombinant families', no longer organised in terms of pre-established gender divisions, are being created; rather than forming a chasm between a previous and a future mode of existence, divorce is being mobilised as a resource to create networks drawing together new partners and former ones, biological children and stepchildren, friends and other relatives. (Giddens, 1991: 177)

We should note that 'recombinant families' in themselves are not new. Hugh Cunningham points out that remarriages constituted about a quarter to a third of all marriages in eighteenth-century Britain. These were the result largely of spousal death (Cunningham, 2005: 96). But what is more recent is the reason for remarriage (i.e. now largely divorce) and the diversity of marital forms (e.g. including lesbian and gay marriages, new forms of co-parenting, and so on). For Giddens, these new family forms are symptomatic of the declining significance of the family as an index of social relationships.

If we look to data from the UK and the USA (namely two countries that might be seen to be at the forefront of processes of modernisation), then, with regard to this argument, that data is certainly ambivalent. In the UK, since marital statistics were first recorded in 1862, the long-term trend is argued to be one of decline in marriage, from a peak in 1972 to an all-time low in 2007 (ONS, 2009). That said, there were 17.1 million families in the UK in 2006, of which 71 per cent were married couples and 14 per cent cohabiting couples. In those families, increasingly both parents go out to work and there are 1.8 children per family (ONS, 2009). In the USA in 2007,

67.8 per cent of children were living with two married parents. Seventy-one per cent of all children were living in households with two parents (whether married, biological or adoptive parents) and 26 per cent were living with single parents (of which the largest group was single mothers, but this figure does not preclude single parents cohabiting with partners). The remaining 3 per cent of children lived with no parents (of which the largest group was living with grand-parents or relatives, rather than in foster care or other forms of guardianship). On the one hand, there is clear evidence that families no longer constitute an idealised nuclear family form (the form that was often reproduced in sociology from the 1930s to the 1970s), that there is slightly more diversity with respect to the patterning of family forms, and that there is more investment in notions of 'self' (whether adult or child) in the negotiation of family life. On the other hand, there is clear evidence that children are predominantly raised in families of one kind or another.

In the second instance, Giddens talks of the increasing impor-tance of the self as a reflexive project, as one guided toward self-actualisation, as one formed through relationships of mutual self-disclosure and one formed through a concern for self-fulfilment (Giddens, 1991: 125). Unlike Donzelot, who accords women no agency (only the status of 'relay') in the networks of power, Giddens construes women as having reflexive agency (see Smart and Neale, 1999: 9). But agency is accorded to all family members. Increasingly, children are construed as having agency in the family. Beck and Beck-Gernsheim refer to this in terms of individualisation (2001). The process of individualisation refers to the increasing formation of identity in 'post-traditional' relations; namely, identity is formed less in relations of fixed employment and class, fixed normative family, fixed religious belief and fixed lifelong geographical belonging than in conditions of flexibility of work, consumption, lifestyle and personal relationships. But it also refers to the role of state agencies in driving the processes of individualisation, and in our case, the individualisation of children as distinct actors within the family. Importantly, a key aspect of this process is that children and young people within families feel that they construct their own lives and shape their own biographies, rather than having their sense of identity and belonging stamped upon them (Beck, 1997; Beck-Gernsheim, 2002). This process of biographisation can be seen, in Giddens' terms, as a form of self-reflexivity in conditions of reflexive modernisation (Giddens, 1991).

In his most recent works Giddens has turned back to 'the family' but in a revivified and idealised form of the democratic family. He states that 'The family is a basic institution of civil society' (1998: 89). Moreover, he argues that

The family is becoming democratized, in ways which track processes of public democracy; and such democratization suggests how family life might combine individual choice and social solidarity ... Democratization in the context of the family implies equality, mutual respect, autonomy, decision-making through communication and freedom from violence. (Giddens, 1998: 93)

He constructs the democratic family as a policy ideal and a political objective. Giddens was a close adviser to the Tony Blair New Labour government in the UK in the 1990s, and his work on the democratic family has been foregrounded in 'Third Way' public policy statements. The 'democratic family' in that sense takes on meaning inasmuch as it both accommodates changes in family form (non-heterosexual families, fragmented families and one-parent families) and also recognises the importance of family in the stability of children's lives (e.g. children are seen to grow up more psychologically secure, better able to achieve academic success, and more confident in sexual and social relationships within a framework of constant non-conflictual co-parenting relations). The ideal of the democratic family is one predicated on emotional and sexual equality, mutual rights and responsibilities, co-parenting, lifelong parental contracts, negotiated authority over children, obligations of children to parents and social integration (Giddens, 1998: 95). And this ideal is set against other sociological typifications of family life (e.g. 'the traditional family', 'the conservative family', 'the dysfunctional family').

Instead of seeing this as a shift from one theoretical position (Foucauldian) to another (broadly Giddensian), we might consider how the agency of children within families is facilitated and supported through governmental infrastructures, as mapped out by Foucault, Donzelot, Rose, Walkerdine and others. The settling of the 'psy' experts (Donzelot) around the family from the late nineteenth century onwards, and the sexualisation, psychologisation and therapeutisation of the family through the twentieth century, serves not to curtail the agency of children in the domestic, but to facilitate their capacity to speak. The speaking child becomes a central figure in the remaking of the modern family as a site of emotional communication and security. The health of the nation and the wellbeing of the family are seen to be dependent on the happy and talkative child. In Lasch's later work on the minimal self, a work that continues but also rearticulates his earlier ideas he argues that

The modern family is the product of egalitarian ideology, consumer capit-alism, and therapeutic intervention. In the nineteenth century, a combin-ation of philanthropists, educators, and social reformers began to uphold bourgeois domesticity as a corrective both to fashionable dissipation and to the 'demoralization' of the lower classes. From the beginning, the 'helping professions' sided with the weaker members of the family against patriarchal authority ... They championed the rights of children, condemn-ing the arbitrary power parents allegedly exercised over their offspring and questioning their competence as well. One result of their efforts was to subject the relations between parents and children to the supervision of the state, as executed by the schools, the social work agencies, and the juvenile court. A second result was to alter the balance of forces within the family. Men lost much of their authority over children to their wives, while children gained a certain independence from both parents, not only because other authorities asserted their jurisdiction over childhood but because parents lost confidence in the old rules of child-rearing and hesitated to assert their own claims in the face of professional expertise. (Lasch, 1984: 185–6)

Although we should be cautious of taking this argument wholesale, it is evident that any democratisation needs to be seen in the context of those infrastructures which both endow children with capacity to speak and the capacity of others to hear their voice. The voice of the child, as it were, is made possible by those 'outside' as well as those 'inside' the family.

Family talk and modernisation

The construction of children with speaking rights, as it were, within the family is closely correlated with a broader narrative of the modernisa-tion of the family. The construction of children as speaking subjects is often seen as a significant lever with regard to the modernisation not simply of the family but also of the social more generally. Thus, Smart and colleagues argue that children should have a stake in the production of academic knowledge. They argue that it is important 'to do research *with* children rather than *on* or *about* them and, in the process, to give their views legitimacy' (Smart et al., 2001: 14); 'children were treated as social equals in the conversations and as co-producers of knowledge and meaning' (185). Bren Neale, one of the researchers with Carol Smart on her family and divorce project, refers to families as being guided by an 'ethic of respect', an ethic which is mutual and concerned with the respect of others (Neale, 2002). Mutuality is increasingly seen as constituting a core ethic for research with children. The endowing of children as co-researchers (i.e. as co-producers of knowledge) suggests a radical rethinking and realigning of what constitutes knowledge and children's role in its production and circulation. But, more than this, emphasis on the construction of children as speaking subjects, on an ethics of mutuality and on the alignment of children as co-producers of knowledge, facilitates a further rebalancing of the relations between children in families and what Lasch refers to as 'the helping professions'.

The idea of children talking on more equal terms in the family is also seen as a key facet of modernisation projects and of a narrative of modernisation across the globe. For example, Cindi Katz, in her research on children growing up in Howa, Sudan, discusses how one of her participants, Muna (whom she has known and researched since she was a child), suggests that her relation to her mother when she was young is very different from her relation to her daughter now. Although Katz disagrees with what Muna says, she settles on Muna's account of how her children are now able to talk about their future hopes (something which Muna says she was unable to do as a child) and how she is able to talk more openly about matters such as henna-ing and smoke baths. It is not clear whether it is the case that this represents a shift in parent–child relations from more hierarchical to more friendship-like relations. Muna wants her children to be educated, but also to know how to do the traditional tasks of farming and tending the land. For Katz, the changes in Howa are correlated with what she calls 'time–space expansion' (rather than David Harvey's 'time–space compression' or Giddens' 'time–space distanciation') through the geography of work (primarily the men in the village travelling from home to work), new forms of consumption and the valorisation of schooled education (Katz, 2004). The changes which

Katz is describing in the Sudan bear some similarities to those taking place in the US and Europe, but with regard to the forms of state, governmentality and marketisation they are very different. It is important, then, both to understand the particularity of particular social formations and not to assume a simple mimetic relation between global north and south within a simple model of development and modernisation and the role of children's talk therein.

These spaces of talk are not only the consequence of historic governmental shifts, they are also traversed by modern forms of governmentality in the here and now, and they are significant sites for the innovation of modern forms of power. We should be cautious, then, of overstating any democracy of the family, not least because even well-meaning statements of intent (as framed in the UK Children's Act of 1989, which supports a place for children having a legal say in decisions of divorce) often play out in practice as vehicles for the will of competing parents or experts (see James and James, 1999). But also, we must recognise that the attribution of voice to children comes with demands as well as rights. As Pryor and Emery state, 'children often do not want to make decisions about adult matters, even when they are deeply affected by them. In our zeal for recognizing the rights of children we may over-interpret their desire to have a voice in family matters' (Pryor and Emery, 2004: 171). This implies having a high degree of sensitivity to children's 'voices' that does not construct an obligation to be responsible. Pryor and Emery argue that

Children often seem to understand that responsibility is the corollary of rights. Young children especially are clear that they do not want to be responsible for major decisions at these times [of divorce]. It may be, then, that adults are well advised to provide a scaffolding structure for children within which they are enabled to foster, maintain, and abstain from relationships as far as possible ... to create and maintain an atmosphere ... within which children can exercise agency in creating their own relationship network and identity. (Pryor and Emery, 2004: 186).

Contemporary forms of governmentality of families, then, need not simply address the parent as the relay of sovereignty but individual family members, namely in our case children, in a manner that allows the interlocutor not only to speak but also to stay silent, to have some control (whether actively or passively) over the conditions of communication and the relations of government.

But any discussion of the family as a space of conversation must also be set alongside a history of violence. Much of the research on the democratisation of families has ignored, or at least failed to properly integrate, the idea of family relations as relations of force, violence and abuse. If the 1970s saw an intensified academic investment in the family as an emotional and sexualised economy, then it was Lloyd DeMause, in his *History of Childhood* (1976), who wanted to talk about that economy as also being an economy of violence and abuse, and who provided a narrative (with some graphic descriptions of cases of the abuse of children by adults) of the development of parent–child relations from a history of infanticide to a present of greater socialisation, care and empathy. His psychohistory has been widely criticised for its model of linear historical development and progress and for its elision of the history of childhood with a history of child abuse. Yet in many ways DeMause is significant precisely because of his insistence on that correlation between family and abuse. Although his psychohistory has overshadowed his major findings, it was his understanding of the everyday casual nature of violence toward children, the correlation of that violence with the very construction of childhood as a social institution, and his understanding that emotional relations of care and intimacy would provide a surpassing of such abuse that set his argument apart from others who were keen to see violence toward children only in the context of a social segregation and children's liberation from the institution of childhood. But we must be wary of seeing in history a reduction in family violence and conversely a growth in love and care. This is a common narrative which reaffirms the 'modern family' as a space of intimacy, shared emotions and communicational harmony.

The relation between violence and intimacy is one that certainly cannot be reduced to an inverse antithetical relation; violence does not necessarily lessen as care increases. The role of intimacy in the demonstration of domestic violence is all too apparent, whether in its most negative presentation of violence as a consequence of decadence or violence as a demonstration of care. Thus it has often been stated that 'chastisement' was done only because it was deemed to be 'good for the child' and 'only because I love him'. Moreover, sexual abuse, as Foucault argues, can be seen as an outcome of the increasing sexualisation of the parent–child relations and the emergence of modern forms of family relations from the eighteenth century onwards (1979). But that said, there is an absence of research on children and violence that understands violence not only as an offshoot of modern forms of power, but as a reasoned form of governmentality. To say this is not to return to monolithic models of violence and patriarchy that were circulated in the 1970s and 1980s, but to suggest that regular, everyday, localised and domesticated violence needs to be made visible in the context of its alignment with forms of reasoned government of children (Larson, 1999). Violence and abuse of children is as much a form of governed care as supervising television viewing or night-time reading or visits for health and development check-ups. The debates in the press, in Parliament, but also among parents in the school playground in the UK about 'smacking' children (and 'reasonable chastisement' or simply leaving a visible red mark) serve as an example. Similarly, long-standing ideas about 'sparing the rod and spoiling the child' should not be read as if they are only the intentions of mean and abusive adults; on the contrary, such declarations should be read for what they are, namely a form of government of children constructed in such a way that aligns physical abuse with parental intimacy and care. And it is this alignment of violence and care that is the problem.

Mediations of family in late modernity

Family practices, understandings of families, and children's agency with respect to the family are all increasingly mediated, not only through localised practices and interactions but also through forms of mediation at a distance. The role of experts and expert systems (such as social workers, doctors and welfare and health systems) play a significant role in modern forms of familial mediation, and modern means of media and communications play an increasingly significant role. Again, the work of Giddens has been highly influential in our understanding of forms of mediation in late modernity. His argument about the disarticulation of space and place and the shift away from social relations as constituted within conditions of co-presence to ones mediated at a distance is one that is taken up by media scholars in order to think about the role of media and communications in familial social relations. Thus, for example, John Thompson, who was at Cambridge with Giddens in the 1980s and 1990s, draws on this work to talk directly about the role of the media in contemporary social life. Other media scholars, not directly drawing on the work of

Giddens, have made similar kinds of arguments. For example, Joshua Meyrowitz (1987) provides a wide-ranging argument about the role of modern media in the dissolution of the sharp boundaries between public and private, between physical and social space, and between the differentiating categories of childhood and adulthood. The electronic media, in this argument, are seen to be at the forefront of the dynamics and processes of modernity and late modernity. What were once highly embedded local interactions have now become mediated and disembedded. Thus a personal conversation about schoolwork between a mother and a daughter might well take place on a mobile phone via text as much as it might via a face-to-face conversation in the kitchen at home. The homework might well be through a dedicated educational website, such that the child inputs data through a screen interface on their computer at home and the teacher, perhaps at school but maybe at home as well, marks the work from a similar interface. Studies looking at the role of video media in South-Asian families in Southall, London (Gillespie, 1995) and the use of the internet by Trinidadian families geographically dispersed across the globe (Miller and Slater, 2000) have documented how media and communications technologies play an important role in contemporary familial social relations.

Notwithstanding the wealth of research on ideological representations of the family in film, television and the print media (see Brunsden, 2000; Haralovich, 1988; Spigel, 1992), research on the social interaction of and interpretation by family members with respect to media technologies and content has been pursued by sociologists and media and communications scholars. Pioneering work by David Morley on the nature of situated family television viewing in the 1980s helped to stage subsequent work by Roger Silverstone and other scholars, such as Eric Hirsch, Sonia Livingstone and Shaun Moores, on the use and interpretation of information and communications technologies in the home (see Morley, 1986; Morley and Silverstone, 1991). Later research, particularly by Livingstone (2002) and Moores (1993), sought not only to consider the use and interpretation of media and communications in the household, but also how that use, interpretation and the technology itself helped to constitute the spatial differentiations, relations and positionings of the home (see also Morley, 2000; Oswell, 2002).

The history of the family has been, in many ways, tied to the history of the built environment of the household. The division of the household into separate sleeping arrangements for parents and children emerges alongside an awareness of the compartmentalisation of adult sexuality and the differentiation of children in terms of the sexual practices of the household (Foucault, 1980). Whereas before children and adults would have slept in a single room, in a household undifferentiated properly by room as defined by its function (i.e. sleeping, cooking, resting), now children not only have separate bedrooms but also occupy the household in different kinds of ways and through different kinds of spaces. The building of children's agency in the context of the family also, then, needs to be understood in terms of the mediation of the household and role of those media and communications technologies in the rearticulation of domestic geographies and of relations across the domestic, the public and the transnational (Livingstone, 2002). Through the use of e-mail, social networking platforms, texting and various other technologies, children and young people have become significant actors in shaping their own personal relations with friends and families within and without the household, but also in using these forms of social and technological networks to reconfigure their position, relationality, authority and expressivity in a family setting (Miller, 2011). Certainly for older children these forms of mediated interaction provide more evidence for considering children as significant producers of knowledge and of circulating that knowledge, sometimes locally, sometimes globally. The readily accessible disclosure of children's everyday lives online, for example, provides an opportunity for commerce to market those lived visible cultural spaces and interactions. Sometimes through observing online chat or activities in virtual spaces and sometimes through directly targeting young people with questions about products and brands, children are brought into loops of knowledge production (although it would be difficult to see this as a form of mutual co-research) (Berriman, 2012). What is also interesting about these domestic spaces (and children's agency within them) is that agency and interaction are mediated not through words alone but through relations with objects. Objects in the home provide points of connection and disconnection; they mark out relations of generation and gender. Bedrooms, for example, are places in which bits of technology are hoarded by teenagers that separate teenagers from the rest of the family but which connect them to others who are outside the built environment of the domestic. Thus, for example, Livingstone's research on children and families in the 1980s and 1990s revealed how cultural practices in the home had become highly differentiated according to generation and that those practices and the spatial differentiations were articulated through the accumulation of media and communications technology, such as televisions, MP3 players, internet connections and so on. The post-war period saw an increasing emergence and development of children and young people's 'bedroom cultures' (Livingstone, 2002; see also McRobbie, 1991). This work helps to frame an understanding of the relation of children to and within families in terms of a notion of what Livingstone refers to as 'living together separately' (Livingstone, 2002). It's not clear that these new forms of spatialisation can be simply analysed in terms of the greater individualisation of children within the home, but this process of separation, and the use of objects and technologies to mark out that separation, certainly helps to construct a form of collectivity which helps to define children and constitutes a space in which they are able to construct a sense of their lives (i.e. to construct their biographies) as a shared space. The material resources which are assembled in children's and young people's bedrooms (but also across other geographies of the domestic) do not simply constitute a set of tools to be used by prior constituted agents; rather, these resources realign and reconfigure that agency as a multiple innovation.

Conclusion

In this chapter we have discussed sociological ideas about the emergence of the modern family in terms of its being framed within a broader horizon concerning the growth of the modern state and the arrangement of relations across family, politics and the economy. We have also looked at the growth of a series of professionals, some of whom were and are aligned with the state, and how this developed to constitute a body of people and a set of practices of care which both put children and families under surveillance and also provided the infrastructure for a growing individualisation of children. This was an individualisation that was importantly projected through an idea of children having a voice (both cultural and political). It is in the context of this governmental arrangement that we can also understand increasing declarations of the democratic family.

It is clear that families in North America and Europe did not suddenly discover intimacy, love and care for the children and for each other in the nineteenth century (or thereabouts). But what we do see is that the affective economy of the family does, from that moment, become a significant register of wellbeing, a means of regulation by internal and external agents, and a site of investment with respect to all family members. Moreover, the capacity of and encouragement for children to speak becomes a defining measure of the wellbeing of both the family and the nation. In addition, the domestic space of the household becomes a key site of investment in infrastructure. Interior decor and design becomes popularised over the twentieth century, but importantly, over this period, media and communications technologies become central sites of investment and infrastructuring. Children are a major driver in the building of the modern home.

But family, household and home can no longer be assumed to be coextensive and to offer an assured stability. The opening up of the family and household through new relations of intimacy, through mixed marriage, through migration, through new forms of media and cultural technology constitute possibilities for these children living in these families and these households. Where historically in the global north philanthropic and state agencies have supported and developed the distributed agency of children, now new forms of media and abstract systems facilitate and innovate with respect to children's collective agency. But this is a particular social and historical trajectory. The formation of capacities and dispositions among family members and the cultural differentiation of familial practices is such that not only does it no longer make sense to talk of 'the family' as a social universal, but what counts as 'family' is dependent on highly complex forms of social and cultural capital and the value of that capital in the context of highly varied fields of experience.

7 | *School and education*

In this chapter we will consider the school, not so much as a site of learning and teaching but as a particular kind of social setting. As a particular kind of institution, it has brought children together and aligned them with regard to their measured and differentiated cognitive capacity. Far from producing docile subjects, modern schools facilitate children's agency, not least inasmuch as this has constituted both an explicit philosophy of the modern school (i.e. learning is through doing) and as this provides the umbrella for a number of innovations regarding children's agency. Moreover, as a social setting, the school has constituted a diagram through which social and cultural practices more generally are, and have been, made intelligible as a pedagology or subject to educational measure, but also importantly through which spaces of innovation and resistance have been constructed.

The emergence and standardisation of a common childhood

The medieval historian Didier Lett opens a chapter on the education of children between the fifth and thirteenth centuries by declaring: 'Contrary to what Philippe Ariès affirmed, people of the high Middle Ages had not forgotten the meaning of education' (Alexandre-Bidon and Lett, 1999: 39). The male offspring of noble families would start doing menial work in the household of another noble family from the age of 11 or 12 years, and would then gradually be trained in the responsibilities of knighthood. Girls would similarly be trained in reading, riding and dancing in the service of relatives (Heywood, 2001: 157). Children from non-aristocratic families would also be sent to relatives or to other households in order to learn through informal apprenticeships or forms of service. Children were instructed in particular crafts and skills; some were adopted into the family and instructed more generally in spiritual and moral matters;

113

others were treated harshly and used only for their labour (Heywood, 2001: 158). As Heywood notes, the education of children through apprenticeship, in which 'each generation merely handed down what it knew from its own experience in a particular calling and region', 'gradually withered on the vine from the sixteenth century onwards'; such a system was suited to a 'stable agrarian society' but was unable to cope with a changing and growing mercantile and urban economy (Heywood, 2001: 160).

The history of schooling in Europe in the early modern period indicates that although there were some schools for girls and although there were some schools in rural areas, most schools were in towns and catered to the education of boys (Cunningham, 2005: 99). Schooling was largely religious in orientation and was concerned with the instruction of Christian (Catholic or Protestant) texts and philosophy, primarily through the catechism. Literacy, in this sense, was tied to religious teaching. Increasingly, Cunningham argues, schools catered to demands for a literate population to administer the growing state offices and to be able to comprehend the growing ordinances that came from that emerging state apparatus; but also, he argues, there was a growing literary culture, which helped to facilitate a demand for print literacy (Cunningham, 2005: 100). There is some evidence, according to Cunningham, for suggesting that young children were sent to school as a childminding service while the parents worked. In all cases, although there were some charitable schools, most schooling required payment, and that indicated both the relative value of a taught education and the disparity between those who could pay (or saw the value of paying) and those who did not. The relative benefits and disadvantages of schooling at this time were reflected in the fact that those children who did receive some schooling often did so for three years or less (101). While elementary schools tended to be available for all, secondary education was largely the preserve of the upper classes. Many of the schools were run as private enterprises and not as state enterprises. They were not well liked by children, but enforcement was encouraged by parents. Increasingly over the course of the seventeenth, eighteenth and nineteenth centuries the role of the state grew (although education was still largely religious in orientation). At the same time, schooling took place less in the homes of families and more within public buildings (119). Increasingly attendance was enforced by church and state through fines and punishments (102 and 124).

Heywood argues that over the period from the late fifteenth to the late eighteenth centuries there emerged the 'first hints of universal literacy' (Heywood, 2001: 164). Over and above the resistance of parents and children alike, the enforcement of a national literacy was important for the shaping of the modern nation-state and its popular culture. In the late eighteenth and early nineteenth centuries schools were seen to be able to provide the means for national identity and unity. Cunningham argues that this was in part a consequence of enlightened absolutist government in Europe (Cunningham, 2005: 122). A single form of education could be provided to a single population under the reign of a single monarch within a single sovereign national territory. The foregrounding of the nation within state-governed education did not mean that the teaching of religious philosophy and doctrine became less important; rather, the latter became more centrally aligned with the objectives of the modern enlightened state. It was in this context that a universal education and compulsory school attendance came to be seen as public virtues, but there were enforcement difficulties and it was not able to be properly funded (i.e. through general taxation) (Cunningham, 2005: 124; Heywood, 2001: 155). The government of children's schooling and its centralisation within a growing national state administration provided the potential means of separation from a Europe-wide religious government centred in Rome (i.e. the papal centre of the Catholic Church).

In the modern period schooling became compulsory and widespread across the national population. The idea of a universal education and the systematic and regulated relationship between the institutions of schooling and the state played a major and significant role in the shaping of children's lives, in constructing normative ideas of childhood, and in the regulation of that normative ideal. Moreover, the consequences of programmatic demands for a national literate population were such that, on the one hand, they helped to form children into a horizontally organised (through an egalitarian principle of reading and writing for all), but increasingly differentiated (by ability, but also increasingly by linear segmentation of age) mass of people, while on the other hand a requirement developed for state investment and the formation of a class of adults increasingly differentiated from ordinary people by virtue of their professional training as teachers. No longer would education take place in family households or be undertaken by those willing to pass on a trade or moral guidance; no longer would schooling by a local schoolmaster be secondary to the everyday demands of familial economy and need (for example, to tend to the crops or put in a day's work in the stable). Modern education has sought to meet the needs of a modern economy to the extent that those needs have been defined by a state administration and the experts that shape its governmentalities, and is not directly the result of the local-ised everyday demands of ordinary people. Schooling in the nineteenth century became the object of increased intervention by educational experts. The emergence of a field of administrative knowledge with respect to children's schooling marked a dramatic shift from medieval apprenticeship to the birth of modern schooling. In the late eighteenth and early nineteenth centuries Andrew Bell and Joseph Lancaster developed, in the context of Anglican and Quaker schools in England but soon to be distributed more widely, a monitorial system of schooling. We will discuss the monitorial system in the following section, but for the moment it is sufficient to state that some historians and sociologists have argued that it was primarily through the development of educational practices and compulsory schooling in the late nineteenth and early twentieth centuries that 'childhood' con-stituted a normative ideal in relation to which children were standard-ised and made to fit that ideal. As John Sommerville has argued:

In the course of the nineteenth century ... [t]he desire to provide a proper childhood for every citizen forced changes both in education and in the public mind. The beliefs that were imposed through the state schools were reduced to those no one had yet doubted. And even liberals began to see merit in eliminating certain prejudices and habits through a standardized education. (Sommerville, 1982: 193)

The school, it has been argued, 'played a pivotal role in the construc-tion of a new kind of childhood' (Hendrick, 1990: 46). This 'new kind of childhood' was both standardised and 'truly national' (Hendrick, 1990: 46). Moreover, not simply an idea or an ideological construction (although it was certainly that too), it was formed through institution-alisation. Hendrick argues that schooling, '[b]y virtue of its legal authority, and on a daily basis through the school attendance officer ... was able to impose its vision on unwilling pupils and their parents' (Hendrick, 1990). And yet, Sommerville has argued that it was precisely because such a standardisation of childhood was an ideal that its institutionalisation and the attempts to shape children to that ideal failed: 'Those who clung to the ideal could only be embittered by the stubborn deviance of so many youngsters' (Sommerville, 1982: 204). The ideal (an ideology of childhood) that was presented in educational discourses, but also in literary and popular cultural texts, in welfare discourses and elsewhere, gave the impression of a standardisation and uniformity that was never actually realised. Moreover, it was this ideological construction of an imaginary ideal of childhood which constituted the object of libertarian critiques of schooling in the 1970s. For example, Ivan Illich states in *Deschooling Society* that

Institutional wisdom tells us that children need school. Institutional wisdom tells us that children learn in school. But this institutional wisdom is itself the product of schools because sound common sense tells us that only children can be taught in school. Only by segregating human beings in the category of childhood could we ever get them to submit to the authority of a school-teacher. (Illich, 1971: 41)

The disestablishment of schools or the deinstitutionalisation of learning harks back to a Rousseauesque view of the natural child learning through nature, but also fails to grasp how thoroughly learning is technologised and how significant the school has been in the development of social technologies.

Scholars have argued that the distribution of educational technologies, such as intelligence testing in the twentieth century, helped to reproduce a society divided by class. For example, Brian Simon, writing on the progression in England from primary education to either a 'grammar school' or a 'modern school' on the basis of examination of pupils at 11 years of age, has argued that intelligence testing 'serves the needs of a class-divided society which is not able to utilise the abilities of all its citizens, and so dare not develop them to the full' (Simon, 1953: 26). He argues that such a system of education distributes children via the psychological measurement of intelligence into one type of school designed to facilitate mental ability and the progression to university and the professions and another designed to train children in the crafts and skills of physical labour. The children who go on to command the leading positions in government, the economy and the professions constitute 'the monopoly of a small group' (26). This argument would suggest that it is from this class of children that teachers come. The intelligence test has a long history that traces back to Galton and others in the nineteenth century (Rose, 1989), but its advocate in the UK in the middle of the twentieth century was the psychologist Cyril Burt. Burt understood intelligence to be largely biological, innate and hereditary. The intelligence test, then, for Burt, simply made visible an innate disposition. The process of testing, classification and selection of children was seen as an efficient distribution of children on the grounds of natural ability. Moreover, some could argue that it was a system that overcame class prejudice precisely on the grounds that the test saw through ostensible signs of class and poverty and simply looked at intellectual and cognitive ability. And thus it could be seen as a meritocratic system that allowed bright working-class children to escape from their class position and to reap the benefits of grammar schools, university life and the professions. A number of commentators have lauded the UK's 1944 Education Act precisely for those reasons. Critics of Burt and of this system of selection, though, were widespread and eventually led to a shift in the UK in the 1970s toward a comprehensive system of secondary education. Nevertheless, attempts to redeploy the notion of intelligence testing on populations in order to govern the distribution of facilities and resources have repeatedly surfaced in the context less of class than of 'race'. Most notably, the issue rose again with the publication in the US in 1994 of *The Bell Curve* by Richard Herrnstein and Charles Murray.

The criticisms of intelligence testing are significant, but they often fall back on the idea of a common childhood, a common people, that is divided and distributed through mechanisms of inequality. In 1953 Simon rightly commiserated with the 'individual heartbreak' and 'disastrous wastage of ability', and declared that

the theories based on 'intelligence' testing, theories which preach the limitation of human powers, the decline of 'intelligence' and the helplessness of men in the face of their inherent defects, stand like a barrier in the way of real educational advance ... Instead, let us recognise that the most valuable capital of society is *people* and that the most important task to-day is to provide for the youth of this country the conditions for healthy, human development and the exercise of ability. (Simon, 1953: 111)

The idea of a common childhood stood as the basis of an ethical and political critique of a system of education and schooling. But the irony was that the institutionalisation of schooling and its standardisation in the nineteenth century provided precisely that ground of commonality, of children as a common people. Such a perspective is not without its problems, and we shall consider those in more detail in the next section.

Discipline and power

In the 1980s research seemed to continue the focus on, and antipathy toward, technologies of standardisation and measurement, but it did so in the context of a Foucauldian model of knowledge and power. In doing so, an anti-essentialist and constructivist notion of the child and of childhood was pursued. Foucauldian scholarship has been able to provide accounts not only for the figuring of the child within the government of and through the family, but also of the extensive canvas of contemporary social life. Foucault himself talks about the monitorial schools of the nineteenth century (Foucault, 1977). These schools were typified by their organisation of children in rows of desks, the regimentation of lessons and the curriculum, the overseeing authority of the schoolmaster, and, importantly, the role of pupils both as learners and as monitors. James Donald refers to a contemporary description by Patrick Colquhoun in his *New and Appropriate System of Education for the Labouring People* (1806):

The province of the master or mistress is to direct the whole machine in all its parts ... It is their business to see that others work, rather than work themselves. The master and mistress, from their respective chairs, overlook every part of the school, and give life and motion to the whole. They inspect the classes [the children sitting in one row] one after another; they call upon the monitors occasionally to bring them up, that they may specifically examine the progress of each pupil. (quoted Donald, 1992: 21)

The schools 'permit an internal, articulated and detailed control – to render visible those who are inside it; in more general terms, an architecture that would operate to transform individuals: to act on those it shelters, to provide a hold on their conduct, to carry the effects of power right to them, to make it possible to know them, to alter them' (Foucault, 1977: 172). The lining of pupils in rows, instituting an observer and monitor who has oversight of that row, coordinating the monitors with reference to a master, and thus facilitating a relationship between those pupils in a row according to their ability or inability to complete the tasks at hand but also with reference to a single standard across the monitorial space and across the collectivity of children constitutes a simple technology of measurement, pedagogic and standardising as much as it is differentiating. This is a technology less aimed at whole individuals than at the eyes and ears of some and the cognitive faculties and dexterity of the hands of others. These body parts are lined up with tools and objects that facilitate writing and desks and benches that permit the orchestration of bodies in lines. The school day is regimented according to clock time and pedagogic tasks are delimited through temporal segments. This is less an 'ideal' or 'ideology' of childhood and more a mixing of bodies, objects, spaces and times. The disciplinary architecture of the monitorial schools was distributed not only across pedagogic institutions, but could also be found in the apparatus of the prison and in the army barracks. The administration of time and space and the organisation of hierarchical observation, in Foucault's analysis, constituted significant techniques in the production of individual and docile bodies across a wide range of social practices and institutions.

This disciplinary architecture of the school remains until the middle of the twentieth century, but it also gets transformed. As we have seen, an understanding of the distribution of intelligence across a population is developed in scientific research from Francis Galton to Cyril Burt. Such understanding has implications for how different sections of the population are conceived and acted upon by government, but it also has a profound affect on the regulation of education according to intelligence difference. The division of schools has not only been according to age, but also with regard to perceived cognitive capabilities. Thus, children are divided into different ability groups within schools, and are also divided across different types of school. The use of regular testing and examination has been central to these distributions. The classification of different levels of intelligence is used to differentiate a population in a way appropriate to wider divisions of work between mental and physical labour (Rose, 1979 and 1985). Although in postindustrial information societies, distribution of children on the basis of cognitive ability is undertaken less with regard to a division between mental and manual than between creative and mundane work, for some, the division of children into school classes is closely correlated to the division of national populations into classes (Walkerdine, 1984). Jones and Williamson argue that

The new domain was defined at the point of intersection of two new ways of making statements about the population which were themselves formed during the nineteenth century, as the result of the constitution of town police forces and town health boards, on the one hand, and as a result of the reform of prison administrations and those of Poor Law institutions on the other. These two new ways of making statements about the population formed a topographical analysis and a historical analysis respectively: and by their intersection defined a new field of objects of analysis, that is to say, the classes of the population. A class was accordingly defined by a web of topographical connections, which also characterised conditions whereby children were trained up as members of a class, and it was this that formed the moral topography of class. (Jones and Williamson, 1979: 96)

Although there may certainly be a correlation between the distribution of children across school classes and the distribution of individuals across socioeconomic categories of class, there are also certainly some major divergences. That said, the deployment of mental measurement across both school and national populations certainly has been connected in governmental imaginations concerning class and classification from the nineteenth century onwards.

The histories and commentaries that emerged from a Foucauldian understanding of education were such that they focussed on the school as one instance among many of a modern form of power, namely discipline. Discipline, as distinct from punishment (which may be seen as the inflicting of pain with respect to the failure to achieve a particular goal or the crossing of a particular boundary), was oriented toward the manipulation of populations and bodies such that their docility would become apparent and such that individuals would be formed through the administration of time and space. In this account, the modern school has an effect of individualising children, but only inasmuch as that individualisation is coordinated within a disciplined grid of time and space. In that sense, the progression through the schooling system, from primary to secondary, and the division of schools according to intelligence, but also the organisation of the school day according to fixed time slots (lessons, break-time and so on) can be seen in terms of the disciplining of children into docile subjects. In this Foucauldian model, the child does not exist prior to its individualisation. The individual child, inasmuch as it is seen and is acted upon, is an effect of such a disciplinary apparatus. In this model, there is no individual child with ability and capability that can be brought forth in the critique of power and standardisation. But also the focus on individualisation downplays the focus on children as a collectivity. Their serialisation within conditions of discipline certainly emphasises and invests in particular children, but only inasmuch as it impacts on all children subjected to this pedagogic technology.

Moreover, many Foucauldians working on children and education were critical of the notion that children were docile subjects. They pointed to the context of modern child-centred classrooms in which children, especially young children, were seen to have significant freedom. And children in contemporary classroom settings were seen to learn not through passive induction but through active learning. The child learner of the mid to late twentieth century was defined through their agency, not through their docility. From the 1950s onwards the developmental psychology of Jean Piaget and others helped to frame a context for the national adoption of a child-centred pedagogy that placed children's freedom at the heart of learning and cognitive growth. Children were now conceived within formal educational institutions as learning through doing. The emphasis within this pedagogy was not on teaching but on learning and the supervising of suitable contexts for learning. The child was produced at the centre of learning. They were seen to learn at their own pace according to the facilitating environment around them. Individual children within the classroom were seen to require different forms of attention as a consequence of their different levels of development. As with pastoral care generally, the teacher, like the priest, was able to care for each member of their class individually. New techniques (such as record cards and student notes) and a new architecture of the classroom (namely the organisation of the room into different learning spaces within an open-plan environment) were deployed (Walkerdine, 1984). Of course, this pedagogic space does not see the demise of teacherly supervision, but rather its reconstruction within a child-centred pedagogy. The teacher has an omniscient vision and the power to organise the children of different abilities and to disperse them appropriately around the classroom in different groups. The teacher is constituted as needing to be able to see each child learning and needing to be able to supervise their learning (i.e. across or through these differences); they need to be able to manage children's learning as a 'supervised freedom' (Walkerdine, 1984). In this sense, then, the Foucauldians argue that there is a continuity between the early monitorial schools (and the disciplinary apparatus within which they were formed) and the regulated freedom of child-centred schools, but they point to a contrast in the two regimes of power, knowledge and subjectivisation inasmuch as the two rest upon different epistemological, administrative and architectural foundations (i.e. they are constituted within different forms of governmentalisation). The two regimes are based on different ideas about the child, different systems of knowledge, and different notions of learning. The architectural spaces of the classroom in the two regimes, for example, are very different. Walkerdine refers to two different diagrams, one of the traditional classroom and one of the child-centred classroom, and she considers how the teacher and his/her relation to the pupils and their learning are very different in each case. She talks about the novel orchestration of learning in the child-centred classroom:

What does 'active learning' mean in this instance? It requires a rearrangement of the desks from rows (listening to the teacher talking) to groups (thereby severely limiting the possibility for instruction of the whole class). The teacher is no longer in front of the class. There are no set textbooks. The 'nature table' has disappeared in favour of 'science'. There is even more room for spontaneity: 'the sudden unpredictable interest that requires space'. (Walkerdine, 1984: 156)

A central tenet of this discourse and its materialisation is the psychological discourse of Piaget and developmental psychology. What is important in these child-centred spaces is that the teacher is not there to discipline the child (although that may be one of their functions), but to facilitate their freedom. Play becomes constructed as a central figure through which children's learning is understood. The Plowden Report on children and primary schooling in the UK in 1967 is a pivotal policy shift in this regard. Moreover, this understanding of children as learning through play had implications for child-centred schooling, but also for modern forms of mothering (Walkerdine and Lucey, 1989).

Children learn on their own terms, through play, through stimulation, not by rote or disciplined 'teaching'. Walkerdine argues that these discourses and practices disclose the child as a subject that is socially and historically specific. The truth of the child – what the child really is – is not external to these practices. The child is not only produced

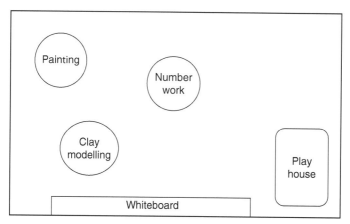

Figure 7.1 Example of a child-centred primary school classroom.

through these techniques, but also through the administration of their bodies in space. And, for Walkerdine, this regulation of children is predicated on class differentiation in terms of the normalisation of a child-centred supervision (to put it crudely, as a form of middle class-ness) and a gendered construction of the normal cognitive subject as masculine (Walkerdine, 1984). But we cannot assume that a Piagetian discourse was simply applied wholesale to educational practices in the UK or elsewhere, and this in turn has implications for how we construe the relevance of an understanding of child-centred pedagogy as a diagram of power and knowledge as described by Walkerdine. Of course, the pressures of being a teacher and the contradictions that might surface in any actual classroom situation (for example, when faced with an unruly child or a child that is too good, or a classroom that is half built, or equipment that is so new that it becomes a fetish for the children) might lead to the playing out a 'regulated freedom' in ways other than those foreseen in the educationalist theorist's eyes (see Lee, 2001: 82).

Social interaction in educational contexts

Methodologically, Foucauldian analysis has often relied on historical documents written by adults, yet many sociologists of children have sought an understanding of children's agency through observation of children present before them and through their words. Exemplary in this respect is Susan Danby and Carolyn Baker's study of children between the ages of 3 and 5 years and their teachers in a preschool classroom setting in an inner city in Australia. In a paper from the study, '"What's the problem?" Restoring social order in the preschool classroom' (Danby and Baker, 1998b), they state that their methodological perspective is derived from conversation analysis and ethnomethodology, that they are interested in conversation and discourse as social interaction, and that they are interested in agency and the capacity for particular forms of agency only in the context of particular social settings, encounters or situations. They are interested in social order only inasmuch as it is constituted in the process of social interaction. In that sense, their work draws on the analysis of Hutchby and Moran-Ellis (1998). They want to provide an argument that suggests that social structure does not pre-exist, as a determining entity, actual social interactions. Structure or power does not stand outside of the interactions of children and teachers; social order is formed within and on the basis of those social interactions. Danby and Baker view children's play in educational settings as part of the 'very serious work of constructing social order' (Danby and Baker, 1998b: 157). They are interested in how the interactions of the young children they observe constitute a peer culture and how those interactions construct and reconstruct the participants of those interactions. In contrast, for example, to a normative model of social institutions, these authors view children as 'competent practitioners of multiple social orders in their relationships with each other as well as with teachers and other adults' (158). But also in contrast to some models of children's social agency, they understand agency only in the context of social interaction. The resources that are deployed have value only inasmuch as they are constituent aspects of that interaction. Of particular importance to Danby and Baker are conversational resources and interactions. It is through talk that social order is accomplished. Sequences of talk form the 'interactional units of *occasioned and situated activity*' (159). This talk is ordinary and everyday social practice.

Notwithstanding the issues regarding how adult researchers might gain access to young children's localised interactions and how they might collect data unobtrusively, Danby and Baker videotaped the interactions across three weeks. Let me here consider two cases of social interaction between a teacher and the children. The first case concerns an interaction between Amelia and Portia (both aged 4), Elana (aged 3) and a teacher. Amelia and Elana are playing. Portia joins in. Portia tells Elana that she is not her friend and Amelia pretends to lock Elana in jail. Elana then opens the door and declares that she has the key. The jail and the key are all constructs of the conversation and have value only in that context. At this point Portia grabs Elana's arm and tries to push her back into the imaginary jail. She says 'The police will get you!' Elana cries, 'No, no!' The second case is of David (aged 4) and John, Colin, Andrew and Connell (all aged 3) and the teacher. Connell, as he is only just 3 years of age, has only just started attending preschool. John and David start picking on Connell. They tell him to go to jail; they say that they'll throw him through a television set; that they will get Batman to help and also the police; and that they will 'piss on him'. Whilst they are saying this, they move closer to Connell until he starts crying. In the first case, the children's social order is unsettled when Elana's arm is grabbed by Portia inasmuch as the pretence of the play is broken and she starts crying. Similarly, in the second case, David's jumping up and down initiates Connell's crying. Thereupon, in both cases, the teacher intervenes.

It is suggested that children are 'political actors' and that they call on the teacher not to settle or resolve a conflict or dispute, but to take sides. It is an attempt at strategic mobilisation. The intervention of the teacher is such that they move close to the scene and then assign responsibility, not for the supposed wrong caused, but for explaining what has happened. Danby and Baker argue that teachers (as with parents) have an ability to asymmetrically intervene. The question 'What is the problem?' is a demand for the child to speak. The teacher establishes 'guidelines' regarding acceptable responses (i.e. regarding 'hurt feelings'). In both cases the teacher does not ask the hurt child for their explanation. That child is not given full speaking rights in the communicative exchange. The teacher, Danby and Baker suggest, may be wanting, less to find out the 'real reasons' as to why the crying has occurred and to settle the children's social order, than to respond to the problem of the hurt child (the 'sad child') and to reassert her teacherly social order. The accomplishment of social order for the teacher is different than for the children. Danby and Baker talk about two cultures (adult and children's), such that the teacher (having sorted out the problem according to her developmental child-centred criteria) then leaves the children 'to restore their unsettled social order' (Danby and Baker, 1998b: 168).

In both cases the teacher intervenes in order to resolve a problem. But, Danby and Baker argue, the resort to crying by Elana and by Connell are different inasmuch as they are articulated in two differently gendered sequences of interaction. Once the teacher has had demonstrated (as a performance) the resolution of the conflict (through a hug between the different parties) and once she has left to allow the child to continue playing, the children themselves need to repair their social order according to their own relation. Danby and Baker comment on the non-verbal repairs that the girls and John do with regard to Elana's upset. The repairing of social order for the girls is very different than for the boys. David is not concerned about making Connell feel better. He does not continue the discourse of the teacher in the same way that the girls do with regard to 'making Elana feel better'. The 'repairing' of social order is highly gendered, such that Portia and Amelia adopt the teacher's discourse of care and consolation, whereas David and the other boys replace the teacherly discourse with their own 'hegemonic masculine version'. Moreover, 'For the girls, the repair restores their connection with each other; for the boys, their repair continues their celebration of masculinity' (Danby and Baker, 1998b: 169).

The question of gender comes up in a more pronounced way in another paper by Danby and Baker from the same study (Danby and Baker, 1998a). In 'How to be masculine in the block area', Danby and Baker compare the scenario between David, John and Connell with an earlier interaction between John, David, Matt and Andrew. For Danby and Baker, both interactions repeat the same sequence of phases, from 'go away', calling reinforcements, resistance, discourse of strength and size, threats of violence, enter the apprentices, repetition of sound and close physical proximity and cry for help, to the presence of the teacher (158). Danby and Baker show how the two groups of boys progress through these phases of social interaction. In each case the level of aggression and the threats of violence increase until the teacher intervenes to diffuse the confrontation. Even then, as we saw above, the intervention of the teacher merely interrupts the social order of the boys; it does not properly take command of their localised masculine order. Danby and Baker show how these interactions are not only about the exclusion of one boy by a group of boys, but also about the inclusion of that boy into a masculine social order inasmuch as such interactions constitute forms of ritualised initiation. Danby and Baker, by taking the case of John, show how a child is transformed from being excluded by a group of bigger boys (in the confrontation with David, Matt and Andrew) to one included in their aggressive and threatening practices (in the scene with David and Connell). They argue that this constitutes a rite of passage in which John moves from being a 'less experienced player to a more experienced participant' and demonstrates how 'selected members of this classroom are initiated into the existing gender relations in the block area' (168). Although Danby and Baker methodologically focus on children's talk and in one sense see talk as a form of action, they also consider such talk alongside children's (other) action. Both talk and action constitute the resources for social interaction. Thus, the escalation of aggression among the two groups of boys discussed above is seen (although not reflexively scrutinised) in terms of the relation between talk and action. Danby and Baker argue that

These boys have taken up the position of assertive masculinity through their use of scatological language and threats of aggression and power. Declarations of male power are manifested as verbal or physical threats and call on outside objects of power (sword, police, robot monster shark). (Danby and Baker, 1998a: 165)

As the researchers suggest, this could be seen as fantasy play, but what is significant for us is the way in which the boys themselves, or at least the principal antagonist, David, refers to his and his compatriots' actions, when asked to account for himself by the teacher, by saying: 'We're just talking to him.' Here the ambiguity of the signifier 'talking' refers both to talk as not-physical violence but also to talk as a form of physical violence. The raising of the boys' voices, the assertion of more cacophonous sounds (such as car noises), is accompanied by the clapping of hands near the younger child's face. As the researchers argue, such social interaction is not dysfunctional but is part of the everyday interaction through which young children negotiate their collective living (Danby and Baker, 1998a: 168). Marjorie Harness Goodwin, a US linguistic anthropologist, in her research on girls' peer group interactions in playground spaces, though, warns against any simple division between the interactions of girls and those of boys. Her research demonstrates that we should be wary of a 'two cultures' approach that differentiates between different forms of aggression along a spectrum of physical to verbal force, such that boys might be seen to be more physically aggressive or, if not, then might be more verbally aggressive than girls. Such a distinction, she argues, is often the result of research that focusses on individual behaviour, whereas research on social and conversational interaction as it happens moment by moment presents a picture of girls' social behaviour in terms of their aggressive demarcation of boundaries and of forms of inclusion and exclusion (Goodwin, 2002).

Conversation analytic and ethnomethodological research, such as that of Danby and Baker, is able to offer detailed observations and insights into children's social interaction. Such microsociological accounts are able to conceive of children as significant actors in their own right and hence are able to substantiate broader claims in the sociology of childhood about children's social agency. But such agency is always situated and composed of the resources to hand within particular social settings. Children's social agency is not conceptualised as an a priori, true for all social settings. There is much value in such research, in that it hypostatises neither agency nor structure. But the methodological focus on the here and now tends to leave unquestioned the historic accumulation of resources and competencies and the consequent asymmetries regarding such accumulated resources and competencies. It is, in many ways, no surprise that the teacher reinforces her social order in the two cases above. Moreover, the concentrated focus on children's situated social interaction, for example in the Danby and Baker research above, tends to fail to recognise the broader discursive, institutional and technical infrastructures within which such interaction is itself situated. Does it matter, for example, that the children are interacting in a preschool setting? What resources are ready to hand as a consequence of that particular institutional and discursive setting?

What we don't learn from Danby and Baker is how the preschool brings together children of similar, but also differentiated, ages, histories and backgrounds and how it provides the infrastructuring of those children through supervised spaces of play but also via mediated conversations and negotiations, emotional struggles and hostilities, and social interactions between children, teachers and other support staff. This is a novel space of interaction for these young children in their personal lives, but it is also (as we have seen earlier) a relatively recent historical innovation. If the boys take up an 'assertive masculinity' and refine their 'scatological language and threat of aggression', then they do so in highly mediated settings and in the context of where certain resources, rather than others, are ready to hand. Why, for example, do the boys resort so readily to linguistic rather than physical aggression? Why is there a threat of 'pissing' rather than a punch?

It is worth adding a note of caution when considering children's conversational interaction and agency, namely, in aligning speech with agency and silence with passivity. Thus, for example, one researcher concludes a paper on children's voice and agency in the classroom by stating: 'The children ... are not passive recipients but active constructors of their classroom community. Their life narratives shape the curriculum' (Etheridge, 2004: 101). In contrast, we might look to the research undertaken by David Silverman and colleagues on the significance of children's silence in parent–teacher interviews. This research shows how interviews between parents and teachers (designed so that teachers can inform parents as to how the child is doing at school and so that the parent can ask questions and raise concerns) are constructed in such a way that the parent and not the child is the designated recipient of the conversational address of the teacher. But when the teacher purports to address the child, the child remains silent and doesn't respond to the question or the invitation to speak. Silverman and colleagues show how such silence is constituted not as the absence of interaction, but precisely as 'an interactive possibility' (Silverman et al., 1998: 238). The non-response is an 'accomplishment in its own right'. It allows the young person neither to agree to the teacherly resolution, nor to disagree. They argue that 'The young person's silence, then, can be seen as a form of interactive work in relation to the design of the talk between parent and professional. By no means is the silent child not a competent child' (239).

Cultural politics of the classroom and popular culture

From the late 1980s and early 1990s a growing body of research emerged from the application and development of a series of ideas and problems concerning culture, identity and power that were associated with the development of cultural studies. Research coming from a cultural studies of education and schooling provided a major platform for the understanding of children and childhood in contemporary society. Two main themes were addressed in the research: different forms of cultural identity formation and identification, primarily concerning gender, sexuality, race and ethnicity; and the relation between power and pedagogy within but more importantly beyond the classroom, in the playground, on the street, in the home and in popular culture.

A central feature of the research on cultural identity formation was that it was highly critical of what it conceived as 'essentialist' theories of identity; namely, those theories of self-identity that presumed (a) that the self was formed as a discrete and whole unit separate from, in the first instance, the social group and the natural world, and (b) the integration of the self into society was through particular mechanisms of socialisation, but that through those mechanisms of socialisation the self remained nevertheless a discrete and distinct individual, and (c) that underlying the individual self were certain key hard-wired features, and although the specific features might be open to contested views, by and large they included gender and sexuality and intelligence as being essential to the make-up of individual beings. In contrast to essentialist assumptions of the self, the research on cultural identity formation put forward theoretical ideas that drew heavily from traditions of thought that were labelled 'post-structuralist'; namely, theories of subjectivity formation that (a) argued that the self (or subject) is always and only ever a cultural construction and that there are no hard-wired traits that determine who the child is or might become, (b) the cultural construction of the self is primarily linguistic or discursive, (c) the discursive construction of the self means that within different discourses different identities are formed such that the subject, or self, is constituted through those different discourses in different, sometimes contradictory, ways, (d) the subject is always plural and never an individual as such, and (e) cultural identity is always in process, never fixed, and is always contestable in fields of power and struggle. Thus in his research on the making of masculinity, Máirtín Mac an Ghaill delineates a shift from the study of the socialisation of children into 'sex roles' to a 'deconstruction of sex/gender identities' that understands subjectivity in the context of structures of power, and in doing so focusses 'upon the confusions and contradictions that are constitutive of the students' construction of gendered and sexual identities in relation to major influences, including increasing central and local state regulation, changing family networks, restructured local labour markets, changing sexual patterns of consumption, peer and leisure group practices and media representations' (Mac an Ghaill, 1994: 13). Mac an Ghaill's research feeds into a broader agenda concerning the social and cultural construction of sexual and gender identities in schoolchildren, including notably in the UK the research of Debbie Epstein. Epstein, in collaboration with Richard Johnson, argues that 'sexuality is intrinsic to the formation of individual and group identities in schools and that schools are sites for the active making of such identities and of meanings around sexuality', and in this sense they are interested in 'the formal sexual curriculum (in the form of sex education)', but also in 'the sexual cultures of both teachers and students, which are intrinsic to the dynamics of schooling, for example in relation to control, resistance and "discipline"' (Epstein and Johnson, 1998: 9).

Some of this research has drawn on, but has radically developed, the ethnographic research of Paul Willis on schooled masculinities and work from the mid 1970s. Willis' research itself was ostensibly a revision, but also a critique, of the Bowles and Gintis (1976) argument that schools had an ideological function, namely to socialise children in order to fulfil the requirements of a capitalist society. Thus, children learned their social position and the skills required for their adult labour. Willis (1977) argued that in the classroom a group of working-class boys, which he called 'the lads' (in contrast to the other main group of boys in the classroom, the boys who worked hard or the 'ear'oles'), did not so much learn the lessons of their future labour in the classroom but rather through their resistance to the teacher and formal education (and their positive construction of a working-class culture). It was in the context of that culture that they learned the kinds of masculine identity required for their future jobs as manual labourers (1977). For Mac an Ghaill, the school classroom is not only productive of a differentiation of manual and mental labour, the lads and the ear'oles, but also of a range of positions: 'the macho lads', 'the academic achievers', 'the new enterprisers' and 'the real Englishmen'. He says that these peer groups (with the exception of the latter) were mixed white, African-Caribbean and Asian and that they were typified by a fluidity rather than a fixed subcultural identity (Mac an Ghaill, 1994: 54–5). For him, this typology was used less as a means of revealing fixed and distinct masculine cultures than as a heuristic device for making visible peer-group identifications (54). In the structuring of these positionalities, there are continuities and discontinuities across generations; thus sons would not necessarily follow in their fathers' footsteps (as in Willis' account). In the context of a social landscape typified by a shift from industrial to postindustrial production, the cultures of working-class masculinities have been shaped by fragmentation and crisis. Thus, for some of 'the lads' any classroom resistance has been an education not for manual labour, but for unemployment (Stafford, 1981).

The correlations across 'race', ethnicity, religion and masculine identity formation have been significant in Mac an Ghaill's research, but also in the research of others, such O'Donnell and Sharpe (2000). In the context of Muslim schoolboys in the UK, Louise Archer's work (2001 and 2003) has been influential in foregrounding the changing identity formation of Asian boys in the context of rapidly changing national and transnational cultures of belonging, territory and identity. The transition from 'soft and weak' to 'hard and strong' masculine identities in the context of the playground and classroom, the shift from 'English' to 'outsider' in the movement from family in the UK to family in Pakistan or Bangladesh, the transnational identification with a global Umma, and the negation of self and group alongside boys, and importantly girls, who are white, African-Caribbean, African, and other ethnicities makes for an empirically complex mix of factors leading to the construction and contestation of modern masculine school identities.

The work of Walkerdine has been significant in these debates; not only her contribution to Foucauldian post-structuralist ideas of children and education, but also her synthesis of those ideas with a psychoanalytic approach to subjectivity that permits an understanding of the articulation of the social and the psychical constitution of the schooled subject. She argues, for example, that the powerful discourse about girls, schooling and rationality that sees girls only ever at best as 'hard workers' and rarely as 'brilliant', 'genius' or 'lazy and troublesome, but highly intelligent' is premised both on the historical construction and alignment of modern educational rationalities and gendered differentiation and on the splitting of gendered subjectivity. On the one hand, this relies on an understanding of 'the child' as a discursive entity constructed and regulated within social practice. In this sense, 'experience' and 'the child' are produced through signs (Walkerdine, 1987: 270). Moreover, the production of signs of the child is such that the child is differentiated according to understandings of 'the normal' and 'the pathological'. In this way, the child is regulated according to such regimes of truth and normalisation. But, on the other hand, the truth of educational discourse and practice is not such that there is a simple division between 'reality' and 'fantasy'. On the contrary, the truth, for example, of child-centred educational discourse is that it is embroiled in both truth and fantasy and that the identifications of both girls and boys are dependent on the psychical structures of fantasy (274). This means, for Walkerdine, that the regimes of truth through which schooled subjects are produced (and for her particularly the gendered construction of girlhood) are always laden with unconscious desire and affect. She states that

If girls' and women's power is a site of struggle, constantly threatening the tenuous grasp of male academic superiority, then any engagement with these issues in practice cannot rest upon a rationalistic base of choice or equal opportunities. Not only must the fiction of the gendered splitting be taken apart, but the psychic struggle engaged in by girls and women to live out the impossibly contradictory positions accorded to us must be addressed, as must the paranoias of the powerful that understand women's success as a (conscious or unconscious) threat to their position of superiority, shaky as it is. This requires a strategy that engages with the educational politics of subjectivity, a politics that refuses to split the psychic from the social and attempts to understand the complexity of defence and resistance and to find new ways of dealing with those for teachers and students alike. (Walkerdine, 1987: 279)

For many working in the sociology of childhood, but also more generally, the engagement with a post-Enlightenment problematic that refuses to separate the claim to truth from the circulation of desire has been a hard task. More often, the claim to truth and knowledge has been held up to fend off the emotional, the affective, and fantasy.

The second major theme within cultural studies research on education and schooling has come from a concerted effort to see education as being not just limited to the school classroom, inasmuch as it is important to consider children and young peoples' playground cultures but also the social and cultural world beyond the school gates. In part, this has been an issue linked with the shaping of the school curriculum and the exclusion through that curriculum of other, local and everyday knowledges and practices. In this sense, the school curriculum is understood in the context of a broader struggle over culture, high and low, elite and popular, and with the elision of that cultural differentiation with a generational differentiation between adults and children, teachers and school pupils. Thus, for example, in the opening pages of their book *Cultural Studies goes to School* (1994), David Buckingham and Julian Sefton-Green state that 'the place of popular culture within the school curriculum has become an increasingly political issue'. And it is unsurprising that these two writers have sought to foreground the politics of this issue in terms of value and the valuing of popular media cultures. They continue by arguing that the 'growing interest in media education at all levels of the education system has re-awakened traditional anxieties about "cultural value" in their most absolutist form' (Buckingham and Sefton-Green, 1994: 1). For these writers, the content of what is taught – especially with respect to the English curriculum – concerns the hegemonic control of both a social order and a national culture. The denial of certain forms of learning and cultural practice on the grounds of 'race', ethnicity, class and political orientation, and the particular promotion of a particular form of 'English' national identity, they argue, 'ignores the changing, multi-cultural nature of contemporary British society, not to mention our continuing economic decline'. Such a conservative view is rooted in 'a mythical golden age that may never have existed' (4–5). Central to Buckingham and Sefton-Green's claim, then, is the idea that 'Con-temporary culture is, by and large, *electronically mediated* culture: the book is no longer the single privileged means of representation that it may have been in earlier times. Literacy in the late 20th century therefore cannot be seen as something that is confined to one particular medium or form of expression' (5). For these writers, as for others, 'cultural literacy' 'needs to be more broadly defined' (1994: 5). The demand for curriculum and pedagogic change is seen to come from an understanding of modernity with respect to social transformation and the role of the media in contemporary social relationality: 'we need to ensure that we are able to engage with those radical and diverse notions of reading and writing that are emerging from current social and technological changes' (213). Forms of media literacy and media education are and have been central to this vision. Moreover, the general thrust of this argument is one that is now widely accepted by both educational, media and government institutions.

Of course, the broader claims about 'critical pedagogy' – that come from the work of the Brazilian radical educationalist Paulo

Freire (1989), but equally the writing on 'common sense' and 'hegemony' that emerges in the context of the writing of the Italian commun-
ist Antonio Gramsci (1971) – have provided part of the genealogical
context for research that has directed its attention to understanding
pedagogy as more broadly framed than within the walls of the school
yard. Gustavo Fischman and Peter McLaren state that for critical and
transformative intellectuals and educators, 'it is not enough to understand any given educational reality: there is a pedagogical mandate to
transform it with the goal of radically democratizing educational sites
and societies through a shared praxis' (2005: 426). Although this has
meant an understanding of the relations of power in the context of
schooling and the demand for the promotion of a critical consciousness
able to resist and change social inequalities with respect to a notion of
the good radical democratic society, work in this field has also sought
to understand pedagogy outside of the context of formal schooling, so
as to include a broader understanding of what Henry Giroux refers to
as 'cultural pedagogy', which he sees as both 'a moral and political
practice' (Giroux, 2001: 6). Cultural pedagogy implies an understanding of the interconnected formation of cultural practices as practices
that shape people in certain ways rather than others, and that do so in
the context of social relations of power. For Giroux, culture is centrally
important for understanding this broader pedagogic and social context, and cultural workers (as broadly defined) are centrally important
to any social transformation with regard to a society based on the
principles of social justice. Thus, he argues, it is necessary, in the
current 'neoliberal' political climate especially, 'to articulate a wider
project that connects artists, educators, and other cultural workers to
an insurgent cultural politics that challenges the growing incursions of
corporate power while simultaneously developing a vibrant democratic public culture and society' (Giroux, 2001: 6). Giroux defines
such a public pedagogy 'as a critical and performative practice' (19).
This might mean that hip-hop, for example, is understood with respect
to the tensions between more commercial and socially conscious artists
and the long traditions of popular cultural workers as educators. This
is to understand hip-hop not only in terms of how schoolteachers
might draw on the music genre, as with other examples from popular
culture, in order to 'engage' pupils in learning, but to understand how
artists, such as KRS-One or Rakim, have seen themselves as popular
cultural teachers, as radical educators of issues and curricula

marginalised and excluded from formal school apparatuses. For cultural analysts such as Greg Dimitriadis, rap and hip-hop constitute public and performative forms of pedagogy that operate beyond the traditional spaces of school learning and teaching (Dimitriadis, 2001: 27). Douglas Kellner, writing on Giroux, states that 'pedagogy needs to be theorized in terms of a variety of public sites that shape, mold, socialize, and educate individuals'. Moreover, it is 'corporate media culture that is shaping our culture and everyday life, as well as institutions such as schooling and cultural sites like museums, theme parks, shopping centers, and the like' (Kellner, 2001: 224). Thus, for Giroux, and others, popular culture is seen as centrally important for understanding children and young people (but in fact for understanding all people) inasmuch as it is a major space in which those people construct and experience their lives and identities. Of course, it is important to understand the articulations of schooling with other cultural practices. But there is also a danger in overstating the case in such a way that we return to a rather outdated notion of 'socialisation'.

Conclusion

Research has pointed to the significant relation between education and the economy inasmuch as forms of education may be seen to be systemically related to particular modes of production. Thus education changes across different social formations, from medieval agrarian to mercantile and a growing state administration, to industrial production and Fordist divisions and specialisations of labour, to postindustrial, post-Fordist symbolic, cognitive, emotional and informational labour. Traversing this rather simple story of economy and education are the invention, emergence and deployment of particular technologies of learning, examination, assessment and judgement, but also the creation of peripheral and cultural spaces of interaction, play, performance, resistance and negotiation. The school classroom and the playground provide the contexts for different kinds of localised interactions between children of similar and different ages and between children and teachers and assistants. The shaping of those interactions is also framed within the built environment of the school, its architectures of both control and learning, but also via the assembling of different objects and relations in different spaces, such as chairs and tables in classrooms (arranged according to particular diagrams of power and knowledge), lines marking out football or netball pitches in play-grounds, climbing frames and slides, and perhaps a sandpit for younger children. Across the interactions, spaces, technologies and knowledges different agencies and resources are mobilised to ensure supervision, examination, development and good behaviour, but also friendships, hostilities and other passions. The modern classroom, in its development from monitorial to child-centred space, constitutes a particular moment in the history of pedagogy. Learning now is formed in the contexts of that history, but is also certainly not contained within the built environment of the school, nor by the authority and expertise of those who work within its borders. At a time when pedagogy happens as much within as it does away from the school, the value of accredited and certificated education has grown (and become increasingly tied to corporate power) but is also more keenly distributed with regard to the contours of socioeconomic class.

8 | *Crime and criminality*

This chapter explores the way in which children and young people have been considered as criminal subjects, but also as the victims of criminality. All of us on a reasonably regular basis commit a criminal offence, whether dropping a sweet wrapper, playing music too loud at night-time, watering the garden during a period of restriction and so on. Some offences are seen to be more serious. Across the range of crimes committed, some people are typified as being more likely to commit more serious crime. Across the range of crimes, some people are more heavily policed and sentenced and more likely to be caught up in the judicial system. The visible range of illegalities that are, and have been, committed by children and young people is large and wide and is dependent on legislation, judicial process, policing, cultural and many other factors. In many cases children are the victims of crime, whether committed by adults or other children. That said, both sociological research and governmental intervention have tended to more consistently focus on a limited range of issues and problems. In this chapter I consider the changing nature of that limited range of problems. I focus on the construction of children and criminality in terms of the figurations of the delinquent (as both 'in danger' and 'dangerous') and the gang. In mapping some of the discussions in these areas, the chapter follows a trajectory that sees marked distinctions, but also continuities, from a criminological and penal discourse in the context of nineteenth-century welfarism, hygienism and moralism to a late modern configuration in the context of neoliberal and neoconservative ideological projects and a series of technologies and technical discourses on risk, probability and prevention. Moreover, each of these strategies of figuration is marked by complex scalings across local, national and transnational, as well as dynamics across expert and popular mediations. Thus, each strategy rests, for example, on highly overdetermined figures such as the neglected child, the youth gang located in the black or Hispanic ghetto, or the genetic and somatic criminal identified in the nursery (which we consider in the following chapter). Of particular significance is the territorialisation of children and criminality as a hybrid confluence of public and domestic.

Origin stories: degeneration, neglect and delinquency

The criminologist Sheila Brown has argued that 'from an early stage, criminology was centrally defined by its concern with the ill-defined concept of delinquency, and with the control of the supposed "problem population" of the young' (Brown, 2005: 29). John Muncie, another criminologist, has argued that the notion of delinquency allows behaviours to be criminalised only by virtue of their being conducted by children or young people. He argues that '"being incorrigible", running away from home, truancy and drinking alcohol in public are considered to be problematic only when committed by young people' (Muncie, 2004: 39). Modern criminology properly begins with the problem of delinquency, but its social and historical aetiology is also rooted in a geographical demarcation of immoral behaviour, hereditary degeneration of the population and familial decadence and irresponsibility. In contemporary society the problems of children's and young people's criminal behaviour are often understood through the ideas of delinquency, urban geography, familial neglect and biological (often 'racialised') hard-wired traits. In 1985, James Q. Wilson and Richard J. Herrnstein published *Crime and Human Nature*, which argued in part that the hereditary features of human nature, and importantly intelligence (as measured by IQ), constitute a significant determining factor in crime statistics. Although there are subtleties to their argument, the explanation (vis-à-vis genetic hereditariness) of a correlation between race and crime has been a major concern. Much of the broader discussion of this work has been framed by a racist and eugenic discourse of crime. In a later work, *The Bell Curve* (1994), Herrnstein and Charles Murray push further a eugenic discourse which considers social stratification, race and intelligence in terms of the formation of a 'cognitive elite'. But instead of treating the problem of crime as either a question of social influence or genetic determination, the government of crime betrays a more strategic and less dogmatic approach to the complex layering of individual behaviour, environment and biological factors.

Hygiene and delinquency

In the nineteenth century the process of industrialisation and the migration of people to the growing cities made visible the problems of urban degeneracy, the concentration of vice, prostitution, violence, theft, abuse – that is, of all kinds of criminalities and immoralities. Certain parts of the city were seen to be outside of society and civilisation. But these places were also seen as the breeding ground for immoralities and crime that would spread like a disease and infect the remaining population if left unchecked, unregulated and unpoliced. The disease would spread through the movement of the poor beyond the slums and within the rest of society, in the migration of ideas of bad example and in the breeding of criminal conduct through the 'transmission of these immoral habits to their offspring who were brought up in an overcrowded, insanitary, atmosphere, forced at a tender age into contact with sights and experiences of corruption and crime' (Rose, 1985: 48). Nikolas Rose talks of the 'grand schemes of social hygiene which attempted to break up these enclaves, to render them accessible to the influences of civilised society and its systems of regulation and police, to disperse these teeming multiplicities, regulate the promiscuous intermingling, eliminate anti-social habits, produce an atmosphere of decency and morality within the home' (48). He argues that in the researches and writings of Charles Booth and others 'one can see emerging a new conception of demoralisation, as a cumulative process with long-term effects upon the quality of the population as a whole' (49). A class of people was being constructed that was 'unemployable', not simply those outside of work but also those who were so thoroughly stained by poverty and degeneracy that they were not fit for industry. Moreover, at the end of the nineteenth century, Rose argues, the 'deterioration of their [i.e. urban] inhabitants was not now seen as a consequence of the effects of conditions of life upon character', but rather 'these forms of anti-social behaviour [e.g. crime, lack of religion, laziness] were seen as the outcome of an inherited unfitness' and the solution to the problem newly conceived was either sterilisation or segregation (53). Alongside moral and religious discourses concerning the good and the bad, a hygienist discourse constructed a correlation between dirt and individual and environmental disorder. At one level this allowed for understandings that construe a child's dirty body living in a dirty environment in terms of high levels of risk both to the individual child and to society more broadly, inasmuch as the child may grow up to commit crime. A hygienist discourse, though, was also more broadly significant in its making visible the individual, the population and their environment, or milieu, in terms of the question of health and thus in making possible the implementation of measures to ensure the good health of individuals and populations. Giovanna Procacci refers to a

group of techniques [that] place their emphasis on hygiene: rules for public hygiene in cities, 'police of dwellings', rules of hygiene in the workplace, hygiene in marriage and procreation (of Malthusian fame): hygiene for these authors is a grid of social relations, a system which serves at once to canalize them and to invent new paths of circulation that are more 'orderly' and more decipherable. (Procacci, 1991: 165).

The translation of moral conduct into medical terms and procedures and the identification of the family as a central site of biological heredity communication across generations has been a long-standing feature of the discourse on crime and children. Rose argues that

Medico-hygienic expertise began to elaborate a set of doctrines concerning the conditions for rearing healthy children and to pose many issues of moral conduct – (drunkenness, debauchery, viciousness, masturbation, insanity) – in medical terms. They not only were detrimental to individual health but arose from weaknesses incurred through faulty government in childhood and could themselves be passed down from parents to children in the form of a susceptible constitution. (Rose, 1989: 128)

A hygienist discourse of crime thus figured both the slum and the family as geographical and hereditary conditions regarding the circulation of immorality, as with a disease. For Rose, the construction and government of this complex of social pathologies is significant in terms of the formation of the psychological individual in the twentieth century and in the figuration of the delinquent. He argues that

In analogy to the new hygienist techniques being developed for minor physical ailments, these disturbances were construed as arising from faulty techniques of child rearing, that is, poor mental hygiene. It now appeared that major mental disturbances in adults, leading to crime and social inefficiency as well as to insanity, had their origins in minor and apparently inconsequential disturbances of emotion and conduct in childhood. Early recognition and treatment were as crucial for promotion of mental health as for physical health. Lack of mental hygiene, like physical hygiene, was a recipe for future social distress. (Rose, 1989: 153)

In the eighteenth and early nineteenth centuries children were by and large imprisoned and punished alongside adults. Children below the age of 7 were treated alongside fools and the insane as *incapax*; over the age of 14 they were treated as *capax* (unless seen to be insane); and between the ages of 7 and 14 the court needed to make a decision as to their ability to have discretion (Rose, 1985: 166). The fact of children being imprisoned with adult criminals gave rise to concern in the mid to late nineteenth century and to the segregation of children who had committed criminal offences from adult criminals. The emergence of the criminal subject in the nineteenth century (in contrast to classical notions of the penal and punishable subject), which demarcates the constitution of criminology as a disciplinary knowledge (Pasquino, 1991), is closely tied to the development of the category of the delinquent and the generational differentiation of criminality across children and adults. The classification of the delinquent in the context of the emergence and development of psychological knowledge and expertise in the twentieth century rests upon the nineteenth-century construction of children as both 'dangerous' and 'in danger' inasmuch as children who roamed the streets committing crimes were seen as already dangerous and children might be seen to be in danger by virtue of parental neglect, poverty or peer group relations with 'bad children'. In the twentieth century this distinction is reinterpreted with respect to notions of instability, difficultness, adjustment and maladjustment. In the context of the juvenile courts, which were established in England in 1908, the young criminal was conceived of alongside the neglected child; thus, criminal 'offence ... was only the outcome of neglect, and neglect, soon enough, would lead to an offence' (Rose, 1989: 153).

In the early to mid twentieth century the delinquent was firmly located in the psychology of the family. The publication of Cyril Burt's *The Young Delinquent* in 1925 is symptomatic of broader shifts that construe the child in the context of the emotional economy of the family, but it also, Rose states, 'staked the claims of psychology, rather than medicine, for the jurisdiction over the behavioural disorders of childhood, on account of their mental origin' (Rose, 1985: 195).

Burt argued that 'the study of the criminal thus becomes a distinct department of this new science, a branch of individual psychology; and the handling of the juvenile offender is, or should be, a practical application of psychological principles' (Burt, 1925: 5). Psychology, he believed, was able to find causes of criminal behaviour and not simply symptoms. The foregrounding of emotional and psychological neglect, as opposed to purely physical neglect, was central to the work of John Bowlby on maternal deprivation. In framing childhood criminality as a mental problem, psychological and psychologised discourses both drew on earlier ideas about family environment, hygiene, immorality and crime, but also rearticulated them in the context of the emotional economy of the family and the psychology of the individual. Bowlby, in major research for the World Health Organisation and in presentations via a series of public talks and populist publications, made the distinction between 'physical neglect' ('dirty and ill-nourished') and 'mental or emotional neglect' ('emotionally starved'). For him, it was not sufficient for health workers to notice the signs of physical ill health or mistreatment (such as dirty skin and clothes, bruising, stale body odour, unkempt hair and so on); they also needed to be aware of the invisible signs of psychological ill health (such as disturbed behaviour, withdrawnness, overly clingy behaviour and so on).

At least two forms of neglect can therefore be recognized – physical neglect and emotional neglect – and, though they may often coexist, it is of prime importance to distinguish them, since they need very different remedies. Broadly speaking, it will be found that, while *physical* neglect is most often due to economic factors, the ill health of the mother, and ignorance, *emotional* neglect is the result of emotional instability and mental illness in the parents. Mental defect may contribute to both. (Bowlby, 1965: 90)

For Bowlby, it was these signs of psychological ill health which were of primary importance and were to be seen to be far more enduring in terms of their impact on children and their development into adulthood. Bowlby's ideas have been widely discussed and this is because this distinction is prefaced by the supposition that good and proper care for the child is necessary for their psychological wellbeing and the form this care should take is that of a loving attachment between child and adult carer (in most cases, between the child and the mother). Hence, the argument that Bowlby – given his research comes just after the Second World War, when large numbers of women were in the public world of paid work – was part of the drive to bring women back into the home (as mothers and housewives) (Wilson, 1987).

Blaming mothers ... and fathers

The attribution of responsibility for criminality – in addition but sometimes in contrast to an understanding of the distribution of crime in the moral topography of the city – has been laid at the door of the family, but particularly the mother. The repetition of this blame is as unsurprising as it is insidious. Notably, the configuration of the 'single mother' within academic and public discourse has been the subject of attention. Criminologist Alison Young has documented some of this discourse. She points to newspaper articles that talk about, for example, the relation between the deprivation of parental care and criminality and of the compounding of poverty through the break-down of the family. She argues that in these discourses 'the single mother lives as a symbolic reminder of difference, of deviation from the marital couplet'. She states that

The legislation of marital discord lies at the heart both of criminological theories of the familial production of delinquency and of governmental policies relating to single mothers. Marital discord is one of the precondi-tions for divorce ... and one of the alleged preconditions for the generation of delinquents in the home. (Young, 1996: 173)

But equally, from the 1990s, the correlation between criminal behav-iour, delinquency and family responsibility has also turned to the problem of 'fatherhood', both in terms of the abhorrent behaviour of fathers (whether directly through the abuse of children or through abuse of the mother) and in terms of fathers absent from the familial care of their children. Controversially, Charles Murray, writing on the underclass, identifies a clear correlation between 'illegitimacy' (which he sees not simply as the birth and care of a child in a one-parent family, but as an 'attitude' of 'irresponsibility') and crime. He argues that

The central problem is that kids tend to run wild in communities without fathers. The fewer the fathers, the greater the tendency. 'Running wild' can mean that young children have no set bedtime. It can mean that they are left in the house alone at night while mummy goes out. It can mean eighteen-month-old toddlers are allowed to play in the street. It can mean children who treat other children too aggressively. (Murray, 1990: 12)

For Murray, the causes of crime do not lie solely with unemployment and single-parent families, but also with the neighbourhood effect. If there are a large number of single-parent families in a poor neighbourhood, then criminal behaviour is likely to occur (Murray, 1990: 12–13). The problem, then, is 'the concentration of the underclass into particular neighbourhoods' (13). In Britain and the United States the problem of 'fatherless' boys is seen to be heavily racialised, and Pamela Abbott and Claire Wallace argue that Murray makes a highly racialised case that sees African-Americans in 'a tradition of male unemployment and female-headed households' that are 'in advance of the trends' (Abbott and Wallace, 1992: 85). These ideas helped to frame neoconservative social policy in the UK and the US. As Abbott and Wallace state, 'The major argument put forward by the New Right is that there has been a large increase in single-parent families, that these (mainly female-headed) families are welfare-dependent, raise children who are trapped into welfare dependency and who do not develop moral values so that they become criminals, drug addicts, prostitutes and so on' (137). The argument was further racialised after the publication of *The Bell Curve*, which argued that poverty (but also criminality) was closely correlated with intelligence and that the gap was increasing between a 'cognitive elite' and an underclass. In doing so, despite denials to the contrary, Herrnstein and Murray returned arguments about poverty and crime to nineteenth-century ideas about heredity, race and intelligence, but in the context of a reworking of long-standing images of errant, now racialised, fatherhood.

Delinquency as an ambivalent sign

The problem of delinquency is thus figured as a problem of degeneracy, uncleanliness and moral topography, as a typification of social scientific expertise, as the consequence of neglect and a familial pathology, and as a product of ethno-racial classification and stereotyping. Delinquency was conceived as a social problem and one such that children who had not even broken the law may be seen to need care and protection (Hendrick, 1990: 43). Hendrick quotes a mid-nineteenth-century author who describes delinquents as 'city Arabs' and as ownerless dogs. The delinquent is

a little student man already – he knows much and a great deal too much of what is called life – he can take care of his own immediate interests. He is self-reliant, he has so long directed or mis-directed his own actions and has so little trust in those about him, that he submits to no control and asks no protection. He has consequently much to unlearn – he has to be turned again into a child. (Hill, 1855: 1–2, quoted Hendrick, 1990: 43)

Delinquency is an ambivalent sign. It figures the child both as 'a child' (i.e. in need of care and protection) and as a non-child inasmuch as the non-child has no controls and no need for protection. The construction of delinquency figures either a demand (as in the quotation above) that the non-child become 'a child again' or a rejection of the non-child absolutely and a casting out of the abject into a land of moral degeneracy. This ambivalent trope is evident as much in nineteenth-century discourses on childhood criminality as it is in contemporary discourses. For example, James and Jenks have argued that public perceptions and contestations of childhood criminality may settle in such ways as to figure crime as pathological to the symbolic construction of childhood. In their discussion of press reporting of a high-profile case in the UK concerning the murder of a 2-year-old boy, James Bulger, by two 10-year-old boys, Jon Venables and Robert Thompson, in February 1993, they consider how public discourse enacts a symbolic purgation of the troublesome ambivalence of children committing murder. The construction of Venables and Thompson in the press as not human, 'evil beasts', but importantly not children (i.e. referred to as teenagers and youth) allowed the media to maintain a version of childhood innocence and hence maintain a certain version of social order. For James and Jenks, the ambiguous figuring of the child as non-child needs to be symbolically purged in order for social order to be secured. They draw on the work of the anthropologist Mary Douglas in her analysis of the purgation of dirt as matter out of place (Douglas, 2010). James and Jenks argue that children who kill are symbolically expelled from the category of childhood (James and Jenks, 1996).

However, we need to be careful with this analysis, not least because it collapses a series of specific but overlapping discourses on childhood criminality and treats it according to just one moral schema, namely that the expurgation of anomaly is defined in the context of a division between the sacred and the profane. Douglas notes the difference in meaning between anomaly (that which 'does not fit a given set or series') and ambiguity ('statements capable of two interpretations'), but declares that such a distinction has no practical purpose (Douglas, 2010: 47). James and Jenks implicitly follow this line of argument. And yet the implication of this is that they are unable to sociologically understand the very major differences in discourse and governmental reaction between, for example, a series of moral populist reactions to the murder of James Bulger, as typified in press and media discourses (which called for the boys to be locked up indefinitely), and a series of paediatric and psychological responses that saw Venables and Thompson not as evil or non-human but as children neglected and in need of proper care (Oswell, 1994 and 1997). In contemporary governmental practice, moral discourses of children and crime tend to be populist, antipathetic to expert knowledge and demanding of punishment, whereas social scientific discourses tend to be rarefied in their governmental circulation and tend to favour processes of care that reintegrate the child into social normality. Venables and Thompson were thus figured not simply as anomalies (in the context of moral discourses of good and evil) needing symbolic expulsion, but also as ambiguities, such that they might be seen to need either punishment or care. In the media reporting and expert deliberation at the time, but also the subsequent excavation of the case, the construction of these two boys as evil was set against their home life and the lack of professional intervention regarding their case. Children and infants are more likely to be victims of crime than its culprits, and the majority of those serious crimes are likely to occur in the family and at home. We know that the public exposure of that fact is often skewed, if not completely invisible (Brown, 2005: 106). The history of the expert reporting of those domestic crimes has been problematic. In the case of sexual abuse, Linda Gordon has documented social work cases in the US in the late nineteenth and twentieth centuries. The victim of domestic sexual abuse was often seen by social workers in terms of the sexual delinquency of the child. It was thus the child, wayward and promiscuous, who was seen to be at fault and who was in itself morally contaminating (Gordon, 1989; see also Pleck 2004). In contemporary high-profile cases of adult abuse of children leading to their death (such as those of Maria Colwell in 1974,

Jasmine Beckford in 1985, Tyra Henry in 1987, Kimberley Carlile in 1987, Cleveland in 1988, and Victoria Climbie in 2000), fault is often lain at the failure of governmental services (social work, medical, law enforcement) to communicate sufficiently with each other (Ferguson, 2004; Laming Report, 2003). Moreover, the systematic failure regarding children in state care and the throughput of young people from care homes to young offender institutions and then prison both indicate at a crude level a relation between childcare (or the failure of it) and criminal conduct. Of course, the relation may be one of the failures of care homes to ameliorate educational pre-existing underachievement, but it may also be that the care home serves to continue rather than amend a history of physical and sexual abuse (Daniel and Ivatts, 1998: 214). Although critiques of social welfare in the 1960s and 1970s rightly noted that concern about children as victims of neglect and abuse was often closely correlated with concerns that these same children may become a future threat to social order (see Dingwall et al., 1983), and hence noticed the long governmental history of the pairing of dangerous children and children in danger, there is certainly a question as to whether more recent concern about children 'at risk' simply follows and continues that older governmentalisation.What is striking is that, despite attempts to strategically reconfigure the child in danger and the dangerous child, the problem of children and criminality returns so consistently to the delinquent as a figuring of the victim–criminal couplet, such that the latter implies the former inasmuch as the one is often seen to follow the other in the biography of the criminalised child. The child criminal is so often seen as the damaged child.

Hooligans, ghettoes and gangs

If the first trope of children and criminality concerns the biography of delinquency as a transition from a child in danger to a dangerous child, the second trope concerns the urban gang, once a neighbourhood phenomenon and now perhaps also a more transnational phenomenon. As a modern phenomenon, it foregrounds relations of agency, generation, territorialisation and representation or mediation. Although the arguments about youth crime as moral panic are part of this discussion, they are only a part of the broader issue.

Hooligans and moral panics

Geoffrey Pearson, in his study of the history of hooliganism in the United Kingdom, talked about the amnesia and lack of communication *between* generations and the communication *across* a single generational cohort. He argued that

The terms and limits within which the problems of lawlessness are understood and acted upon are established within a form of public discourse which has been with us for generations, each succeeding generation remembering the illusive harmony of the past while foreseeing imminent social ruin in the future. The 'timeless' raw materials of the human condition – whether the feelings of nostalgia or the facts of youthfulness – provide some basis on which it is possible to understand how the immovable vocabulary of 'law-and-order' complaint is able to construct and re-construct itself across these broad acres of time. These raw materials do not constrain human possibility by universal decree, however, and nor do they predetermine the formidable constancies of this preoccupation with social ruin. Rather, they are recruited and harnessed in a much more specific way within public discourse – as ideology. (Pearson, 1983: 229)

Over and above questions about the 'raw materials of the human condition', the idea that perceptions of children's and young people's criminality are shaped by public expressions of structural generational difference is one that appears in a different form in the work of Stuart Hall and Tony Jefferson, including their edited volume *Resistance Through Ritual* (1976). Importantly, the contributors to this volume foreground generational conflict inasmuch as it is articulated with class. They talk about how youth subcultures are subordinate to the parent cultures of a dominated working class. They discuss how youth subcultures have a relation not simply to any dominant hegemonic culture, but also to parental cultures in their symbolic expressions of class and the generational struggle. Often crime and youth are collapsed and left unquestioned, as if children's and young people's lives and cultural expression constituted an undifferentiated threat. Dick Hebdige has talked about 'a symbolic violation of the social order; such a movement attracts and will continue to attract attention, to provoke censure and to act ... as the fundamental bearer of significance in subculture' (Hebdige, 1979: 19). In a later work Hebdige states that

When disaffected adolescents from the inner city, more particularly when inner city *unemployed* adolescents resort to symbolic and actual violence, they are playing with the only power at their disposal: the power to discomfit. The power, that is, to pose – to pose a threat. Far from abandoning good sense, they are acting in accordance with a logic which is manifest – that as a condition of their entry into the adult domain, the field of public debate, the place where real things really happen, they must first challenge the symbolic order which guarantees their subordination by nominating them 'children', 'youngsters', 'young folk', 'kids'. (Hebdige, 1988: 18)

Much of this work, though, talks more about youth than it does about children. In the context of questions about crime, this distinction is significant, as the division can easily mark a clear break between 'troublesome youth' and 'innocent children'. In many ways, perceived historic threats have focussed more on youth than on children and childhood. It is noticeable that the generational differentiations of geographical space have tended historically, in the context of crime and criminality, to construe youth as a problem regarding public space and children as a problem regarding private space. Children in the home were very much conceived within the purview of dangers, neglect, deprivation; youth on the street were conceived as the active pursuers of crime. Of course, this geographical separation is one that is heavily gendered, as has been argued by Angela McRobbie (1976). That said, it is noticeable that the gendering of youth criminality has increasingly figured young women, not necessarily as more masculinised but certainly as more present as a public threat (Schaffner, 2006). Young women on the street have recently either been construed as gang members (and are constructed in terms of the changing violence and aggressivity of young women) or they are constructed as drunks (bawdy, but also vulnerable sexually). This separation and spatialisation of crime has meant that public spaces – such as streets, shopping centres, playgrounds and so on – in some areas are very much seen by young people themselves as spaces of threat and danger. A consequence of this has been that there is an increasing tendency for young people to pursue their activities, friendships and leisure pursuits at home (Livingstone, 2002). Some commentators have suggested that it is predominantly middle-class children who are fearful of public spaces (James, Jenks and Prout, 1998: 51).

Stuart Hall, Chas Critcher, Tony Jefferson and John Clark in their investigation of youth crime in the 1970s state that 'The first

phenomenal *form* which the "experience of social crisis" assumes in
public consciousness, then, is the *moral panic* ... the cycle of *moral
panics* issues directly into a law-and-order society' (Hall et al., 1978:
323). In their neo-Gramscian analysis, the narrative of moral panic
takes form through the mediatisation of a public panic about the
'black mugger'; this ideological construction is pushed and mediated
by particular 'moral entrepreneurs' (churchmen, politicians, campaigners, lobbyists and others) (Becker, 1966); legislation is enacted
and then, as its outcome, we see the emergence of a social formation,
racist and concerned with law and order. Hall and colleagues localise the ideological perception of 'black crime' within the territory of
the ghetto. Mugging was seen as a crime 'peculiar to black youth in
the inner city ghettos' (Hall et al., 1978: 329). Michael Keith, in his
reading of this text, talks about how the authors use the metaphor of
the 'black colony' in a way that figures it as 'both victim of racist
practices of criminalisation *and* (apparently) social reality' (Keith,
2005: 67). He talks about how there is a 'repeated elision of the
ghetto as metaphor and the ghetto as reality: a fictional black colony
that signifies criminality in racist discourse and a factual black
colony of subordinated communities' (68).

Hegemony and offensiveness

In the sociology of childhood the ethno-racial spatialisation of crime
has been downplayed in favour of an emphasis on hegemonic constructions and contestations between adults and children. Thus, James
and James understand criminal offence in the context of the threat
'the rebelliousness and non-conformity of the young' poses for 'the
hegemony of adult order and values'. They argue that

the offending behaviour of the young challenges not only the power and
authority of the adult generation to control children but also valued
and often idealised notions of childhood. It is interesting to pause, in
passing, and consider that if we talk not of criminals but of child or young
offenders, it raises the question of what else it might be they offend against
other than criminal law. Our answer would be that their offence is also
against hegemonic adult perceptions of what childhood and children are.
Part of these is how they should behave and in this sense, their offending
behaviour is also an offence to adults. Thus, as well as the identification of
the particular needs of children as a corollary to the emergence of

childhood as a separate social status, we have also seen the increasing identification of crime as being a particular problem associated with childhood. (James and James, 2004: 167–8)

The visibilisation of crime as a correlative of childhood and youth and the pathologisation of children's and young people's behaviour has led to some stark posturing and to media declarations of the need to purify public space of unruliness. Some scholars in the discipline of geography have talked about the hegemonic control and contestation of space. Gill Valentine has argued that

All of these attempts to segregate or police young people's use of space can therefore be seen as attempts to draw or reinforce boundaries between adults and the demonised young (and by implication their 'failed' parents). These measures therefore demonstrate first, the taken-for-granted nature of adult spatial hegemony on which these controls are predicated; and second, the importance of space to adults' ability to (re)produce their authority. Third, several measures (re)produce the notion that parents 'own' their children and that the state has the right to step in and act *in loco parentis* where parents are perceived to be not governing their children in public space in 'appropriate' ways. (Valentine, 1996: 596)

She continues:

Underlying adults' contemporary anxieties about other people's dangerous children appears to be an assumption that the streets belong to adults and children should only be permitted into public spaces when they have been socialised into appropriate 'adult' ways of behaving and of using space. Autonomous young people appear to be automatically perceived to disrupt the moral order of the street. In the climate of panic about 'dangerous children', adults (parents, the police, the state, the media, and so on) appear to be articulating a need for greater spatial controls to be exerted over young people in order to maintain the boundaries between 'us' and 'them'. (Valentine, 1996: 597)

In some ways, this repeats a critical 'moral panic' discourse in the context of geography, and we should be wary of simply assuming that such a problematisation of space is 'moral' as such and should be equally wary of reducing the spatial organisation and containment of young people to a cognitive and identitarian apparatus (that labels, classifies and is mobilised ideologically). In many ways, responses to crime are not cognitive, but emotional. Adult fear of young people on the streets, or their images circulated through media channels, is often an affective response to a complex social situation (see Skeggs and Wood, 2009). But in other ways, what becomes apparent in these writers is that agency cannot be assumed (as in moral panic theories) to reside in the state or in adults and that children and young people cannot simply be assumed to be the object of representation. Instead, the figuring of children and criminality constitutes a significant representational space in which children and young people have, and are seen to have, a stake inasmuch as their agency is played out and negotiated as a question of both representation and territory. But it is race, ethnicity and class, not only gender and generation, which are, and have been, key markers in this discourse.

Media typologies

Media and governmental concerns about children's and young people's occupation of public spaces of the streets and shopping centres have been significantly inflected by discourses of both race and class. What is striking is that race and class have in media but also expert discourse often been presented in terms of style and consumer culture. In these discourses there is often a collapse of criminal conduct on to forms of dress in such a way that the styling of the self is disclosed in the context of new taxonomies of criminal personality types. Although there are certainly differences to the use of documentary, portraiture and photographic technologies (see Tagg, 1988) in the classification of criminal types of person in the nineteenth century, the circulation of video and photographic images of 'hoodies' (young people wearing sweat tops or coats with hoods) or 'chavs' (working-class kids dressed in particular kinds of branded sportswear and stereotyped as drinking excessively and being loutish in public; see Tyler, 2006 and 2008) continues to feed the loop of representation and control. But also, public media circulation of these images invests the young people with capacity – to occupy public space, to threaten, and to ward off any potential incursions. Moreover, while contemporary images of hoodies and chavs certainly repeat the tropes of nineteenth-century juvenile crime (Pearson, 1983) as well as the long history of iconic figurations, contemporary iconographies of criminal youth are caught more systematically within consumer culture. In this sense, the signs of criminality are not necessarily signs of exclusion. For example, the criminologist Jock Young looks to Carl Nightingale's ethnographic research on the Philadelphia poor (see, for example, Nightingale, 2003). He states Nightingale's argument that the culture of the ghetto is not one of 'isolation and alienation' but 'a whole-hearted yet desperate embracing of mainstream American values', which are defined in terms of 'consumption and immediacy', 'machismo', 'use of violence as a preferred means of settling problems' and 'racist stereotypes and divisions' (Young, 2007: 51). For Nightingale, Young argues, this is a means of compensating for 'the pains and humiliations of poverty and racism'. Young is critical of a seeming psychological causality implied in Nightingale's argument, which he sees as returning to earlier ideas about delinquency, but he holds on to a notion of the two stigmas that the poor face 'that of relative deprivation (poverty and exclusion from the major labour markets) and misrecognition (lower status and lack of respect)' (51). This humiliation of poverty finds its form in the essentialisation of gendered, ethnic and territorial division. Hence, the confrontations between gangs defined through territorial demarcation and the use of derogatory language, such as 'nigga', 'pimp', 'motherfucker' and so on. For Young,

> the humiliation of poverty finds its 'magical' solution in the cult of con-sumerism, in children who learn the trademarks BMW, Nike, Gucci from an early age, who value designer labels, watches, and blatant jewellery ... The American poor eat their way to obesity in pursuit of the American dream. Yet they are flawed consumers, the market welcomes microconsu-merism just as it flaunts wealth while excluding the poor ... it is not simply that structures oppress the agents, but that the social agents themselves contribute in a pyrrhic fashion to their own exclusion and oppression. (Young, 2007: 52–3)

Racialised ghettoes

That said, although the offence of childhood criminality (as James and James might put it) is seen to have spread across the social landscape, youth crime has been most consistently seen to be generated within particular ethno-racial urban containers. In much popular and expert discussion of children and young people's crime, it is the black (but also Hispanic) ghetto in the US major cities (Chicago, Detroit, Los Angeles), rather than the nineteenth-century Victorian slum, that is seen as a significant contemporary point of social origin. The origins of the contemporary US black ghetto are seen in terms of three significant factors: unemployment, lack of two-parent family structure, and the evacuation of middle-class African-Americans from poor neighbourhoods (Jencks, 1993; Wilson, 1987). These factors are seen to be sociostructural and dependent, in large part, on the transformation of urban space and its populations in the context of post-Fordist restructuring from the 1970s onwards. In US sociology and social policy the ghetto has a particular privileged place as the container of poverty, crime, but also of a racial underclass. William Julius Wilson, in *The Truly Disadvantaged* (1987) but also in other works such as *When Work Disappears* (1996), has been a significant interlocutor with regard to our understanding of the contemporary formation of the black US ghetto. For Wilson, it is the historic, rather than contemporary, forms of racism and the structural impact of changes in the economy that shape the black ghetto. For us, it is also the fact that these places have a high percentage of young people (Wilson, 1987).

Loïc Wacquant, onetime colleague, co-researcher and co-author with Wilson, analyses a contrast between what he calls 'the communal ghetto' of the mid twentieth century and 'the *fin de siècle* hyperghetto'; whereas the former was 'compact, sharply bounded and comprising the full complement of black classes bound together by a unified collective consciousness, a near-complete social division of labour, and broad-based agencies of mobilization and representation', the latter is 'a novel, decentred, territorial and organizational configuration characterized by conjugated segregation on the basis of race *and* class in the context of the double retrenchment of the labour market *and* the welfare state from the urban core, necessitating and eliciting the corresponding deployment of an intrusive and omnipresent police and penal apparatus' (Wacquant, 2008b: 46 and 3). For Wacquant, the growth of the ghetto as a deproletarianised space is an effect of neoliberal social and economic policy that places the ghetto alongside the prison as parallel spaces of containment and carceral power (Wacquant, 2008a). The ghetto, the prison and low-paid, precarious forms of postindustrial and post-Fordist labour form a complex of interrelated factors that constitutes a new form of the government of poverty (see also Procacci, 1991). It constitutes not simply a reaction to crime but a new form of state and social policy and policing (Wacquant, 2008a). A central platform, especially in the USA, has been the removal of welfare programmes under both Democratic and Republican administrations since the Clinton regime in the 1980s. Informal economies became more consolidated amongst what was now referred to as 'the underclass' (see Jencks, 1993; Murray, 1990). The punitive ideologies and government programmes of the 1990s were, according to Wacquant, not so much a reaction to an '"explosion" in youth delinquency', than a new government of social insecurity. The lack of jobs and the growth (and in part privatisation) of the prison sector in the 1980s and 1990s ensnared 'the marginal populations of the metropolis in a carceral-assistantial net that aims either to render them "useful" by steering them onto the track of deskilled employment through moral retraining and material suasion, or to warehouse them out of reach in the devastated core of the urban "Black Belt" or in the penitentiaries that have become the latter's distant yet direct satellites' (Wacquant, 2008a, 18). For Wacquant, then, concerns about children's and young people's crime is seen as an ideological screen that hides this structural dynamic.

Although Wacquant talks about the translation of this carceral and economic regime to Europe and elsewhere, he is careful not to collapse the spatialisation of urban poverty in the US with apparently similar spaces elsewhere. In a comparative analysis of France and the US, the differences between the urban banlieues in France and the ghettoes in the US are explored, not least in terms of the very different levels of crime and insecurity in each location and the corresponding levels of policing, but also in terms of the different levels of state welfare intervention and the different forms of community (homogeneous or diverse in terms ethnicity and race). But what is important for us are his comments on youth, not so much his dismissal of political and ideological statements about youth delinquency, but his description of everyday interactions of young people on the streets. He states that 'If the impact of delinquency on daily life in La Courneuve [a suburb in the north of Paris] is felt mainly at the level of representations and collective sentiments, violence in its most brutal forms – including assault and battery, shootings, rape and homicide – is so intense and prevalent inside the hyperghetto [the particular reference Wacquant is making here is to the Chicago South Side] that it has forced a complete reorganization of the fabric of daily life' (Wacquant, 2008b: 210).

Sudhir Venkatesh's sustained ethnography of one of the gangs of the Chicago South Side reveals a less dramatic and more liveable picture of the everyday precarious lives of young people in one of the most notorious and now demolished housing projects in the US. Although the built environment of the Robert Taylor Homes Project had all the hallmarks of a contained urban space (inasmuch as it was couched the other side of a major freeway and effectively sealed off from the rest of the city), Venkatesh (who was a student of Wilson's at the University of Chicago) humanises the forms of social organisation in this ghetto in terms not so much of their conforming to a stereotype of 'the gang' or 'the black ghetto', but their making do, their local forms of justice, the helping out and solidarity, the making of money and the complex politics (Venkatesh, 2009). He is keen to stress the lineages of gang life not to a black hypermasculinity or to the history of migrant protection and violence (as is often told of Irish gangs and Italian mafia), but to forms of social movement and political organisation in terms of community action, black rights and gender equality (see Venkatesh, 1998; also Schaffner, 2006). In these accounts there is an emphasis on the resources and accumulation strategies of those without immediate access to formal, state-defined and controlled forms of authority and power. What is brought out in this later research is not only the repeated banality of masculine violence, but (in Mike Davis' phrasing) 'mint[ing] power for the otherwise powerless from their control of small urban spaces: street corners, slums, playgrounds, parks, schools, prison dormitories, even garbage dumps' (Davis, 2008: xi).

Olawale Ismail argues that in Lagos, Nigeria, neoliberal policy in the shape of the International Monetary Fund and World Bank initiated structural adjustment programme (SAP) rolled back the state and deregulated and privatised services. This led, he argues, to the deskilling of young people (through lack of training programmes, apprenticeships and employment), a 'boom in informal economic activities' and the growth in young people's involvement in criminal networks. He argues that 'All this made the economy of Eko, as well as that of Nigeria, largely a patchwork of uncoordinated, splintered and informalized activities' (Ismail, 2009: 470). For Ismail, what are significant are the cultural and spatial sites of intensity and organisation around 'bases' and 'junctions'. The former are neighbourhood meeting places where young people socialise, discuss politics and sports; the latter are spaces of largely illegal economy at the junctions of roads. The young who hang around these spaces are 'area boys'. These spaces are largely improvised, innovative, 'textured by emergent terminologies associated with the redefinition of identities and spatial boundaries'. The bases and junctions 'embody emergent social modalities'. They are laboratories of social solidarity and change (464–5). There are clearly differences across the locations of South Side Chicago and Lagos, but also striking similarities. The neoliberal withdrawal of the welfarist state from the city, the geographical exclusion from the formal labour market (through the stigma of place, but also the socialisation of the wrong skills or none at all), and the strategy of policing and incarceration create spaces of emergent solidarities and precarious social and economic innovation.

Despite populist and political talk of gangs spreading across the US or across the Hispanic diaspora (e.g. from the US and Latin America to Spain as in the case of the Latin Kings), much of the evidence points to highly localised forms of organisation. The symbols, names and insignia of gang identity certainly travel far and wide and often gangs with no actual organisational connection adopt a gang name and insignia (Hagedorn, 2008). Certainly also, some gangs are formed through family and ethnic connections forged through migration. But there is little evidence to suggest that children and young people have mobilised gangs which in organisational form are transnational. These forms are largely local. They are restricted by the capital (of different forms) that young people are able to mobilise. Economic poverty, precarious infrastructure and geographical containment consolidate an enforced localism. As Alcinda Honwana and Filip de Boeck argue in the context of Africa, 'the possibilities of becoming seem constantly curtailed by cultural, political, and economic constraints that work hegemonically to pin them down to localized place and imprison them in a precarious and fragile state of being' (Honwana and De Boeck, 2005: 7).

Representation and governmentality

Let me return to the question of representation and mediation. The misrepresenting of crime with respect to young people is an important factor (Halsey and White, 2008). For example, the almost daily reporting of knife and gun crime in the UK is often slanted in a way that figures black youth in ethnically codified urban spaces (e.g. 'Brixton', 'Hackney', etc.) as the core of the problem. A recent report from the London-based Runnymede Trust stated that most youth stabbings and gun crimes are not committed by black or ethnic 'minorities' (see Alexander, 2008; Hallsworth and Silverstone, 2009; Wood, 2010). What is at stake is not only misrepresentation but the distribution of power or agency across representation and territory and the accumulation of capacity with respect to both. Wacquant is highly critical of empirical descriptions of 'ghetto life' that fail to provide adequate theorisation of the ghetto as an analytical category (Wacquant, 2002). In particular, he is critical of forms of moralisation that see the inhabitants and forms of social organisation of these urban spaces not in negative terms, but in terms that humanise and positively evaluate their daily existence. But this epistemological hierarchy of 'the ghetto' (into analysis and description) effectively excludes certain spokespersons (including children and young people) from having any equal stake in the coalescence of factors that accumulate to constitute the problem and the solution of the ghetto. Children and young people by and large are not able to accumulate intellectual resources and sustain those resources over time in such a way as to counter the accumulation of resources and time available to an academic such as Wacquant (i.e. the logic of analysis which Wacquant typifies as 'analytical' requires a certain form of training and constitutes a particular form of labour). Those marginal youth, those folk scripts and those ideological forms need to be factored into the complexity that is the agency of representation, and not simply bifurcated into a myth–reality or analysis–description binary. As Michael Keith has argued (although not in the context of children in particular), 'the stories they [those who populate the ghetto, or as Keith puts it, 'the protagonists of gun crime and itinerant migrant labour'] tell about the spaces in which they live are not isolated from the representations of the ghetto in the scripts of the bureaucrats, policy makers, politicians and academics whose temporalities may have more distant horizons'. Keith argues that 'a more iterative relationship between folk-naming of city spaces and their official or analytical cartographies might aid and not detract from an understanding of the carceral imperatives of contemporary ghetto urbanism' (Keith, 2005: 63).

Conclusion

Contemporary understanding of children and criminality to a large extent still rests on the historical figuring of the delinquent. The delinquent is presented as a couplet, 'dangerous child'–'child in danger', which consistently burdens any explanation of young people's criminality in terms of a biographical relation between victim and perpetrator. And the splitting of this couplet offers no simple solution inasmuch as victim–perpetrator is seen through the ambivalent lens of both moralism and care. Although the construction of the second figuring of the urban gang (often seen as black or Hispanic) draws on the discourse of delinquency and on the family (inasmuch as the gang constitutes both the other of the family and also its symbolic return), it foregrounds the relations of agency, territory and representation in such ways that it insinuates children's agency in iterative processes of government. This does not suggest a simple message of hope, but it does mean that any understanding of children and criminality needs to account for the collective agency of children in the shaping of governmental epistemologies.

9 | *Health and medicine*

Much of the sociology of childhood, as I have already indicated, has sought to offer an account which, although it acknowledges the biological immaturity of the child, considers the child as a social being. Much of the criticism has been directed to biological accounts of the child's body (in terms of growth and maturation) and to psychological accounts of the child's mind (in terms, primarily, of cognitive development). But in children's everyday lives there is no single bifurcation of the social and the natural. When children brush their teeth in the morning or forget to do so, when they go to the dentist every six months or fail to do so, and when their teeth fall out and they are given silver coins from the tooth fairies, there is not a keen division between social conduct, habits and regularised routines, on the one hand, and the work of the human body, either passive to the social or steadfastly determining, on the other. Over the course of a young lifetime, a child with a chronic illness, whose regimen of care dictates the taking of different pills over the course of the day and visits to the paediatrician for examinations regularly over the course of the year, does not disclose the natural or the biological more than any other child. Nevertheless, what is clear is that a sociologist, a psychologist, a psychiatrist or a paediatrician is often interested in different bits of the child's body, different forms of movement, different relations of bodies and different relations of scale. They all certainly understand these through different rationalities, methods and methodologies. But sociologists over recent years have become more interested in the movement of a disease or the habits of a medication in the context of different scales of materiality and association (Fraser, 2001; Mol, 2002; Rosengarten, 2009). In this chapter, then, we explore how children's bodies and movement become disclosed as an object of medical science and as an object of concern regarding health. And in particular we inquire as to how our understanding of this disclosure might lead us to reassess our understanding of agency with respect to children.

Experimental observations

In 'A biographical sketch of an infant' (1877), Charles Darwin provides an account of the activities of his young children. His notes are detailed and yet they lack overconceptualisation. He provides, as he says, a sketch of the infant which is both ordinary and commonplace. And yet his account of the conduct of his children has a precision and a measure regarding their ages in terms of days, the nature of the movement of actions and feelings, the objects of attachment and association, and the organs and parts of the body motivated. His description is focussed on the development of the infant and in particular on the relation between habit and instinct. At one level in his description there is a clear distinction between experience (the experiential and habitual association of actions and ideas) and instinct, between will and reflex. And yet, in the example he gives of the nervous disposition of his 66-day-old son after experiencing the sneeze of his father, Darwin states that for an hour afterwards his son started at any slight noise, but also that for some time afterwards he started and winked more frequently. Darwin states that the winking (a response to shield and protect the eyes) 'had not been acquired through experience' (Darwin, 1877: 286), and yet the context in which the winking and starting occurs and the role of memory in the repetition of the response suggests that a distinction between will and reflex (habit and instinct) is less than clear cut.

Darwin presents the child as an open book. He does so in a manner which assumes that the body of the child will deliver its meaning in clear and demonstrable terms. The evidence of 'swimming eyes', for example, is assumed to imply pleasure for the child while sucking. Smiling is assumed, similarly, to imply pleasure. Of course, you may say, smiling and 'swimming eyes' are indicators of pleasure. The infant is devoid of speech, and so Darwin 'knows' what he knows only on the basis of analogy. We know the inner feelings of the infant by analogy with ourselves. But such an epistemological stance assumes a priori that adult observer and infant are similar in such respects (i.e. a simple unfettered continuity between infant and adult) and thus voids the philosophical basis for an empirical investigation of the infant. An assumption is made, then, to treat the infant as semiotically transparent – they are what they show – and bodily signs, in this sense, are not deceitful and do not lie. Moreover, their assumed semiotic transparency is linked in Darwin's paper to the transparency of both their instinct (as interpreted by the adult scientist) and will (as assumed to originate within the child).

Claudia Castañeda has argued that Darwin in this paper treats the development of the child through a Spencerian narrative which progresses from simple to complex, savage to modern. In doing so, Darwin in this 1877 paper offers a model which is at odds with the model of evolution that we ordinarily now take for Darwinism. In 'A biographical sketch' the child is taken as a sign of the ancient and it is from this savage that instinct emerges (Castañeda, 2002). Castañeda argues that such a narrative, derived in part from Spencerian biology, is a racialised narrative which mimics the colonial discursive opposition between savage and European man. This is a narrative which we certainly see in many places from the eighteenth century onwards, as, for example, in Rousseau's discussion of the natural contract. The little savage transparently displays their nature. Nevertheless, significant in Darwin's paper is the difference he marks between the younger infant and the older child. Darwin tells the story of his son Doddy, at just over 2½ years old exiting the dining room with pickle juice staining his pinafore. Of interest to Darwin is the fact that Doddy has attempted to conceal his actions. The child is seen to be able to lie, and such lying is understood in moral terms. No longer then is the child at this age typified by their semiotic transparency, but by their disarticulation of image and meaning and by their deliberate and wilful dissimulation.

The account Darwin provides could be not only of his children, but of any children. Through his observations of the growing child and through a detailed writing of the minutiae of their activities, he is able to take account not only of the particular children in front of him and the considerable differences of the 'period of development of several faculties', but also of the developmental process of all children (Darwin, 1877: 19). What is significant about this is not so much the observation in itself (as this is typical of many parental views of their own or other children), but the documenting of the observations and their recording in a form (writing on paper) which will endure through time, the units of measurement in that documentation, their publication in a journal of science and the authority of their author. In documenting children's conduct and commenting on their growth, and in circulating this paper among a community of scientific peers, Darwin makes available these observations for further detailing, scrutiny and refinement. Moreover, the community of peers to whom the paper is circulated has implications as to how the observations are read and used. In contrast, a parent watching their child play in a playground and then commenting to a friend sitting next to them about a gesture that their child makes has little consequence. They are words said and gone. They may matter to the parents or they may matter fleetingly to the friend, but they would often have little enduring significance.

We know also that over seventy years earlier Jean Itard had kept detailed notes on the habits and conduct of the wild boy Victor. Victor's eating and sleeping habits were observed, as were his table manners, his likes and dislikes, his feelings and so on (Malson and Itard, 1972). Importantly, though, Itard's documentation of what Victor is able to say or not to say provided his peers with an understanding of infant language acquisition in the context of physiological growth. Similarly, at the beginning of the seventeenth century the royal physician Héroard provides an account of Louis XIII's life from birth to death in such detail that he comments on the subject's eating, his sexual habits and his defecation, among other things (Marvick, 1993). Certainly by the end of the eighteenth century and beginning of the nineteenth century children's bodies and movements were more regularly observed, not only by physicians but by parents as well. Carolyn Steedman notes that

The observation of children was an Enlightenment injunction, and parents of the polite classes of society had long been told to keep 'remarks made on the progress of their children in a book kept for that purpose, in order that they might attain a more distinct view of human nature' ... The injunction was, indeed, to observe the unfolding of the human mind, and those mothers who left records paid most attention to the development of language and of the moral sentiments of their children. (Steedman, 1994: 68)

By the late 1820s the focus had shifted towards signs of sickness and the interior of the body. Steedman states:

The new type of 'mothers'' guide that was published from the late 1820s onward advised attention to the child's body, especially so that the signs and symptoms of sickness might be read (many of these books advertised themselves as home doctors); and whilst they may have built on a habit of domestic observation, they directed attention to the body's interior in a way that broke with eighteenth-century practice ... Because of the established practices of child observation, the reading of signs in children seems to have been taught to nineteenth-century parents long before it was recommended to doctors in training ... In urging on mothers the daily watching of children's heads, tongues, cries, gestures and faeces, Edward Cory introduced the idea of 'la sémiologie physiognomique' to British readers ... By the end of the century this semiology of infancy had spread far beyond the home and the general practitioner's surgery. (Steedman, 1994: 68–70)

There are two issues that are significant here: firstly, a circuit of information begins to form between medics (but later psychologists and others) and parents (mainly mothers), such that observation in itself becomes subsumed within the accumulation of observations, their documentation, analysis and discussion and, moreover, the language of expertise itself circulates among parents in a way that shapes subsequent observations; and secondly, the form of observation brings into being simultaneously both the positionality of the 'expert' and the parent. For Donzelot, this move places the mother as an ally of the doctor and as a relay in the government of the family. Before the mid eighteenth century, he argues, 'medicine took little interest in children and women', yet over the eighteenth and nineteenth centuries the 'discreet but ubiquitous mother's gaze' amongst various other tactics is directed toward the maximal growth of the child and its protection from harm or corruption (Donzelot, 1979: 19). For Steedman, though, what is important is that the figuring of the child becomes a way of pursuing a puzzle about growth and disintegration in such a manner that 'children become the problem they represented; they become the question of interiority' (Steedman, 1994: 79).

As we move into the twentieth century we see new forms of observation in relation to the growing knowledge of psychology (particularly developmental and cognitive psychology). We see forms of observation that take place outside of the home, in the laboratory proper, and a clustering of expertise around the laboratory. At the same time, we see the parent (mother) still construed as an observer of the child (in matters of health and wellbeing), but increasingly being denuded of expertise. We also see the development of centres of calculation and knowledge production and the emergence of new spaces and architectures of observation concerning the growing child. Arnold Gessell is one notable psychologist who devised a means of observation that involved putting a child into a large glass dome, within which there were domestic objects (depending on the age, a cot, toys, and so on), and through which the scientists could observe the growing child in a 'naturalistic setting'.

The one-way vision screen is a device which permits an unseen observer to see. It enables him to *see* many things which he could not otherwise see at all, and brings him closer to the realities of child behaviour because it removes the distorting and disturbing influence of the observer. It is not merely a laboratory gadget but an adaptable technique which has many practical uses both for controlled and naturalistic observation and for educational demonstrations. It is a contrivance which combines intimacy of observation with detachment.

The principle of the one-way screen is relatively simple. Perhaps you have had an experience like this: You walked down a sunny path of a garden; you opened the screen door of a porch located at the end of the path; to your surprise you found in the shadow of the porch someone whom you had not noticed at all while you were in the garden. Yet all the while this person could see you plainly ... one must imitate these conditions. (Gessell, 1943: 370)

As with Bentham's panopticon (as described by Foucault, 1977), the idea was to observe without being seen, thereby maintaining certain relations of power through relations of seeing–being seen.

The location of the observer's station is of critical importance. The station should be as dark as possible ... Care should be taken so that direct light from windows or from lamps will not strike directly through the screens. Such direct rays of light tend to reveal the observer's eye-glasses and light coloured objects. Invisibility is increased by wearing dark clothes ... The walls of the observation station should be painted black or midnight blue. Dark carpeting draped on the walls and thick carpeting on the floor serve to silence sounds inadvertently made by the observers. Placement of plate glass behind the screen excludes sound but interferes with ventilation. Strict silence is an extremely important rule. Our injunction to the observer ... is 'Be absolutely quiet'. (Gessell, 1943: 371)

The child is always constructed as the object of the gaze, never its subject. The relations of seeing are also relations of knowledge. The child is always the object of knowledge, never its subject. It is the apparatus – as an apparatus of power and knowledge – that secures such a relation. This kind of apparatus involves a fair amount of financial investment. The building of the dome, the staffing of the observations, the documenting and filing of notes and much more is such that not everyone can afford to have a Gessell dome, and as with the physical sciences, there is often an accumulation of authority that attaches itself to such investment (e.g. as with big well-equipped laboratories). Nevertheless, the apparatus of scientific observation was one that travelled more lightly as well. For example, Albert Bandura, in his well-known experiments on the nursery children of Stanford University staff, placed infants and small children in a laboratory made to look like a family sitting room. The children watched filmed sequences of aggressive behaviour and then were allowed to play with some nursery toys (including a Bobo doll). In the corner of the room psychologists watched the children surreptitiously and made notes. The laboratory, which was made to look like a domestic setting, allowed Bandura to make claims about the causative influence of film violence and children's aggressive behaviour (Bandura et al., 1961; see Oswell, 2002). This standardised process of observation, documentation, accumulation and discussion of data was such that it could be adopted across multiple locations in such a way that the experimental setting did not require the built environment of an actual laboratory.

Although visual forms of observation predominated in contexts of understanding children as physiological, social and psychological beings, other sensory forms of expert experience and documentation should not be ignored. For example, Harry Ferguson talks about the role of smell in social work practice throughout the twentieth century. He refers to a case of neglect from 1909 in which was reported concern about four children aged 1, 3, 10 and 13 years. The family were inspected and a report stated:

> The woman and two youngest children were at home, but for more than twenty minutes she refused to open the door, she simply cheeked me through the window. But, when she did open it and I went inside the hot musty and dirty stench drove me out again and I had to have the back door open too. The woman and two children were as black as tinkers.

Moreover, the inspector reported that he had caught fleas from the children. Other officials were equally appalled by the family. The County Court Bailiff stated: 'The smell of the house is so disgusting that I am compelled to smoke to keep the taste out of my mouth.' A doctor who visited the family also reported: 'the stench was abominable and I had to ask the Inspector to try to open the window' (quoted in Ferguson, 2004: 64–5). Ferguson argues that before the end of the nineteenth century these kinds of smells were not indicative of moral and psychological failure, but in the twentieth century they increasingly come to signify abnormality, pathology and danger. A discourse about moral and physical hygiene that circulates in the late nineteenth century begins to change not simply how we see children and danger, but also how we smell them, how we feel them and how we hear them. Even our seeing becomes more 'haptic' (i.e. more local and short-sighted) (Deleuze and Guattari, 1988). As Ferguson states:

Visuality, literally 'supervising' and setting eyes on children and families, remained central to the ideals, the 'vision', of child protection. But in addition to the gaze, in practice smell and touch took on increased significance in sensuous hierarchy in ways that were more important even than what professionals were prepared to hear from parents and children about their experiences. Smell in some respects organized sight. But in many respects they complemented one another ... smell can be taken as a useful metaphor for the contingent and unpredictable nature of child protection as a modern practice. (Ferguson, 2004: 69)

Across these different practices and different moments of history, children's bodies are disclosed and observed in relation to a series of adult bodies and the material bodies of laboratory equipment, the architectures of buildings and rooms, and so on. It is within these practices and forms of observation, among others, that we witness the growth of the body of the child and the growth of its mind.

Charting physical and psychological growth

A consequence of the acceptance, by some, of Ariès' thesis regarding the social invention of childhood in the modern period has been to similarly think that children prior to the eighteenth century were not regarded in terms of their bodies, in terms of their health and in terms of the care and treatments of them in their sickness as separate and distinct from adults. As I have already noted in Chapter 2, historians have certainly contested Ariès' thesis, and it is no exception in the history of health and illness. Hannah Newton, in her research on a 'children's physic' from the late sixteenth to the early eighteenth centuries, makes the argument that certainly from that time onwards and also before children were understood as having a different physiological constitution to adults and that the treatment and care of them at times of ill health was also often different (Newton, 2010). She argues that, as with medicine generally in this period, medical understanding and the treatment of children was based on ancient Greek Hippocratic and Galenic traditions. In these traditions, living bodies were conceptualised in terms of the four basic qualities of heat, coldness, moisture and dryness, and it was thought that these qualities corresponded with the four humours (or liquids): blood (which is warm and moist), choler (warm and dry), phlegm (moist and cold) and melancholy (dry and cold). Newton argues that medical texts at this time showed how different ages of personhood were characterised in terms of the distinct mix of these qualities and humours. The division of age into infancy, youth, adulthood and old age accorded with long-standing divisions of age, which were not only medical. Children were characterised as being like soft wax and they were 'tender, moist, and warm' (Newton, 2010: 470). Medical understanding and the treatment of children was different from that of adults on that basis, but also inasmuch as children were not, by and large, distinguished in terms of gender, whereas adults were. Children were understood to be more prone to certain diseases, such as smallpox, epilepsy, diarrhoea, nightmares and teething (Newton, 2010: 461). Children were similarly treated differently in terms of their relative weakness and humoral constitution.

Certainly from the late eighteenth century, with the decline of Galenic medicine and the development of modern forms of anatomical and physiological medical knowledge and clinical practice, the child's body was seen less as having a distinct constitution and more as differentiated according both to its size and its stage within a process of development. Children begin to be measured according to height and weight from the late nineteenth century and on a regular basis from the early twentieth century. The institutionalisation of such measurement occurred in part due to concerns about malnutrition. For example, in the 1910s in the USA public health workers measured children's weight in schools and churches. Weight was seen to be an indicator of health, and after the First World War there was seen to be 'an epidemic of malnutrition among US children' (Brosco, 2001: 1385). For a few years before this time infants were weighed on a regular, often weekly, basis; in doing so, health workers had records of weight over time and could thus assess appropriate weight gain or loss.

But in the 1910s weight was measured on one-off occasions (e.g. at weighing festivals aimed at reaching large numbers of the infant population) and was assessed according to a standard norm. As a consequence, a large number of children were now deemed to be underweight and malnourished (Bosco, 2001: 1386). Weight began to be measured against height in terms of a standard rule. The Emerson rule dictated that malnourishment constituted 7 per cent under the average weight for height. Nevertheless, paediatricians argued that children's health, growth and development could not be assessed by untrained people, but could only be done through a range of tests, devices and indicators (not simply weight measurement) by professional medically trained experts. It was only in this context that child malnutrition could be properly diagnosed. The care of the child by specially trained physicians was focussed not on the ill child, but rather on the 'well child' initially, in newly constructed 'well-child clinics', but then in infants' own homes. In the clinics a range of tests and immunisations were conducted on children as part of a widespread preventative health programme. In the 1930s the American Academy of Pediatrics was established. Paediatricians could claim an expertise with regard to children's health, while paediatric knowledge could facilitate the construction of a 'scientific motherhood' (Bosco, 2001: 1388–9).

Both weight and height charts were deployed as mechanisms of measurement across clinics, schools and homes. At a specific age, the weight and height of the child could be mapped. These figures were then charted and assessed according to normal percentiles (in this case, growth lines) according to low, medium or high rates of growth. Every child could be measured and every child could be assessed according to normal rates of growth. Moreover, those children whose height or weight was below the low or high percentile could also be noted, closely monitored and assessed for physical abnormality, family pathology or dysfunction. The case of a child who is obese might be monitored in relation to whether this is a continuing problem and if so, to what extent the problem is a result of physical abnormality (hereditary disposition) or due to family dysfunction. A simple test and standard could set off a whole discussion of possible pathologies regarding unhappiness at home (and eating as compensation) or habituated family practice of unhealthy eating (due to lack of appropriate dietary knowledge or wilful gluttony) or lack of physical exercise. The measurement of weight and height is institutionalised alongside the inspection of children on a regular basis, not simply in terms of their physical growth but also their psychological growth (Armstrong 1995 and 1983). Developmental tests, which would ordinarily take place in the first few years of an infant's life, are conducted by a qualified person (for example, a registered health visitor, nurse or sometimes a GP doctor). In the past the tests would be completed at home or in the GPs surgery by one of these experts. Now, although the tests are still conducted formerly by these experts, parents are encouraged to take a greater interest in the developmental health of their child and hence are given developmental charts to complete. The parent is expected to notice signs of abnormality and to report any concerns to the local GP or health visitor. Over the course of the twentieth century the measures might include head size in infancy, waist size or body mass index (BMI).

As with all these tests and forms of measurement, the normality/abnormality of the child is measured according to the whole population (i.e. from statistics from across the whole population and also in comparison with other national statistics). Normal development (i.e. that which is assumed to be internal to the growing body of the child) is a generalised norm, a trajectory of points on a series of graphs that are assembled from a collective body, from the whole population. The gathered data is categorised according to a notion of age (i.e. measured daily, monthly and annually). The division of age provides us with a constant and against this constant we can differentiate according to expectations at particular age periods, or stages, and we can accord these age periods a 'biological' norm. These differentiations are different from the marking of ages, for example, on a wall or chart at home; domestic charts tend to be done in a more arbitrary manner (i.e. without a uniformity of temporal spacing) and are understood in relation to more localised, less expert knowledges (i.e. Charlie was taller at 6 years than Alice, etc.). Moreover, those children who at certain times do not match up to the normal and who are classified as abnormal are only designated as such on the basis of arbitrary decisions about what distance or area is acceptable around the normal line (i.e. what constitutes 'high' or 'low' on the weight–height chart is not a biological 'given', but an agreed 'standard', as arbitrary or conventional as a 'pass mark' in an examination). The standard is based on conventional wisdom at the time and changes according to that conventional wisdom and to social policy demands. The statistical mapping of children's health feeds into national social policy. The healthy child population is defined through indicators which are increasingly global. The profile of a population is a point of comparison with other national samples. Yet these indicators have significance in the context of national particularities and exigencies. Thus what might constitute a health problem at one time may not at another time. For example, recent concerns about obesity can be seen to be correlated with other policy concerns (concerns about absenteeism at work, NHS costs, an aging population, etc.). The normal curves are constructed according to concerns about the collective, but they also function according to the responsibilities they place on the individual (child or/and parent). The curves are constructed in terms of how they make visible certain sites of intervention at a personal level. Although obesity due to heredity facts might involve drastic measures regarding medication and so on, in most cases it is framed according to what the child and the parent can do. Social policy is predicated upon things that can be done. At an individual level, due to the shifting of responsibility downwards to the parent and the child, the normal curve becomes an instrument for understanding what should be done. Of course, a parent/child can always not do what is required and often there are few consequences to these actions. But sometimes, and in relation to certain areas, the not doing what should be done results in the parent/child being caught in the loop of expertise. Those who don't do (i.e. who don't recognise a developmental health problem) are further pathologised (i.e. lack of recognition is seen as lack of concern and thus as a sign of neglect).

Interiority and development

Over the twentieth century the measurement of height and weight was institutionalised alongside forms of psychological measurement. The emergence and embedding of developmental psychology across schools, hospitals and homes has been central to an understanding and assessment of children's growth. Of particular importance has been the work of Jean Piaget, who understood children's development in terms of their ability to act and interact with the world. Piaget was primarily concerned with cognitive development such that the child's knowledge of the world is not innate, nor is it simply socially determined, but rather it is dependent on the child's 'doing' in the world.

This is an interactive relationship dependent on two processes of accommodation and assimilation that are in balance or equilibrium. According to Piaget, the child develops cognitively (in terms of how they know and interact with the world) according to a set and structured passage across specific stages. These stages mark the transition of the child toward a normal adult rationality. These stages are sensori-motor (birth to 18 months), pre-operational (18 months to 7 years), concrete operational (7 years to 11 years) and formal operational (12 years onwards). Broadly speaking, the progression is from, as it were, hands-on thinking to abstract thought. At each stage there is an expectation that the child will be able to perform different capacities and dispositions and that the temporal succession of developmental stages is set within a linear and teleological model.

The measured and standardised temporal ordering of the child emerged at a time when 'time' itself was emerging as a major problematic. Across the natural and social sciences in the nineteenth century, 'time' was foregrounded as a key issue and central motif in the understanding of who we are as human beings. This is what differentiates Darwin from the 'natural historians' of the late eighteenth century. It is at this time that we see the figure of linear development and progress stamped not just in relation to the question of human growth, but in relation to the growth and development of nations and civilisations. From the amassing of huge amounts of empirical data (from skulls to rock formations), the temporal ordering of the world and of civilisations within it could be charted. At the height of European colonial power the world was mapped, in its images, through its time line. This was a naturalised temporality that was internalised not just on the body of the world, but also on the body of the child. And thus a correlation could be observed and regulated between 'primitive peoples' and the 'primitive' stage of human infant life. Castañeda talks about this in relation to Darwin. She argues that development is coded with regard to social power through 'temporal distancing'. She notes Darwin's use of 'savage' to differentiate between a biographical time of the human and an ancient time of the species. She draws on Fabian's (1983) notion of 'temporal distancing': 'what could be clearer evidence of temporal distancing than placing the Now of the primitive in the Then of the Western adult?' (Fabian, 1983: 63; cited Castañeda, 2002: 13). Castañeda argues that 'As the infant biography suggests, the Now of the primitive was not only placed in the time of childhood, but also in the child-body: the child was seen as a bodily theater where human history could be observed to unfold in the compressed time-span of individual development' (Castañeda, 2002, 13). We have already noted that this correlation of the temporalisation of civilisation and the temporalisation of the child is common to a range of texts in the nineteenth century, from Spencer to Charles Fourier. But what concerns us here is not so much the social construction of the biological body, but the relation between different forms of regulation and ordering and the historical shift which occurs such that the growth of the child is seen to be internal to its body, as a self-regulating organism (Canguilhem, 2000).

Carolyn Steedman's historical analysis of the figuring of the child as a central image of growth in the nineteenth century is significant for us. She considers how the notion of the interiority of the child has been a determining characteristic of modern childhood. The life of a child is somehow internal to itself. The child grows and develops like a tree grows from a seed. But what typifies the growth of the child, at least from the nineteenth century onwards, is a notion that internal to the child is some kind of 'motor' that enables the child to physiologically change over time in such a manner that the transformation is seen as an advancement and that enables the growing child to acquire knowledge and develop the skills and capacities for knowledge acquisition. A range of discourses assembles to construct the child in this way, as the quintessence of human life and growth itself (as we've seen in relation to notions of the development of society or civilisation, as an entity that progresses to a certain end). Steedman takes the story up to the nineteenth century with her discussion of physiology and cell theory. The child becomes the figure upon which internal growth is imagined. She says:

The building up of scientific evidence about physical growth in childhood described an actual progress in individual lives, which increased in symbolic importance during the nineteenth century, whereby that which is traversed is, in the end, left behind and abandoned, as the child grows up and goes away. In this way childhood as it has been culturally described is always about that which is temporary and impermanent, always describes a loss in adult life, a state that is recognised too late. Children are quite precisely a physiological chronology, a history, as they make their way through the stages of growth. (Steedman, 1994: 37)

As the child is increasingly taken to be the site through which the problem of generation can be investigated, others (including natural historians and philosophers) begin to talk about the life of the species and the life of society in terms of a linear temporal progression that is coded through the metaphors of human life (birth, childhood, maturity, old age and then death). The growth of the child is a biological and psychological development, and this notion marks a stark difference from ideas of preformationism, such that the child is preformed from conception, or of the continuity of the soul as an indivisible form.

The notion of development is central to the story of modern childhood, to modern child psychology and to modern paediatrics. David Armstrong, for example, considers the emergence of paediatrics in the UK. Paediatrics was seen not to be a specialism of general medicine, but rather was itself a form of general medicine, including a range of medical disciplines and expertise. The argument was more for the establishment of children's hospitals, which could house these different specialisms (including urology, ophthalmology, dentistry, psychiatry and so on) within the general study of children in health and disease (Armstrong, 1979: 9). Paediatrics relied on the classification of life into different stages (for example, infancy, childhood, adulthood and old age), but it also provided the basis for the emergence, in the 1920s and 1930s, of a distinct discipline studying children's health and diseases. Children were seen to be different, with different physiological and institutional needs. Paediatricians studied not only diseases in children, but also diseases of children. In that sense, the study and classification of diseases of children could not be subsumed within a general classical nosography. Children's bodies were seen as growing and developing bodies that required not a comparison with a standard and static chart or measure or table of classifications, symptoms and diagnoses. On the contrary, their growing bodies required a reference to the biography of the child, to their life history. As Armstrong states: 'Paediatrics replaced the nosography of traditional medicine with a multi-dimensional property space whose main axes were temporal. Medicine was taken from its compartments, from its form of reduced abstractions and opened out; no longer was the model strongly classified and static, instead the intersection of the axes of human growth and development and of the full natural history of disease in all its manifestations provided the space in which paediatricians could use their skills' (11). For the child, normality was not a fixed standard, a discrete pathology, a 'static ontology', but a series of 'active on-going processes'. Normality at one age and with one set of conditions may not be so at another age and with another set of conditions. In contrast to critiques of 'development' which formed the basis of the new sociology of childhood in the 1990s, Armstrong shows how the consolidation of paediatrics relied precisely on not treating children as miniature adults. He quotes John Apley from an article in the *Lancet* in 1965: 'Childhood can neither be understood nor taught simply by extrapolating back from adults' (quoted Armstrong, 1979: 10). Paediatrics, then, in the UK as in the USA (as evidenced by Brosco, 2001) emerged as a predominant form of expertise and authority with regard to children's health, disease and lives because it was able to claim that children required more than a reduction to abstract measurement. Paediatricians were, precisely because of their training and their singular focus on the life of the child, able to account for children unlike no others. As Armstrong argues, the paediatrician alone decided 'whether the derangement from the average is of quantitative importance' or whether a boy is 'below average height and should ... be given testosterone' or a girl's obesity 'constitutional, endocrine or emotional' (quoted Armstrong, 1979: 10). The question was thus: 'Is the child growing normally?' (quoted Armstrong, 1979: 10). And such a question was precisely not reducible to static measurement, but to a form of expertise and care oriented to a particular type of personhood as defined by its futurity. Development, then, unlike growth, which had extension and could be measured in quantitative terms, was governed by a qualitative epistemology. Development was not defined according to a single scale, but was by its being intensive and qualitative. Difference and change were defined in qualitative terms in the context of becoming or development.

A biomedicalisation of children's everyday lives?

Paediatrics moved out of the hospital and into the population at large. It was concerned not simply with disease and illness, but with health and wellbeing. It was concerned not with the spatialisation of illness in the clinic (Foucault, 1973), but with the lives of individuals in a national population and with the risk and probability of ill health in the community. Armstrong talks about a general shift from 'hospital medicine', which was dominant as a form of medical organisation from the end of the eighteenth century, with the rise of hospitals as an institutional form in Paris, to 'surveillance medicine' in the twentieth century (Armstrong, 1995). The former was organised around what Armstrong refers to as three spatialisations of illness: a primary spatialisation according to symptom (which was the subjective experience of illness), sign (the interpretation of illness through the expert eyes and examination of the physician) and pathology (which was thus diagnosed as the basis of medical interpretation in the patient's body); a secondary spatialisation that allowed the patient's body to be understood as a three-dimensional object within which the pathological lesion could be identified and importantly in the context of which medical techniques of examination (through sounds and observation) could be invented and developed; and a tertiary spatialisation that was formed within the clinical space of the hospital itself, such that the clinical space constituted a neutral and clean space of observation and treatment. In hospital medicine, Armstrong argues, the illness is observed, examined and treated in the context of the clinical space. But with the advance of surveillance medicine the issue was not to bring the illness within the hospital, nor even necessarily to treat illness as such, but to act on the population in the context of its normalisation. For Armstrong, the child is central to the extension of surveillance medicine, particularly the child as a developing subject. The child is examined and observed not only in the clinic, but also in schools, in nurseries and at home. Medics and health workers are able to go out into the community in the context of preventative health programmes and not simply to cure disease. Such programmes required a constant surveying and examination of the population, but also the promotion of campaigns aimed at, for example, diet, exercise, sex and so on. Medicine in this sense was embedded in the everyday conduct and lives of people inasmuch as it provided a means of understanding and acting in the interests of the health and wellbeing of the population. As such, it was not the relation between symptom, sign and pathology that was of importance, but the probability of illness or ill health. It was thus through a concept of risk that wellbeing was now governed, not in the clinic but across the land. Such a medical concept of risk meant that illness did not reside within the body of the patient as observed and examined in a clean clinical space. Rather, illness was seen in probabilistic terms in the context of an aggregated series of factors and not simply within a unitary human body as such (Armstrong, 1995: 401).

Of course, the growth in what Armstrong refers to as surveillance medicine constitutes one aspect of what Michel Foucault and others have uncovered with respect to more general shifts in the nature of modern power. Foucault considers the huge changes in government occurring from the eighteenth century onwards in terms of a generalised shift in knowledge and power. He lists the emergence of a series of issues that arise at the end of the eighteenth century – concerning rate of births, fertility of the population, rate of deaths, epidemics, endemics – that are concerned with the life and wellbeing of a population. Mortality and the propensity to illness are conceived of in terms of a general care for the population, in terms of what Foucault refers to as 'biopolitics' and 'biopower'.

These are the phenomena that begin to be taken into account at the end of the eighteenth century, and they result in the development of a medicine whose main function will now be public hygiene, with institutions to coordinate medical care, centralize power, and normalize knowledge. (Foucault, 2004: 244)

For Foucault, the family, but also importantly the child, is central to the growth of biopower. Thus, in a discussion of the medicalisation of the family and the positioning of the child therein, he states:

The family is no longer to be just a system of relations inscribed in a social status, a kinship system, a mechanism for the transmission of property. It is to become a dense, saturated, permanent, continuous physical environment which envelops, maintains and develops the child's body. Hence it assumes a material figure defined within a narrower compass; it organises itself as the child's immediate environment, tending increasingly to become its basic framework for survival and growth. (Foucault, 1980a: 173)

The concern with health and hygiene can be seen in the rise of a discourse of eugenics in the nineteenth and twentieth centuries, such that the control of reproduction was seen to be essential to the wellbeing of the species. Nikolas Rose makes this clear when he argues:

Attempts to act on reproduction were widespread, ranging from popular advice on the choice of marriage partners, through the development of children's allowances and welfare benefits for mothers, to segregation and sterilization of those thought to be physically or morally unfit. Infused with a

more or less virulent racism, eugenic policies of forced or coerced sterilization of those considered threats to the quality of the population – notably
inhabitants of mental hospitals, the 'feeble-minded', and those deemed incor-
rigibly immoral or antisocial – spread across the United States, Europe, to
Latin America and beyond. (Rose, 2007: 61)

For Rose, as for Foucault, a discourse of eugenics was visible in the
broader conceptualisation of a biopolitics of health. Rose continues:

The specificity of the biopolitics of the first half of the twentieth century
lies ... in the links established between population, quality, territory,
nation, and race. It involved more than the idea that, other things being
equal, healthy individuals were more desirable than those who were
unhealthy. Health was understood in terms of quality – of the individual
and of the race – and quality was understood in a quasi-evolutionary
manner, as fitness. (Rose, 2007: 62)

The implications for such an understanding of health and medicine are
wide-ranging, but it is sufficient for us here to stress that from the
eighteenth century onwards the health of the child is increasingly
considered in terms of both individual and societal wellbeing.

   Certainly, much has changed since the eighteenth century in terms of
a shift from classical mechanical and geometric conceptions of the
body (as anatomy and physiology), even from simple electro-chemical
neurology, toward notions of communication and genetic coding (see
Canguilhem, 1994). Advances in medical knowledge, practice and
technology have shifted the terms of both understanding and also
government. Sarah Franklin thus states that

We are currently witnessing the emergence of a new genomic
governmentality – the regulation and surveillance of technologically assisted
genealogy. This is necessitated by the removal of the genomes of plants,
animals and humans from the template of natural history that once secured
their borders, and their re-animation as forms of corporate capital, in the
context of a legal vacuum. This dual imperative, to take evolution in one
hand and to govern it with the other, is a defining paradox of global nature,
global culture. (Franklin, 2000: 188)

Rose typifies this in terms of a 'molecularisation' of biology and
biopolitics (2001). Life has become re-engineered, Rose argues, on
what is now a molecular scale. But also, and not necessarily coextensive, the production of knowledge of life and its forms of government
have an increasingly political economic dimension. Not only with

regard to the capitalisation of 'the global genome' (Thacker, 2005), but across various forms of life as molecular processes, personal biography and individual conduct, the biomedicalisation of children's everyday lives involves the forceful presence of commercial interests.

In the field of psychiatry we see a striking shift, not in terms of the tropes of infantilism but in terms of the language of the molecular and the deployment of neurochemical treatments. Regarding infantilisation, Foucault has argued that the separation of childhood from adult maturity constitutes a significant development in the discipline of psychiatry. He talks about the case of Henriette Cornier, who as a child had been happy and cheerful but from adolescence onwards had become sad and quiet. She grew up to a difficult life and was imprisoned for murdering and chopping up the young baby of her next-door neighbour. Foucault argues: 'Childhood, then, must be separated from the pathological process so that the latter can effectively function and play its part in the deresponsibilization of the subject. You can see why the signs of infantile wickedness were a stake and the object of an important struggle in the medicine of mental alienation' (Foucault, 2003: 302).

In contrast, Foucault recounts the case of Pierre Rivière. He talks about how the signs of wickedness in the young Rivière (including the 'torturing of frogs, killing birds, and burning the soles of his brother's feet') may be seen to prefigure his killing of his mother, brother and sister. Foucault argues that instead of seeing a difference between childhood and adulthood, psychiatry notices a continuity between, for example in the case of Rivière, the signs of wickedness and the later adult criminal insanity. He argues: 'Childhood as a historical stage of development and a general form of behaviour becomes the principal instrument of psychiatrization' (Foucault, 2003: 304); and continues:

far from considering childhood as new territory that is annexed to psychiatry at a certain point, it seems to me that it is by taking childhood as the target of its action, both of its knowledge and its power, that psychiatry succeeds in being generalized. That is to say, childhood seems to me to be one of the historical conditions of the generalization of psychiatric knowledge and power. (Foucault, 2003: 304)

He elaborates on this as follows:

The presence of any kind of trace of infantilism is enough for conduct to fall within the jurisdiction of psychiatry, for it to be possible to psychiatrize it. As a result, inasmuch as it is capable of fixing, blocking, and halting adult conduct and of being reproduced within it, all of the child's conduct is in principle subject to psychiatric inspection. Conversely, all adult conduct can be psychiatrized inasmuch as it can be linked to the child's conduct in one way or another, whether through resemblance, analogy, or a causal relationship. Consequently, all of the child's conduct is thoroughly scoured since it may contain an adult fixation within it. Conversely, adult conduct is scrutinized for any possible trace of infantilism. (Foucault, 2003: 305)

Not only were the lives of children scrutinised with respect to symptoms of adult psychopathology, but also toward the end of the nineteenth century children were increasingly disclosed as themselves having significant psychiatric problems.

In recent discourse there has been a focus on genetic disposition. Jeremy Rifkin, for example in *The Biotech Century*, has talked about 'the troubling social and economic consequences of shifting to genetic causation as an all-encompassing explanatory model' (Rifkin, 1999: 158) in the context of the NIH Human Genome Project conference 'Genetic Factors in Crime', which, after initial cancellation due to public concern about racist science, took place in 1995. Rifkin states: 'By making violent crime a health problem, the public debate shifts from environmental factors that affect crime, like lack of educational opportunity, joblessness, and poverty, to genetic "errors" that can be controlled or weeded out' (159). Of course, as he notes, such a view when mapped on to existing demographics of crime and the over-representation of African-Americans in US prisons, serves a racist and anti-poor agenda.

Research into serotonin levels has been linked with impulsive and aggressive behaviour (Rifkin, 1999: 159), but equally psychologists such as Jerome Kagan have argued that people with lower heart rates and blood pressure (i.e. those calmer under pressure) may be more prone to violent crime (160), and Rifkin goes on to claim that in the near future scientists will be able to identify children with violent tendencies through genetic testing (160). The use of PET scans and other brain visualisation technologies (such as CT and MRI) have been significant in demonstrating violent tendency in particular areas of the brain. Rifkin noted: 'Legal scholars believe that the courts will increasingly rely on brain scans in determining sentencing and making parole decisions' (160). But as Joseph Dumit has argued, the use of PET scans functions as a form of persuasion in that by pairing brain images from 'normal people and those with disorders, and through images of treatment's effect on the brain, people may be persuaded that mental illnesses are, in fact, biological' (Dumit, 2004: 155). The ambiguities of the image and the work of interpretation are occluded by the insistence of the factual nature of the brain image showing us the abnormal brain. Dumit's work makes it clear how the link between the brain and social behaviour is mediated by molecular biologists, psychologists and other brain scientists, but also by journalists, filmmakers and others. As such, he shows how early public discourse on the discovery of a gene for crime, for example, was caught up and deeply embedded in the marketing and fictionalisation of scientific claims (185). It should be noted, though, that those scientists (molecular geneticists, neurochemists and neurobiologists) looked not for a 'gene for crime', but at impulsive, violent and aggressive behaviour (Rose, 2007: 225). The courtroom has been a key site for the articulation of biosocial and penal discourses and expertise (Rose, 2007: 229). Rose has argued that, regarding the use of this expertise in legal trial, 'Present evidence thus suggests that biological and genetic defences have largely failed to displace older conceptions of responsibility within the practice of the criminal law, at least in the United States where one might expect such developments to be furthest advanced' (Rose, 2007: 234). Moreover, he says, although PET scans may have 'greater rhetorical force' than expert witness from psychologists or psychiatrists, these 'physical inscription' devices are often subjected to legal scrutiny in the courtroom in such a way that any simple truths are exposed as a 'messy complexity' (234). Against Rifkin's narrative of the success of the molecular biological and neuroscientific knowledges in shaping legal process, Rose offers a more sanguine stance, stating that it is unlikely that these arguments would 'not be subjected to the same destabilization if they begin to enter the criminal trial process on a regular basis' (235). Rose argues that where these knowledges have an effect is not with regard to arguments about diminished responsibility or free will, but with regard to the determining of the kind of sentence meted to the condemned. He argues that it is with reference to 'public protection' that biological knowledge is used to justify the long-term containment of the pathological person. These persons are thus incarcerated – not only in prisons but also in other forms of medical-carceral institutions – due to their being considered a threat to society (235). Biological explanation is now put forward in

the context of societal protection and a series of questions about risk
factors (238). And criminality is understood in terms of the probability
as to what might happen in the future and hence the need to control
persons with respect to tendencies demonstrated at an early age and
with respect to family and genetic history. This, Rose argues, despite its
apparent similarity, is a far cry from the kinds of eugenics arguments
put forward by people such as Charles Murray.

David Healy, Professor of Psychiatry at the North Wales Department of Psychological Medicine, Cardiff University, and a leading
international psychiatrist, in a review of a book on the history of
ADHD has stated:

> It seems clear that a dam has been breached and that a taboo on giving drugs
> to children has gone. Indeed, children, almost more than any other party in
> the USA, are probably most at risk of ending up on physical treatments
> and indeed combinations of physical treatments for behavioural problems,
> where little more than a decade ago this would have been inconceivable ...
> ADHD is the most visible symbol of the bio-medicalisation of childhood
> disorders ... (Healy, 2006: 177–8)

In the nineteenth century the combination of inattention, hyperactivity
and impulsive behaviour in children would have been understood and
acted upon largely in the context of moral terminology and control,
but such a combination of behaviours is now understood in the context
of the American Psychiatric Association's *Diagnostic and Statistical
Manual of Mental Disorders* (DSM) or the World Health Organization's *International Classification of Diseases Manual* as attention
deficit hyperactivity disorder (ADHD) or hyperkinetic disorder. Across
different countries there are differences in diagnosis and treatment, but
the core features include: easily bored, easy loss of interest, preoccupied by moment-to-moment attention, behaviour inappropriate for
particular situations, and inconsistent, sometimes rude and lazy
(Tucker, 1999: 217). These core features are themselves seen to
'exhibit a significant degree of co-morbidity with other early childhood
risk factors, most notably conduct disorder and cognitive deficits' and
thus increasingly a link between ADHD and children's criminal behaviour is made (Savolainen et al., 2010: 443). For example, ADHD is
often seen as a contributory factor in the exclusion of children and
young people from school on the grounds of disruptive behavioural
problems, and yet in making such prognoses other, more enduring risk

factors (such as sustained family socioeconomic disadvantage and poverty) are seen as secondary or symptomatic of a genetic hereditary disposition (see Bynner, 2001). ADHD is seen as a disorder that is located in the prefrontal cortex, which is part of the cerebellum and the basal ganglia, and can be explained, it is argued, 'very largely by genetic factors'. Children with ADHD have genetic malfunctions in the parts of the brain that use dopamine as a neurotransmitter in order to relay communications (Tucker, 1999: 218). Although ADHD may be treated by careful and constant expert supervision in order to modify behaviour toward situationally appropriate conduct, the cost of such treatment is high and demands the commitment of expert support teams (including parents, health workers and psychiatrists). Since the rapid rise – initially in adolescents, but increasingly in much younger children – in the diagnosis of ADHD in the USA but also in the UK and other countries, the disorder has largely been treated through the prescription of methylphenidate (or Ritalin), but also with dexamphetamine (or Adderall), which acts on the dopamine transporters and increases the time dopamine binds to its receptors (Tucker, 1999: 218). A disorder that is seen largely in the USA, largely since the 1980s, and largely in the context of behaviour seen to be inappropriate in an educational schooling context, ADHD is treated through an amphetamine-like drug, a drug with effects similar to cocaine, which increases motivation and attention. The production of Ritalin, which is consumed largely by the US market (which accounts for 90 per cent of the world market; Breggin, 2000), rose by 450 per cent in the early 1990s (Transit, 2003; see also Rose, 2007: 209). It is prescribed by paediatricians and family practitioners rather than by psychiatrists (Schachar, Tannock and Cunningham, 1996), and in most cases the initial referrals are made by teachers. This chain of events is what has moved the classification and government of children's impulsive, distracted, disruptive behaviour from disorderly conduct to a clinically labelled psychiatric disorder (Rafalovich, 2004), and it is in this sense that some critics have argued that teachers act as 'sickness brokers' for ADHD. Of particular significance is the role that pharmaceutical companies play in educating teachers about the disorder with regard to its identification and referral (Phillips, 2006). Phillips argues that such brokerage is not necessarily a disinterested activity for the teacher, since the referral can become a device for managing disruptive conduct in the classroom (Phillips, 2006). What has become a worrying trend is that it is no longer adolescents who are being diagnosed with ADHD, but increasingly younger preschool children. We should be wary of simply arguing that ADHD is largely an effect of psychiatric labelling or the result of 'moral panic' (Miller and Leger, 2003), inasmuch as the reduction of such conduct to a biological disorder and the determination of its aetiology does not necessarily dictate the form of treatment (i.e. inasmuch as biological diseases might be treated through psychotherapy or behavioural relearning), but also inasmuch as those directly affected by the disorder might find comfort in its naming and in the support networks (clinical, family, friendship and political) facilitated through such naming.

Although ADHD has dictated a huge amount of coverage regarding the biomedicalisation of children's lives, all the recent indicators of children's and young people's health have identified a rise in the number of young people suffering from behavioural and mental health problems (e.g. WHO European Ministerial Conference, 2005). Twenty per cent of children and young people across the world are seen to be suffering from disabling mental health problems (WHO, 2001). Increasing in significance is the diagnosis of bipolar disorder. In July 2000, the US newspaper, the *Star Telegram*, reported that the mother of Heather Norris, a 2-year-old child who had been diagnosed with ADHD, had requested that her doctor rediagnose her daughter's condition as a bipolar disorder after reading Papolos and Papolos's *The Bipolar Child* (see Healy, 2006b: 443). Two years later, in August 2002, *Time* magazine ran a cover story on the increase in paediatric bipolar disorder in the USA. Healy argues that there is now 'a surge of diagnoses of bipolar disorder in American children' (443). This, he argues, is largely dependent on subjective criteria and judgements (namely, through reports of parents and other family members) and on the basis of these judgements pharmacotherapy is prescribed. The prescription of Zyprexa, Risperdal and other antipsychotic drugs, which are more likely to be prescribed by psychiatrists, has risen dramatically since the 1990s (*New York Times*, 6 June 2006). These are drugs designed initially for adults and with little proper testing regarding dosages or effects for children. They are increasingly used for treating preschool children (443). This is similarly the case with the diagnosis of childhood depression and the prescription of SSRIs (selective serotonin re-uptake inhibitors such as Seroxat and Prozac). Large pharmaceutical companies, which spend large amounts of money developing a drug for adults and with little commercial incentive to redevelop and retest the drug for children, market antipsychotics, antidepressants and stimulants to children. Drugs originally designed to treat one disorder are remarketed with regard to a collection of disorders which are themselves labelled and designated in the *DSM*. The relationship between *DSM* labelling, pharmaceutical marketing and the growth in children and young people suffering psychiatric disorders is not always clear cut (Rose, 2007: 209–15; Applbaum, 2006). But also, the growth in citizen and patient groups, which are aligned to forms of disorder and treatment, has been significant in recent years, giving rise to what Rose has called 'neurochemical citizenship'. Although some activist groups are certainly shaped by the anti-psychiatry movements and philosophies of the 1960s and 1970s regarding the social nature of mental health problems, others not only accept but promote the biological nature of the disorder as a positive point of political identification and mobilisation and social and empathetic support. Some of the groups are directly funded by pharmaceutical companies. Many exist largely in online environments and their political mobilisation and support networks are conducted via the internet. In doing so, new forms of agency and solidarity are formed as a consequence of new pharmacological knowledges, medicines and new communications technologies such as the internet and social media platforms.

Realigning children's agency

Before concluding this chapter, I want to look at the significant and influential early work of Pia Christensen, in order to foreground more clearly the implications of our earlier discussion for an understanding of agency with respect to children. Christensen's research comes more directly out of the new sociology of childhood paradigm which emerged in the late 1980s and early 1990s. This work, which was presented in Chapter 3, stressed the role of children's agency in social relations and particularly in terms of the dynamic structuring of structure through agency. Children aren't simply determined by social structure, but are themselves productive of those structures. Christensen's research in the field of health and illness has focussed at different times on children between the ages of 6 and 13 years at home, school and in after-school centres in Copenhagen, Denmark.

Her research has been largely ethnographic and included observations, but also interviews and other forms of data collection, including children's drawings. I want to consider two arguments that she makes in two research papers, from 1998 and 2000.

In 'Difference and similarity: how children's competence is constituted in illness and its treatment' (1998), Christensen considers children's competence. She argues that competence is not a psychological property of the individual, but a relation between social persons in contexts of negotiation. The question for her, then, is not what children are able or not able to do, but how their competence about illness is performed and in the context of what kinds of social interactions. She considers illness and therapy in the context of everyday interactions and looks at how symbolic boundaries between illness and health are constructed in social interaction. She is also keen to investigate how children's negotiated competence adjusts our understanding of the deployment of formal medical hierarchies in the family inasmuch as children might ordinarily be viewed in terms of their lack of competence and knowledge in contrast to an adult, professional expert medical knowledge. She argues that adults tend to construe themselves as 'rational' and rely on 'mediating devices' (such as thermometers). Christensen argues that 'children's competence becomes suspended; their subjective experiences of their own bodies do not qualify them as "speakers of fact"' (Christensen, 1998: 198). Duration acts as 'an important boundary marker between a well or an ill child' (191). For example, parents are prone to saying, 'Go and sit down for twenty minutes and let's see if you feel better.' Adults use time as a means of judging children's claims to be ill. They may assume that a child is faking illness and that a child would not be able to sustain the performance of illness for any length of time, or they may assume that the child may want attention, or maybe that they lack the competence to judge for themselves whether they are really ill or not. Of course, sometimes also illness (as demonstrated through a high body temperature) may arise at night and subside by morning. Body temperature is a key issue for both children and adults. But for adults, the testing of temperature is significant in ascertaining the authenticity of the illness and in objectifying the illness. Taking someone's temperature is seen alongside other forms of adult competence conduct, such as opening medicine (who opens the bottle? who is allowed to go into the medicine cabinet?), and determining the medicine, dose and therapy. For

Christensen, the relation between adult and child and the use of mediating devices is seen in terms of adults' and children's relation to objectified and authorised knowledge and, inasmuch as children are not deemed reliable speakers of objectified truth whereas illness mediated by a thermometer does constitute a form of objectified truth: '[i]llness classification indicates the position of the child as incompetent (as well as dependent, passive and subordinate) while the adult is seen as competent, active and in charge' (193). These forms of conduct concerning examination and medication rely on the complicity of the child. Children need to act and agree. For Christensen, then, the negotiation and mediation of children's illness is seen primarily in terms of the relationship between children and adults, not such that these are defined and differentiated as prior categories, but rather as relational positions formed through the practices and objects in which competence is performed. We should note at this point that Christensen's account does not attend to children with chronic illness, who are more likely to have control and responsibility for their medication and therapy (Clark, 2003).

In a second paper 'Childhood and the cultural constitution of vulnerable bodies' (2000), Christensen starts by considering the distinction between the exterior (surface) and the interior of the child's body. She considers how vulnerability constitutes a penetration of the body (literally, a wounding). Christensen draws on the work of Ronnie Frankenberg to make a distinction between the 'somatic body' and the 'incarnate body'. The somatic body is an 'objectification of the body beyond subjective experience "revealed at a particular diagnostic instant ... A partial, often technologically mediated, clinical view, restricted in time and space"' (Frankenberg, 1990 quoted Christensen, 2000: 45). The incarnate body is 'a unity of past, present and future simultaneously experienced from inside and outside ... The perspective of the incarnate body lacks the boundaries in both time and space and is permeable to the world' (Frankenberg, 1990 quoted Christensen, 2000: 45). Whereas adults want to objectify and unify the child's body, the child talks more about experience and relates illness to acts. Illness for the adult is conceptualised with respect to symptoms, names of symptoms, measures and technical therapies. For the child, illness concerns, for example, the disruption to daily routines (e.g. not being at school, being at home, not being with friends, etc.). Children talk with respect to a notion of the incarnate body and adults talk with respect to a somatic body. Moreover, the adult conceptualises the child's body as divided (interior and exterior). Thus, attending to the exterior body (clothing, washing, etc.) is reflected in a contented and well interior body. Moreover, 'an intact exterior body is indicative of the well-being of the child' (Christensen, 2000: 49). Christensen states:

Children's accounts showed that experiencing vulnerability also related to the experience of losing their social position, activities and relationships and changes to their environment. This suggests that, from children's perspectives, they *are* their world and did not see themselves as separate from the part they take in processes and events and their experiences of them. Children, then, spoke from the perspective of the body incarnate, the body as experience, in action, involved with the environment as well as in interactions with others. (Christensen, 2000: 47)

In this later paper we see that illness is performed not only with regard to the adult and the child as they are relationally defined, but also through the binary of technology–experience. A division is thus set up between a system world (of expertise, knowledge, technology) and a lifeworld (of experience). The former is sociotechnical and technocratic; the latter is more phenomenological. This gives rise to the question of the bifurcation of adults and children and to the anomalous status of the child with chronic illness. It also suggests that experience is itself not always mediated through devices (whether linguistic, medical or other). It figures the child as the site of an almost pure experience, which is itself denied the status of truth.

This is a powerful way of describing the lives of children, but we should question its analytical validity. We might want to question Christensen's tendency to treat children's experiences as if they themselves were innocent and unmediated, and also the notion that children can simply speak *from experience*. Christensen, too, readily reads medical terminology and adult practice not simply as different, but as different in kind. For her, adults' actions with regard to children's illness are not simply actions predicated on experience, but actions that seek to control the experience of another. Although Christensen and others help us to think about the agency of the child in the context of social interactions with other children and with adults, we need to locate such ideas not as a critique of new forms of biomedicalisation (as if we could simply situate the social agentic child as separate and distinct from social and technical processes, including those which construct subjectivities), but in the context of biopower in such a way as to explain the new, differing and distributed forms of agency available. Moreover, in this context we would want to have an understanding of the plurality of agencies, negotiations and devices. The teenage child with HIV, for example, does not stand in opposition to adults and adult objectifying technologies, but rather their regimen of care is distributed across paediatricians and nurses in the clinic, the daily dosage of medicines, and their own responsibilities (with regard to treatment, sense of self and relation with others) (Boulton, 2012). The experience of 'body' is so thoroughly mediated by devices and measures, experts and others, that it may seem to make little sense to mark out a space for the authentic child's body unless only as a space that surfaces at particular moments to contest others, as a political space of resistance in the assemblage.

Conclusion

Children's bodies have been disclosed through the invention and development of particular technologies of observation, measurement and standardisation. The tabulation of the child's physiological and psychological growth is understood through graphs and charts, but also through photographs. Children's interactions with the material world of objects and other people are mapped and recorded. Their health, illness, wellbeing and increasingly also happiness (largely recorded through the negative indicator of mental health problems) are not only points of surveillance and normalisation, but also sites of negotiation and mediation. Children's lives are sites of experience and experimentation. Their health cannot simply be defined in terms of a singular experiential body and medical therapies. Children's bodies are multiple, as Mol might say (Mol, 2002). But they are neither holistic nor fragmented. There is no single child's body that may be held up as a totalising image. There are instead aggregated bodies statistically assembled through huge amounts of testing over many years that help perform normalisations of size (height and weight) against age. But these don't produce a single adequate image. The paediatrician draws on this data not to reduce the child before them into a single uniform mould, but to deliver a form of care which is particular to that singular body. And yet the treatment of that body, albeit framed within a form of professional care and ethics, is directed to particular body parts. The governance of children with respect to the biomedical has grown and intensified. It has spread from the clinic to the everyday and across a huge array of different forms of classifiable conduct.

10 | *Play and consumer culture*

The major economic significance of children's role in consumption is with regard to the purchasing of everyday domestic items (such as soap powders and breakfast cereals) or large household items (such as cars, houses and holidays). Many of these items are manufactured by a small number of global corporations (such as Procter & Gamble or Toyota), who produce global brands that are sold through the main supermarkets and other retail outlets in conjunction with the main global advertising agencies. Advertisers often refer to the role of children in these household decisions in terms of 'pester power'; sociologists tend instead to talk of agency and negotiation. However, instead of considering this, in Chapter 10 I want to look at how, from the mid eighteenth century onwards and rapidly developing in the twentieth century, there has been a convergence of investment in children's play, consumer culture and the media industry. This chapter looks at the importance of children's play and at how it has become a site of invention and innovation. It considers how the central tropes of play – freedom, growth through interactive object relations, and performance in and through friendship – provide the basis for the massive development of a consumer culture of child-hood and its extension and mediation across many forms of everyday life (in the context of both adults and children). I will start by looking at a psychologist's account of play, a psychoanalyst's account of the child's interaction with objects, and a sociological account of play as peer-group interaction. I then set this in the context of a social and cultural history of play, paying particular attention to the close relation between commerce, toys and play from the nineteenth century onwards. In contrast to a standard account of the encroachment of the child's developmental space by commerical business, what we see is that the marketisation of play has been a site of productive innovation in children's agency, in terms of both building capacity and also in proliferating and multiplying its forms.

Recent advances in robotics, artificial intelligence and thinking about biological life have had an interesting synergy with developments in the toy industry and in reconstructions of play spaces and forms. But to look at the issues in this way is certainly not to ignore any very serious concerns regarding market dominance by a few global corporations and centres of knowledge, technology and capital accumulation, and the differential impact on children and adults in this respect.

Toward a sociological account of play

A standard textbook understanding of play is offered by the psychologist Catherine Garvey in her book on the subject: 'Play is most frequent in a period of dramatically expanding knowledge of self, the physical and social world, and systems of communication; thus we might expect that play is intricately related to these areas of growth' (Garvey, 1977: 7). She argues that something as seemingly simple and frivolous as play is actually something that is of the utmost importance to the healthy development of the child. Children's play is not chaotic and ungoverned, but rather rule-governed and well regulated. Its ordering and consistency are not always obvious to observers or to the children themselves. Garvey lists what she sees as the significant descriptive features of play:

1. Play is pleasurable, enjoyable ...
2. Play has no extrinsic goals. Its motivations are intrinsic and serve no other objectives. In fact, it is more an enjoyment of means than an effort devoted to some particular end. In utilitarian terms, it is inherently unproductive.
3. Play is spontaneous and voluntary. It is not obligatory but is freely chosen by the player.
4. Play involves some active engagement on the part of the player ...
5. Play has certain systematic relations to what is not play.

(Garvey, 1977: 10)

On first viewing, these descriptions may not seem contentious, but on closer inspection we may want to question some of them. The context for these definitions, in part, comes from Huizinga's anthropological definition of play and from Piaget's cognitive developmental one. Garvey doesn't make any reference to Huizinga, but we can clearly see how his work provides an important frame. Play is, for Huizinga:

> a free activity standing quite consciously outside 'ordinary' life as being 'not serious' but at the same time absorbing the player intensively and utterly. It is an activity connected with no material interest and no profit can be gained by it. It proceeds within its own proper boundaries of time and space according to fixed rules and in an orderly manner. It promotes the formation of social groupings which tend to surround themselves with secrecy and to stress their differences from common world by disguise or other means. (Huizinga, 1949: 13)

More apparent is the Piagetian debt. Very crudely, Garvey maps out a Piagetian frame which identifies three forms of play corresponding to the child's development across cognitive stages:

(a) Sensori-Motor (infancy–2 yrs old) – Play involves repetition of movement, sound, and so on; it involves the child's mastery over motor skills and experimentation with touch, sound and sight; and there is a pleasure in making things happen.
(b) Two to Six Years Old – Play is symbolic and representational; it encodes experience in symbols; and it demonstrates a symbolic creativity and use of imagination.
(c) Six Years and Over – Play is with rules; it involves games and organised sport, often including competition, co-operation, and teamwork; it involves strategic and objective thinking.

(Garvey, 1977: 13–14)

Writing, as she was, in the mid 1970s, Garvey's work is framed by Piaget's theoretical understanding of children's development, but her departure toward a better understanding of social context and social interaction is fairly typical of the period (see Donaldson, 1978). Piaget is seen to offer a rough and ready schema of development, but instead of making cognitive development the primary issue, Garvey reverses this and emphasises the social nature of play. Interaction with others becomes a central motif. Garvey's account is typical inasmuch as a whole range of infant behaviour – from baby smiles oriented to others, to externalisation of fantasy in make-believe worlds, to formal games and pastimes – is understood as play. The specificity and singularity of the behaviour is reduced to a universal orientation toward play with others understood along developmental lines.

We can place this alongside an account of play which comes out
of the psychoanalytic literature (notably from Melanie Klein and
D. W. Winnicott) on children's development and relationship to their
mothers. Winnicott, who was a paediatrician and psychoanalyst,
offers perhaps the most interesting account in his analysis of the role
of toys in facilitating the separation of infant from mother and in the
construction of play as a therapeutic site. Winnicott's concern is not
toys per se, but the function of what he terms 'transitional objects':
namely, those objects that carry the emotional investment of an infant
for its mother in the process of separating from that mother. Transitional objects are phenomena that designate an 'intermediate area of
experience, between the thumb and the teddy bear' (Winnicott, 1986: 2).
In the separation from the mother, the infant is formed as a separate
being and the world is constructed as a world of independently
existing objects. Transitional objects constitute that realm
of objects between need and desire, inside and outside, reality and
fantasy. The sucking of thumbs, blankets, teddy bears, favourite
dolls, an old sock with holes in it can all function as transitional
phenomena inasmuch as they provide the infant with a sense of a
world external to itself and the mother, but not quite external or
'real'. Winnicott argues that

Transitional objects and transitional phenomena belong to the realm of
illusion which is at the basis of initiation of experience ... This intermediate
area of experience, unchallenged in respect of its belonging to inner and
external (shared) reality, constitutes the greater part of the infant's experience ... It is not the object, of course, that is transitional. The object
represents the infant's transition from a state of being merged with the
mother to a state of being in relation to the mother as something outside
and separate. (Winnicott, 1986: 16–17)

Winnicott understands play through this understanding of the infant's
relation to transitional phenomena. Play is not a psychic phenomenon,
but equally it is not properly external and real. Play takes place in a
'potential space'. The objects of play are presented as if in a dreamlike
world (of 'make-believe') and the objects are invested with affect and
manipulated accordingly. This interactive space is not purely cognitive
(although this is one aspect); it is emotional and bodily. Moreover,
play is directed toward satisfaction (i.e. the mobilisation of agency is
motivated by desire) (60–1).

The sociology of childhood has investigated the phenomenon of play broadly in terms of, firstly, considering it as a means of differentiation from adults and, secondly, as a central topic for understanding children's peer-group interaction. Firstly, play is seen as something that children do, but adults don't. Thus Berry Mayall refers to a child who says, 'Adults are a bit boring ... they don't really play football or nothing like that ... They just go to work most of the time, and when they come home they just want their dinner and then sleep afterwards' (quoted in Mayall, 2002: 133). She states:

Young people do not refer to a developmental need for play (as learning) but they do refer to their need for a break from the adult-oriented day; and for them the function of play is to enable them to experience delight and fun, usually, but not necessarily, in company with friends. (Mayall, 2002: 135)

Secondly, play is understood in terms of peer-group relations and friendship formation. For example, in Allison James' discussion of friendship she states:

Friendship is not simply a cognitive relationship of affectivity. It must be affirmed, confirmed and reaffirmed through social action. This explains how the emphasis on 'sameness' and conformity in children's social relationships – wearing the same clothes, eating the same food, liking the same football teams – works to mitigate the significance which any differences might have. It represents one visible demonstration of friendship, for it is through such public performances that children evaluate and acknowledge their friendships with one another: being friends must not only be experienced but seen to be experienced. (James, 1993: 215)

In this context, children's play is seen in terms of forms of inclusion and exclusion within peer-group cultures (see also Sanders and Freeman, 1998), but it is also a significant factor in the performative relationality of play. Play is something which is experienced and done, but it is also commented on and constantly stage-directed. Play as social relationality is both experienced and rehearsed. Thus children spend much time setting up what is going to happen and talking through what is about to happen just before and during its happening. It is a highly reflexive form of social relationality.

Social and cultural histories of childhood play

Across the disciplines there are clearly – over and above superficial similarities – major differences in understandings as to what constitutes play. The different phenomena that are understood as play – within the different perspectives outlined above – would suggest that any history of play and its association with childhood is far from a simple matter. For example, if we take Winnicott's analysis, we would have to assume that play is a human universal and occurs even when there are no demonstrable objects named as 'toys' or 'playthings'. And yet, it is commonplace within the sociology of childhood to talk about the invention of childhood in the seventeenth century in terms of the distribution of play on the side of childhood and work on the side of adulthood. The historian J. H. Plumb talks of life in the Middle Ages:

> There was no separate world of childhood. Children share the same games with adults, the same toys, the same fairy stories. They lived their lives together, never apart. The coarse village festivals depicted by Breughel, showing men and women besotted with drink, groping for each other with unbridled lust, have children eating and drinking with the adults. Even, in the soberer picture of wedding feasts and dances the children are enjoying themselves alongside their elders, doing the same things. (Plumb quoted in Kline, 1993: 46)

Of course, the originator of this perspective was Ariès in his *Centuries of Childhood* (1962). Ariès talks about the abundance of images and statuettes from the Middle Ages and before that have been interpreted by toy historians and doll collectors as 'toys'. He argues that they were objects of religious significance, 'objects of a household or funerary cult, relics from a pilgrimage ... miniature replicas of familiar objects placed in tombs'. Moreover, he argues: 'I am not suggesting that in the past children did not play with dolls or replicas of adult belongings. But they were not the only ones to use these replicas; what in modern times was to become their monopoly, they had to share in ancient times, at least with the dead' (Ariès, 1962: 67). Ariès also talks of how miniatures of people and things in daily life were used in magic, and also played with by adults as well as children.

> By 1600, approximately, toys had become an infantile speciality, with a few differences of detail with regard to present-day usage ... There was probably some connection between the infantile specialization in toys and the importance of infancy in the ideas revealed by iconography and dress since the end of the Middle Ages. Childhood was becoming the repository of customs abandoned by the adults. (Ariès, 1962: 68)

A series of objects once shared by all (including the dead) take on new meaning through their congregation around young children. Ariès qualifies this statement, though, by saying that the specialisation of toys and pastimes did not extend beyond infancy (i.e. 3 to 4 years old) at this particular time. But as the centuries rolled on this age period extended upwards and downwards. Ariès' version of the history of childhood and its relation to play, toys and pastimes is far from uncontested, however, and many historians now argue that children across the ages played with toys (Orme, 2001).

Nevertheless what is uncontested is that since the end of the nineteenth century we have witnessed an intensification of investment in the relation between children, play and toys. As Gary Cross has argued, 'Before the second half of the nineteenth century, toys were rare and often served the needs of adults more than the play of children. The modern toy is a distinct product of a new kind of toy business and a new childrearing ideal' (Cross, 1997: 12). What is central to this is not simply the rarity or abundance of toys, but that, by and large, toys in the 1700s, for example, would have been hand-made by the player or a family member or someone close to hand. When in 1760 Laurence Sterne describes Tristram Shandy's Uncle Toby playing toy soldiers, these figures are ones he has made from the lead from household window weights (Brown, 1996). Some toys (such as metal figures, dolls and rattles) were mass-produced in the medieval period (Orme, 2001), but over the course of the next two hundred and fifty years they became manufactured in larger numbers and in greater variety, in conditions which were industrial, market-oriented, technological and global. The toy industry reflexively constructs, invests in and changes the nature and conditions of play. In the late nineteenth and early twentieth centuries we see an expansion of toy makers, a reaching out to a mass market and the use of advertising to appeal to parents (as the main purchasers of toys for their offspring). The growth in the market for toys, a massive innovation and development, has been a cause of pleasure, but also of concern. We should remember that despite this huge intensification and proliferation of investment, children and parents still make toys from scratch and that toys both handmade and bought are played within creative, 'local' and embedded spaces. We can easily punk up a Barbie's hair; we can turn a hairdryer into a ray gun; and we can mix teddies with Action Man in a game of intergalactic ice-cream wars.

The dedifferentiation of childhood and adulthood?

Alan Prout has claimed that 'the boundary between childhood and adulthood, which modernity erected and kept in place for a substantial period of time, is beginning to blur, introducing all kinds of ambiguities and uncertainties' (Prout, 2005: 34). Such a claim is based on long-standing arguments that in the latter part of the twentieth century advances in visual cultural technologies and their growth and commercialisation have meant that the distinctions and differentiations between childhood and adulthood are either blurring or disappearing. The most resonant form of this argument comes from the sociologist and communications scholar Neil Postman (1994). Postman makes an historical argument that draws on the work of Ariès with regard to the notion that childhood is a social invention emerging in the seventeenth century, but he frames it in relation to major changes in communications technology. For Postman, the Middle Ages is a time of openness. There are no distinctions between adults and children; work is conducted by both adults and children; sex and violence are visible to both and the hardships of life are not concealed from children. But with the invention of printing with moveable type (signified by the publication and distribution of the Lutheran Bible) there develops an adult culture different from that of children. Print allows certain forms of abstraction that are not possible within oral culture. Print allows certain forms of reflection (i.e. the ability to read, but also to reread). It allows certain forms of complexity (Ong, 1982). Moreover, whereas oral cultures are public (i.e. stories, such as the *Iliad* from ancient Greece, are told to audiences sitting before a story-teller), books and pamphlets and printed documents are read on an individual basis. Print constitutes a culture that is not readily accessible to everyone. Books can be used to keep secrets, to keep things from children, to encode knowledges that are not accessible to the illiterate. But print also requires certain forms of apprenticeship or certain forms of training and learning. Certain forms of institutionalisation emerge to facilitate this training (i.e. schools) and certain forms of power relation are established on the basis of this training (i.e. between teacher and pupil, holder of knowledge and the ignorant). Print brings about 'adulthood' as a new form of consciousness and culture. And in this sense, childhood is that which is excluded from the world of adulthood. Thus the development of print technology brings about new forms of consciousness (abstraction, reflection, individuation), new forms of knowledge, new forms of exclusion, new forms of training and new forms of culture.

In the twentieth century with film but especially with television and other visual media everything, Postman argues, is accessible; there are no adult secrets, no way of separating children from that adult world. Postman states that

Television … is an open-admission technology to which there are no physical, economic, cognitive, or imaginative constraints. The six-year-old and the sixty-year-old are equally qualified to experience what television has to offer. Television, in this sense, is the consummate egalitarian medium of communication, surpassing oral language itself … The most obvious and general effect of this situation is to eliminate the exclusivity of worldly knowledge and, therefore, to eliminate one of the principal differences between childhood and adulthood … Children are a group of people who do not know certain things that adults know. In the Middle Ages there were no children because there existed no means for adults to know exclusive information. In the Age of Gutenberg, such a means developed. In the Age of Television, it is dissolved. (Postman, 1994: 84–5)

Postman refers to television as 'a total disclosure medium'. It constitutes forms of knowledge and access to knowledge that are readily accessible to everyone. Although framed in different terms, this is also the argument Joshua Meyrowitz makes regarding the transition from 'print culture' to 'television culture' due to the latter's inability to properly differentiate between age-related people (Meyrowitz, 1984 and 1987). Of course, these arguments about television culture seem to be potentially exacerbated in the context of internet and mobile communications. There seems to be little if any regulation of content, and despite a large amount of textual navigation, everything is visible.

One of the problems with this account is that it is technologically deterministic. There is an assumption that print, television and oral culture have set meanings or functions. But what we know of communication technologies is that they are open to different interpretations and to different forms of use (see Grint and Woolgar, 1997; Silverstone and Hirsch, 1994). But equally, Postman's argument assumes that in order for print to differentiate between adults and children, the difference between those with literacy competence and those without is akin to a division between children and adults. In fact, what we know is that levels of cognitive intelligence (and perhaps even more so media literacy) do not exactly correlate with age. A bright 10-year-old is just as likely to be literate as a dull 50-year-old. If print were to differentiate between adults and children, as if there were a clear division between the two on the basis of literate–non-literate, then such a differentiation could only be on the basis of a prior cognitive division between children and adults. What we know is that things are much more complex. What we know is that all media (print and television included) require 'reading' and that the pedagogies for accessing media are both formal (and institutionalised, for example, in school) and informal (i.e. learnt through popular culture, friendship networks and so on). We know that television, far from being readily accessible to everyone, is actually something that requires forms of literacy to understand it. Children of different ages with different media competencies read programmes in different ways (Buckingham, 1993).

The cultural critic John Hartley put forward a variation on this theme initially in a paper on the institutional construction of audiences in television (Hartley, 1987). He put forward a thesis that similarly leads to a dissolution of the boundary of generational distinction, not in terms of the adultification of children, but in terms of the infantilisation of adults. The term that he uses is 'paedocratisation'. Hartley, as Postman does, focusses his argument on television, but unlike Postman's thesis, his argument can be deployed in relation to a range of media (not only visual), including novels (as with the popular reception of the Harry Potter books), theme parks (as with Disney World and Parc du Futuroscope) and computer games (as with *Lara Croft* and *Grand Theft Auto*). There are three elements to his argument: that the audience is an imagined community; that a commercial logic drives a demand for audience maximisation; and that childishness constitutes a universal imaginary. Firstly, for Hartley, the television audience is a fiction or an imagined community. There is no real audience waiting to be discovered. It is something that is wholly constituted within the discourses of the television institutions. The television audience qua audience is only ever a representation. Secondly, for Hartley, a commercial logic is geared toward audience maximisation and profit maximisation and the figure of the child is seen to provide media and consumer industry with a means of addressing audiences that may be divided demographically by class, gender, 'race' and so on. Thirdly, then, Hartley argues that in addressing something that is supposedly universal (i.e. childhood), we can all potentially buy into such an imaginary figuring. Moreover, the child-like audience is one that is addressed through the lowest common denominator (i.e. to a base level of intelligence). Thus, in the television industry storylines are told and retold in a single episode of a soap opera or sitcom; characters are developed to allow maximum identification; any complexity is ironed out. And thus the industry, which was once on to a good thing, now reproduces that which seems to work and a productive cycle multiplies this paedocratisation.

As with Postman, Hartley doesn't take account of how television is used and interpreted at a local level (Billig, 1997). In lots of ways his argument seems dated. It seems to come from an era when television was the most significant media industry and at a time when audiences were primarily defined in terms of their 'mass'. Television media certainly are still important alongside internet and social media, but from the 1990s onwards the commercial logics have shifted away from profit maximisation by way of massification and toward niche but global markets. And yet even in the context of these changes, there is still an appeal to 'childishness', which remains a persistent feature of the contemporary play, media and consumer cultural landscape. Hartley, in looking to forms of infantilisation, offers an explanatory model for understanding what is at stake in contemporary adult childishness. How do we explain the impact of adults playing computer games, going paintballing, dressing up in fancy dress, and so on? Although the commercialisation of adult entertainment may in some cases lead to its paedocratisation, to the hailing of the lowest common denominators that we were all and still want to be children, or at least childish, it is unclear whether there is a single market logic which is able to explain a massification of audience or market in the manner of pitching to a notion of the lowest common denominator, a common base intelligence and emotional responsiveness. It is worth noting here that some critics discuss paedocratisation in the context of adult narcissism, and hence there is a clear correlation with Giddens' work and that of others on the transformation of intimacy in late modernity (e.g. Giddens, 1992; Lasch, 1984). Pat Holland is concerned about and critical of such paedocratisation inasmuch as it leads, she argues, to adult irresponsibility (Holland, 1996). If adults are behaving narcissistically and childishly, then who is going to care for the children themselves?

In both Postman and Hartley there is an understated but central theme regarding the centrality of play as the basis upon which children and adults have been and are differentiated and distributed. Postman states, for example, in his concluding chapter: 'There is no more obvious symptom of the merging of children's and adult's values and styles than what is happening with children's games, which is to say, they are disappearing' (Postman, 1994: 129). His contention is that proper children's games are ones that evince a freedom and spontaneity and that are unsupervised by adults. In contrast, he gives an example of children's baseball leagues in the USA, which are being thoroughly supervised by adults, thoroughly invested in by adults and thoroughly controlled by adults. He says: 'For adults, play is serious business. As childhood disappears, so does the child's view of play' (Postman, 1994: 131). Postman seems oblivious to the obvious contradiction in his argument inasmuch as children's reading is nothing if not a thoroughly adult-produced and orchestrated affair (see Rose, 1984). For Hartley, on the contrary, play is the basis of a common appeal; paedocratised audiences are formed through an 'appeal to the playful, imaginative, fantasy, irresponsible aspects of adult behaviour ... a fictional version of everyone's supposed childlike tendencies which might be understood as predating social groupings' (Hartley, 1987: 130).

Both Postman and Hartley in their discussion of modern visual culture treat representation in a manner that simplifies questions about mode of address, marketing, forms of identification, patterns of use and communities of interpretation. For example, they fail to understand that a single text, computer game or other form of entertainment may appeal to both adults and children alike, not because it addresses a common childish identity, but, on the contrary, because it constitutes a form of what Marsha Kinder has termed a 'transgenerational address' (Kinder, 1991). For example, she argues that films such as *Home Alone* combine the generic conventions of children's farce (e.g. in the manner of *Bugs Bunny*) with those of the vigilante movie (e.g. such as *Dirty Harry* or *Die Hard*) with the effect of 'a transgenerational hybrid that enables kiddy spectators to grow into the more mature action genre and their parents to enjoy a non-saccharine children's film with a cutting edge' (Kinder, 1995: 81). Whether *Home Alone* actually achieves this effect is another matter, but Kinder makes clear a long-standing argument within literary and media analysis that texts are never transparent and that they constitute ambiguities at the level of text, interpretation and use. Media texts, consumer texts, and play texts open up rather than close down and dictate meaning and use.

But there is a problem with framing children's relationship to consumer culture as if it were a matter of meaning and symbolic differentiation or dedifferentiation. Both Postman and Hartley agree inasmuch as they present a picture of the blurring of the boundaries between childhood and adulthood in terms of the symbolic, or representational, nature of this generational distribution. Thus, Postman states that his argument has been 'directed at describing how the symbolic arena in which a society conducts itself will either make childhood necessary or irrelevant' (Postman, 1994: 120). Although he seeks evidence from different sources (the media, taste and style, and social facts regarding drug use, alcoholism and so on), this 'evidence' is mobilised inasmuch as it has an effect on the symbolic level. But to focus solely on the symbolic precisely fails to account for the more hybrid mixes of the human, the technological and the natural (see Prout, 2005). Over and above a division of representations into childhood and adulthood, the distributions of people and things offers a subtlety and complexity which needs to be explored, not least because if there has been a convergence of play and consumer culture, then it has been largely driven by the huge investment in children's toys and the object relations within which play is constructed.

The marketisation of children's culture

Stephen Kline's account of the growing interrelationship between television media and toy manufacturing is one that presents children's play as something that has been increasingly colonised since the 1950s. He states that

Commercial television's main cultural impact therefore is connected with the way it privileges fiction as a cultural form and the fantasy mode of consciousness and expression. And nowhere is this tendency to amplify the dominion of fiction more evident than in the new approach to communication resulting from the link forged between children's television and toy industries. (Kline, 1993: 317)

He continues:

Television permeates children's daily activities and conversations: when we observe them arguing about G.I. Joe's firepower, or simulating World

Wrestling Federation bouts, or staging mock battles based on Ninja Turtle heroics, or even when they tell us that they can't fall asleep without their Care Bears or that they want to grow up to be as beautiful as Barbie, synergy between television and children's wants and play fantasies is abundantly evident. (Kline, 1993: 321)

Kline is concerned about the limitations that are placed on children's imaginations and the way in which children's culture is usurped by the toy industry.

One notable case that condensed many of the concerns dates from the early to mid 1980s and surrounds the production of what were then called 'programme-length commercials' (PLCs). PLCs were children's television programmes made by independent television production companies, but which had a close relationship with the toy companies and which presented stories containing characters based on characters sold by those companies. Two widely debated PLCs at the time were *He-Man and the Masters of the Universe* and *Thundercats*. The former featured toys produced by Mattel and the latter by Hasbro. These were, and still are, the world's two largest toy companies.

Due to television deregulation in the early 1980s in the US and corresponding deregulations in the UK and elsewhere, a greater relationship between toy companies and production companies could be facilitated. In the US, Filmation – an animation company that had made *Fat Albert* (written by Bill Cosby) and had a reasonably sound reputation – made He-Man. As Cross states,

The PLC reversed the traditional relationship between licensed characters and toys. They were not simply entertainment featuring characters that gained popularity and thus a market for licensing as toy concepts. These programs were 'originally conceived as a vehicle for providing product exposure to the child audience'. (Cross, 1997: 1999)

In response to PLCs, children's television campaigners in the US (Action for Children's Television with Peggy Charren) and in the UK (British Action for Children's Television with Maire Messenger Davies, Philip Simpson and others) campaigned for the enforcement of tougher regulation. Child psychologists and other child experts were lined up on either side of the battle. Filmation hired specialists to defend the company, but also to check the content before it was syndicated. And the campaigners drew from the ranks of

academia to bolster their credibility. The battle was won by the campaigners, but it has certainly been lost subsequently. Indeed, it was
certainly lost even before it began. For example, if we consider a very
different kind of animated film, such Raymond Briggs' short film *The
Snowman*, then this was a huge critical success and was often lauded as
a contrast to animations like *He-Man*. But in fact *The Snowman* could
only be made because of the promise of future merchandising deals (i.e.
because of the revenues that it could be seen to earn). Animations are
hugely expensive to make, and so money needs to be found to finance
them: toys are an obvious place to look for revenues, but equally
important are other forms of merchandising deal (clothing, school kits,
and so on). This relation is not new. It certainly goes back to *Muffin
the Mule*, the first children's television programme in the UK in the late
1940s, if not before.

One of the standard responses to this marketisation and commercialisation of children's culture is typified by a recent paper by Jennifer
Ann Hill, who states: 'it is the ubiquitous power of media and its
concomitant consumerism that has spread across continents and cultures alike, infiltrating childhood with each pass'. She continues: 'many
children are being deprived of a "full" childhood or series of experiences that distinctly differentiates them from that of the adult world
and meets their needs as children' (Hill, 2011: 348). For Hill, children
are vulnerable and unreflexive with regard to such global corporate
power. It is worth contrasting this view with that of David Buckingham, whose report on children's wellbeing and commercialisation for
the Department for Children, Schools and Families was written when
Labour was in government in the UK. He states that

Research on 'consumer socialisation' suggests that children gradually
develop a range of skills and knowledge to do with the commercial world
that helps prepare them for adult life. They are neither the helpless
victims imagined by some campaigners nor the autonomous 'media savvy'
consumers celebrated by some marketing people. Their engagement with
the commercial world is part of their everyday social experience and
is very much mediated by other social relationships with family and friends.
(Buckingham, 2009: 8)

Both the approaches mentioned by Buckingham tend to construe the
child as a discrete being which is either tainted by commerce or resistant to its effects. Whereas Buckingham finds a balance in terms of a set

of questions about children's mediated use and meaning-making practices, what concerns me in this chapter is the question of how, for better or worse, consumer culture has been a central site of innovation regarding children's agency. The services and things sold to children make a difference not only in terms of their meaning as texts (i.e. as if consumer culture were about 'reading' culture; see Fiske, 1989), but also in the way that the objects have meaning, affects and affordances of use. Imagine a world divided by children with tiny books, the size of matchboxes with very small print, and those with huge encyclopaedia-sized books with huge typeface. Even if the same content is published in both large and small size, the meanings of the artefacts will be different, the uses different and the impact different. Will children with small books tend to sit to read; will they have problems with their eyesight and hence require glasses? Will those with large books tend to huddle on the floor to read, or will they develop very large and muscular forearms from carrying such volumes across the room?

The marketisation of children's culture works in two main ways: firstly, in multiplying the age and lifestyle differentiations of children; and secondly, through pluralising the forms of children's agency. With regard to the former, Daniel Thomas Cook's argument about the retail clothing industry is instructive. He argues that this industry brought about changes in the early twentieth century in the commercialisation of the child and childhood and that this fed into a broader transformation in the cultural construction of the child and childhood. Cook looks at how 'children's commercial selling spaces' were created in US department stores (Cook, 2003). He considers the building of child-friendly spaces in the 1910s. These were spaces of in which children could be left. They were spaces of play, but equally a child could be occupied with a haircut. In the meantime, mothers were able to shop elsewhere in the store. These rooms were decorated and constructed with all the 'images and iconography of childhood' (Cook, 2003: 153). At this time, there were no separate children's clothing departments; clothes were sold according to size, not age. But over the next twenty years retailers began to market their products directly to children. Retailers began to classify their clothing according to age but also to gender. In the 1920s retailers, Cook argues, began to treat the child both as a customer and also as an independent person (155). Retailers began to study the agency and conduct of children in consumption. Young teenage girls, for example, were seen not to want to be addressed as children and so would be catered for in a separate "Twixt-and-Tween' section of the store. Cook states:

Thus, the separation of age-graded sections took into consideration differences between age groups as much as the similarities within them. These sections, taken together, offer something of a gendered, spatial biography of commercialized childhood, designating an appropriate path to follow requisite for specific age ranges. It is a pattern which becomes a model for the design of juvenile clothing departments in the 1930s, and other child commercial spaces thereafter. (Cook, 2003: 156)

Age-graded differentiations were mapped out according to different stages along a teleological path. Children's development thus matched the progression through different products and services and through different commercial spaces. The desire to be older and to be seen to be older facilitated the movement from one stage to another. Consumer desire thus built in both progression and obsolescence. Although these spaces and products were, and are, made by adults, they are iterative spaces which are recognised and taken to be children's own (Cook, 2003: 161).

The processes and forms of organisation which Cook discusses are familiar across other industries oriented toward children. In broadcasting, for example, radio from its earliest days in the 1920s had separate programmes for children, which were in turn divided into programmes for the very young and those for older children (Oswell, 1998). With the advent of television and its popularisation, children's programmes were further differentiated according to age (Oswell, 2002). These were spaces specifically oriented to children and which marked their identity as distinct and separate from that of adults. In the 1980s and 1990s the differentiation of childhood by age took into account much younger children of 2 to 4 years old (e.g. *Teletubbies*, Ragdoll Productions) and 1 to 4 years old (e.g. *In the Night Garden*, Ragdoll Productions). Programming for age segments of the children's market relies on there being a sizable and sufficiently profitable market, on the ability to distribute across that market, and on synergies across media and across products (i.e. through merchandising agreements). In the case of both *Teletubbies* and *In the Night Garden*, these programmes were sold internationally, audiences other than the 'intended audience' watched the programme, and there was a huge amount of merchandising; it was only because of these factors that a programme such as this could be made ostensibly for such a small age group. In this sense, then, the differentiation of children's markets is dependent more, in the first instance, on economic rather than developmental factors. In this case, market segmentation relies on globalisation. That said, the process of segmentation is productive with regard to forms of identification and constructions of spaces for children. Cook argues that

childhood itself is commodified. It acquires exchangeable values in that the very transitions between life stages create perpetual and market-necessary forms of scarcity. Children do not encounter the marketplace as if somehow separate and distinct, but come to realize self, others and perhaps the very idea of childhood itself through commodity form, their identity and personal agency emplaced vis-à-vis merchandising categories. (Cook, 2003: 165)

Moreover, for Cook, there is a fusion between biography and consumption in such a way that 'the boundary between person and commodity is increasingly irrelevant' (Cook, 2003: 166; see also Cook, 2004). Children's agency is not set against commercialisation, but facilitated through it. It is through marketisation that children have been endowed with greater personhood, Cook argues, 'a partial (that is, non-exhaustive) and progressive process of extending to children the status of more or less full persons, a status most concretely realized when children gain recognition and adjudication as legitimate, individualized, self-contained consumers' (Cook, 2004: 3).

   In the second instance, the marketisation of children's culture has led to a pluralisation of agency. Market-driven play innovation facilitates new kinds of interaction among children and between children and things. In such spaces of interaction, different resources and competencies might be drawn on. The negotiation of protocols and the sites of pleasure for an 8-year-old playing *Moshi Monsters* online are very different from imagining doll play face to face in a bedroom. Such innovation and pluralisation of agency produces a tension with the investment in consumer personhood that Cook discusses. There is not simply a bolstering of children's agency as if the articulation of biography and consumption were contained within the individual child. Toys and play environments facilitate situated competencies dependent on the situated interactions assembled across different body parts, social encounters and technologies. Children are assembled as the compilers of jigsaws, the drivers of cars, the builders of houses and castles, the makers of fantasy worlds, and so on. These toy spaces are the spaces upon which agency is constructed; they are the spaces of invention and a multiplication of investment. They allow the big toy corporations to harvest huge profits, and children's lives are inextricably entangled within the iconographies, meanings, pleasures, technologies and materialities of them.

In relation to the early years of infancy, there are new codifications of intelligence, new spaces of facilitation for the developing child. For example, in the 1990s the Lamaze 'Cot Bumper' and accompanying booklet for parents or guardians offers a glimpse of how the infant's visual and tactile experience is seen to be coded. Certain things attract the infant's vision and touch and hence stimulate 'interaction'. This is a toy for the very young child, to be played with in their cot. The visual and tactile experience is coded according to stages of progression: 'sensory awakening', 'birth of exploration', 'birth of doing' and 'pretend and discover'. Two internationally renowned child developmental psychologists, Dorothy and Jerome Singer, are stated to have assisted in the design of this and other toys, and are quoted as saying:

Newborns, infants and toddlers play as they grow and grow as they play with the Lamaze® Infant Development System®. Lamaze® toys are specially designed to encourage developmental 'firsts.' The system's four phases gently guide baby from milestone to milestone and help you select the Lamaze® toy that is most appropriate – and enjoyable – for your child at each stage of development.

From another range of toys, Tiny Love Soft Developmental Toys, we can see a similar discourse. For example, the literature on the packaging for a cot toy (a 'Symphony-in-Motion 3-D Developmental Mobile') states that it is 'Designed by a team of baby development experts including psychologists and musicologists'. It talks about the infant in terms of its development, not only of cognitive capacities but also of musical intelligence, spatial intelligence, linguistic intelligence, logico-mathematical intelligence, bodily-kinesic intelligence and emotional intelligence. What was once described as 'hothousing' (i.e. the placing of child into an intelligence incubator, a hothouse) and defined in relation to a small number of overly ambitious parents is now addressed as a common practice for all parents. These toys are not simply sold as educational toys, but as generators of better forms of personhood facilitated through novel forms of interaction. This indicates a collaboration, across scientific expertise, commerce and

technology, in the codification of novel forms of interaction. It is
important to be wary of the claims of market discourse, but it is equally
important to recognise how such toys, just as much as the codification
of the colour palette or alphabet letters correlated with pictures or
word cards, have constituted innovations in social technologies for
children.

In the context of artificial intelligence, artificial life and robotics life,
toys sit on the interface of product development, huge capital investment, leading research and reconceptualisations of the relations
between the human, the technological and the natural. In the big
academic and commercial scientific research laboratories in Japan,
Europe and the US (e.g. at Rodney Brooks' lab at MIT; Sony Computer
Science Laboratories in Tokyo and Paris) new toys are invented to
advertise the technologies, to generate new consumer demand and new
capital investment, but also to facilitate new forms of interaction. Some
of the online and increasingly mobile toys come out of a context of
research on the slippage between 'protein-based life' (i.e. human
beings, animals) and 'silicon-based life' (i.e. dependent on computers
and computer networked technologies). There is talk of the extension
of biographies across new substances and the articulation of new
knowledges of life (Kember, 2003). Some of the discussion is science
fiction, but some is science and often the development of toys works on
this interface between scientific and science fiction imagination. There
are seen to be mutual benefits to playing up the confusion between the
two. 'Wetware' (e.g. attempts to create artificial biological life through
building unicellular organisms in test tubes), 'hardware' (e.g. constructions of robots and other embodied life forms), and 'software' (e.g.
creations of computer programs that instantiate emergent or evolu-
tionary processes) constitute key areas of development. An early UK
example of the fusion between first and last mentioned above was the
computer-networked software game *Creatures* (1996) designed by the
scientist Steve Grand (see Kember, 2003). In robotics, the Sony Computer Science Laboratories created Aibo, a robotic dog which is sold as
a toy but which is also emblematic of leading research. The MIT
laboratories have produced the emotional robots COG and Kismet
(Brooks, 2002; Turkle, 2011) and these have been developed alongside
more commercial spin-offs such as Mattel's Miracle Moves Baby and
Furby (designed by Caleb Chung). For Sherry Turkle, who observed
and researched the interactions with Rodney Brooks' COG (1993) and

Kismet (with Cynthia Breazeal), it is precisely in the development of these kinds of emotional and social robots that we come to define who and what we are as human. She said in 1995: 'Today the controversy about computers does not turn on their capacity for intelligence but on their capacity for life. We are willing to grant that the machine has a "psychology", but not that it can be alive' (Turkle, 1996: 84). But although children's humanness might be asserted against the machine in front of them, it is precisely in the interactions with such robots (in talking, cuddling, caring, and so on) that the robot itself is endowed with humanness and the form and nature of talk, love and care correspondingly change. Talking about new forms of pet, or 'companion species' (Haraway, 2003), Nigel Thrift has argued that 'the advent of software-driven entities modelled on biological assumptions is a significant event that has the potential to decisively change everyday life by adding in a new range of cohabitees'. Moreover, he adds that 'it is quite clear that these animals can be made more or less lively and more or less threatening by the lines of code that animate them – not just in their capacity for surveillance (which is substantial) but also in their capacity to pass on and inculcate behaviours that may be inimical (for example, all manner of corporate dictates)' (Thrift, 2005: 210–11).

Conclusion

Huge commercial investment in children's play, the expansion of play across both adults and children, and the convergence of the toy industry, new and old media and children's consumer culture lead us to believe that the central tropes of children's play have been reworked in quite dramatic fashions. Play as a form of free expression, as a relation with objects, and as the performance of both friendship and self has been transformed over the course of the last century, and the rate of change has massively accelerated toward the end of the twentieth and the beginning of the twenty-first century. Cook has argued that

The market-culture of childhood represents a monumental accomplishment of twentieth-century capitalism. The rise and expansion of a child-world of goods, spaces, and media over the last century signifies a development above and beyond the opening of merely one more market similar to others. The child market stands apart from others because childhood is a *generative* cultural site unlike any other. Childhood generates bodies as well as meanings which grow, interact, and transform to the point of creating new childhoods, new meanings, and quite often new markets, and in the process effectively ensuring the movement and transformation of exchange value beyond any one cohort or generation. (Cook, 2003: 2)

Not only have the symbolic frontiers of childhood or the meanings associated with consumer culture become intense sites of innovation and change; so, too, have the very infrastructures of children's agency itself.

11 | *Political economies of labour*

Viviana Zelizer eloquently described a shift in the value of the child from a subject that labours and contributes to the domestic economy to one that is 'economically "worthless", but emotionally "priceless"' (Zelizer, 1994: x). Zelizer's argument, which we will consider in more detail later in this chapter, provided an explanation of how children from the 1870s to the 1930s in the USA came to be taken out of paid employment and moved into classrooms and playgrounds, and showed how the correlative of this was an investment in children by adults as emotional centres of family and social life. In 2002 she provided a reconsideration of her original argument and suggested that if we look to children's experiences of economic relations, and not simply at adults' perspectives on children, then we are able to see how children are in fact 'active economic agents' in processes of consumption, distribution and production (Zelizer, 2002: 377). Zelizer's reinterpretation of her earlier work is significant inasmuch as it picks up on a broader range of studies, interest and reinterpretation of children's work and their relation to the economic that some writers see as emerging in the mid 1980s (Abernethie, 1998). In this chapter we will consider children's labour in the context of industrialisation and will look at the framing of arguments against children's labour in the late nineteenth century. We will then consider contemporary arguments about children's labour in the context of broad shifts in socioeconomic organisation and discursive realignments around children's human rights. Of importance is the construction and valuation of children's labour in a global context.

From preindustrial to industrial labour

In agrarian and early mercantile societies the fact of children working was, and is, commonplace. Children and young people helped out in the family economy as they became able and as best they could. There was no clear division and point of transition from non-work to work as a transition from childhood to adulthood. As children became more physically able, boys helped out in the fields and tended to the animals, while girls were often put to work in the kitchen or in the home, sewing or weaving (Orme, 2001: 307; Heywood, 2001: 125). Historian Colin Heywood argues that 'Despite the grisly images that loom large in textbooks, much of the work done by children in the past was casual and undemanding' (Heywood, 2001: 123). Many children in the medieval countryside were serfs, as were their parents. They were 'bondmen' tied to the lord of the manor and unable to freely leave the land. Many children from a very young age were sent away to work (sometimes only to a neighbour on a daily basis, but also for longer periods) and many were sent into service and were servants of a household. The category of 'servant' referred to any person between the ages of 7 and 70. The various terms for 'servant', though, carried strong age connotations, whatever the actual age of the person (e.g. 'page', 'child', 'maid' and 'groom'; Orme, 2001: 309). Servants might be involved in a range of work concerned with the upkeep of an estate and the day-to-day care of household members. Fewer children – ordinarily from about 14 years old and primarily of higher-status families – went into apprenticeships, learning a trade. In both cases the relationship between servant or apprentice and master and his family was an intimate affair and could very well be equally either abusive or greatly beneficial inasmuch as servants, for example, were sometimes bequeathed gifts in their master's will (Hanawalt, 1993; Heywood, 2001: 156–60). Children's moral and social life was closely governed, for example, regarding their drinking in taverns, sleeping with prostitutes, gambling, getting married without permission and having sex with other members of the household. But the master of a household also had an obligation to care for their servants or apprentices and to provide patronage (which would include helping to find a job once service or apprenticeship was completed). Most children worked for societal elites, large aristocratic households, the gentry, the clergy and those who approached the gentry in rank who owned large farms (Orme, 2001: 310). Towns presented an attraction inasmuch as they offered different kinds of work opportunity, but there was also danger with regard to disease and crime (Orme, 2001). Many young people drifted to the towns, and so laws were formulated to keep people on their manor of birth and to restrict movement without the lord's consent (Orme, 2001: 311).

It would be easy to imagine children of all ages working, whether in their family, with a local neighbour, on a farm, in service or learning a trade. But historian Hugh Cunningham argues that 'In fact many children, unless there was a local industry, were frequently idle' (Cunningham, 2005: 84). Heywood notes that the systems of service and apprenticeship were largely conservative inasmuch as they only allowed the transmission of experience from one generation in one locality with respect to one kind of occupation. He states that this may have suited agrarian societies, but was less suited to urban and commercial societies (Heywood, 2001: 160). And he makes this observation in the context of a comparison with modern forms of schooling, which, we might add, allow for the accumulation of knowledge and skills, for their abstraction and distribution outside of particular localities, and for their refinement, development and innovation with respect to different kinds of deployment and employment.

From the seventeenth to early nineteenth centuries across north-western Europe the transition from feudal agrarian to industrial urban economies is often referred to as a process of 'proto-industrialisation' (Medick, 1976). It is argued that, for example, in Germany and England families became involved in spinning, weaving and knitting. Trade in these industries increased and children were a source of labour (Heywood, 2001: 129). But rather than seeing this negatively, many commentators at the time saw it as a positive solution to the problem of idleness in children (Cunningham, 2005: 88). Over the late eighteenth and nineteenth centuries industrialisation located work less in the family home and more in the factory. In the early nineteenth century there was widespread use of children in textiles, dressmaking, mining, agriculture, domestic service, shipping and navigation, metalwork, light engineering and toolmaking (Hendrick, 1990). Industrialisation introduced regularity and repetition to the work schedule on a day-to-day basis (i.e. work patterns were no longer determined by the 'natural' cycles of the seasons and weather) and a clear division between work and non-work (i.e. inasmuch as at one age one was at home and then at a later age at work, but also inasmuch as the factory constituted a particular locale of industrial labour). Furthermore, whereas in the past work had been overseen within families (although not necessarily one's own), now the factory constructed a relation between child worker and supervisor which was distanced and impersonal (Cunningham, 2005: 89). The growth of the textile industries continued to draw on children within these new conditions of work. In some mills children under 13 years of age constituted nearly half the workforce (Heywood, 2001: 131). Both girls and boys did similar work; mining, however, was boys' and men's work. By and large the work conducted by children was ancillary, and many worked as assistants to adults (131). Historians have argued that during the period of industrialisation in Europe and the USA, children constituted a significant source of labour. This also meant though that they constituted a source of competition for work within families (i.e. fathers, mothers and children all competing for the same work; 130).

Many commentators have talked about the exploitation and brutal conditions in which children worked, and particular industries, such as textiles, mining and chimney-sweeping, have figured largely in the popular contemporary imagination as sites of concern. Many assume that the natural innocence of the child would have disclosed the harshness of these conditions to all that were willing to look. But the reality was that children were regarded very differently. Moreover, it is precisely as a consequence of those campaigns in the nineteenth century over the working conditions of children that our understanding of the child and childhood has changed. As Harry Hendrick argues: 'In campaigning to restrain this form of child labour, reformers were in effect arguing about the direction of industrialization, the meaning of progress, and the kind of childhood necessary for a civilized and Christian community' (Hendrick, 1990: 40). Over the course of the nineteenth century there were a series of pieces of legislation in England designed to regulate the factory system and children's working conditions. These factory acts, and other acts, aimed to reduce the number of hours children worked, to place lower age limits regarding particular industries, to delimit the types of work performed by children and to restrict certain forms of labour, such as 'gang labour'. For example, the 1819 Factory Act prohibited children under 9 years from working, the 1840 Act prohibited children from chimney-sweeping and the 1842 Mines Act prohibited children under 10 years and women from working underground in the mines. There were similar acts of legislation across Europe and the USA at this time

(Heywood, 2001: 141–2). The factory acts were not necessarily productive forms of state intervention (Heywood, 2001: 121–2). Campaigns against child labour drew on the support and slogans of anti-slavery campaigners; banners at demonstrations, for example, called for 'No infant slavery' (Hendrick, 1990: 41). But the campaigns and acts of legislation were not intended to abolish child labour; campaigns were not based on the banishment of all child labour, but only on certain forms of it (Heywood, 2001: 135). Diana Gittins has argued that we also need to consider that the campaigns against child labour were against public forms of labour and not those based in the home. She states:

It was primarily *public* labour (or labour that was seen as such) that concerned the middle classes in relation to children, while the 'private' realm of family household was left uncriticised, uninvestigated, because that realm was defined as sacrosanct by the middle classes themselves. Such views largely let the middle classes 'off the hook' as regards their own widespread employment and exploitation of young girls as servants. (Gittins, 1998: 64)

Some employers viewed some of the factory acts as intending to provide them with a better quality of labour (Heywood, 2001: 141). There is also evidence that the decline of children's factory labour starts to occur before legislation (140). In the 1900 US Census, one in six children between 10 and 15 years old were identified as working. Zelizer argues that this was an underestimate, as it didn't include children under 10 years and those children who worked for parents on farms and in textiles before and after school (Zelizer, 1994: 56). By the 1930s the number of children working had dropped dramatically. Zelizer considers a whole set of possible structural reasons for the decline of children's factory work, including: (i) growing demand for skilled labour, hence children in schools; (ii) rising incomes, so no need for child labour; (iii) a rise in the standard of living, so families could afford to keep children at school; (iv) institutionalisation of the family wage, thus a father earned enough for the whole family; (v) new cheap labour due to an increase in immigration, hence children are not competitive and thus the social problem of their presence is addressed in terms of putting them in schools; and (vi) new technologies in the workplace replacing the jobs that children had done (62–3).

As children's factory labour declined, so their attendance at school rose. But rather than see a direct correlation between the two, as if the campaigns against one might be seen as linked to campaigns for the other, sociologists and historians point to the broader social, cultural and political mobilisation of an emerging ideology of childhood. Hendricks, for example, argues that 'The campaign to reclaim the factory child for civilization was one of the first steps in what might be described as the construction of a *universal* childhood. The arguments against children's labour focused very much on their perceived "nature"' (Hendrick, 1990: 41–2). Zelizer argues that child labour reformers held a sentimental view of the child and it was the mobilisation of this image of childhood that is significant; it was not an issue of those for or against children's work (Zelizer, 1994: 57). She argues that the struggle between reformers and others was about 'conflicting and often ambiguous cultural definitions of what constituted acceptable work for children. New boundaries emerged, differentiating legitimate from illegitimate forms of economic participation by children' (58). She states that the boundary between legitimate work and illegitimate work centred on whether the work was a form of exploitation (58). In relation to England, Hendrick argues that

In opposition to laissez-faire capitalism, there could be found the Romantic image of childhood which opposed the unremitting debasement of children through long hours, unhealthy conditions, corporal punishment, and sexual harassment. But there was a conflicting perception of children, which also opposed their economic exploitation. This emanated from the combined (and often contradictory) influences of Evangelical opinion about human nature, the gathering pace of the bourgeois 'domestic ideal', and fears about the social and political behaviour of the working class. It saw the brutalization (including alleged precocious sexual awareness) of children as contributing to the dehumanization of a social class and, therefore, was to be avoided. (Hendrick, 1990: 41)

But there was certainly no clear division between the child labour reformers, who were interested in the welfare of the young, and the capitalist bosses, who were only interested in profit. Zelizer quotes the Reverend Dunne in the *Chicago News* who argues that restrictions on child labour were 'a curse instead of a blessing to those compelled to earn their bread by the sweat of their brow' (quoted Zelizer, 1994: 66–7). If children worked, then they would not be tempted by the sins of idleness, of crime and poverty. In contrast, those wanting to bring in reforms were, according to Zelizer, 'determined to regulate not only factory hours but family feeling' (72). The campaign for the useless child, as Zelizer typifies it, was also concerned with the valuation of children in terms of their affective labour, domesticated and familial.

Fordism, post-Fordism and postindustrial labour

It is easy to see the problem of children's work in terms of saving children from harsh experiences and in moral terms of children's salvation from depravation. But sociologists are interested in questions that problematise children's movement from the factory to the school and that seek to investigate how the shortfall of children's contribution to economic value was made up after they were evacuated from the formal labour market. Some of that discussion has turned to the type of social and economic formation that was emerging in the twentieth century and to the centrality of schooling to that formation. Nick Lee, in his theoretical discussion of children in the context of dependence/independence and completeness/incompleteness, talks about 'the historical growth of two figures: the "standard adult" that is understood to have all the properties of an independent human being, and the "developmental state", which is a model of proper relations between states and their population within which children are understood to have all the properties of human becomings' (Lee, 2001: 5–6). In making this connection between children's development and the developmental state, Lee is able to make a theoretical correlation between sociological accounts of state formation (particularly forms of statehood in the global north in the twentieth century) and dominant theories of childhood socialisation and psychological development. Thus the structural functionalism of Talcott Parsons can be seen alongside the work of Jean Piaget but also alongside theories of socioeconomic organisation and statehood. Lee discusses the latter in terms of theories of Fordism, namely the form of socioeconomic organisation and regulation that takes its name from the organisation of work in the construction of Ford motor cars in the early twentieth century and its relation to capitalist development. Fordism is understood in terms of the development of a system of mass production, such that the products built were standardised (i.e. any colour as long as it's black) and built according to Taylorist principles of efficiency (i.e. division of labour and specialisation), the assembly line and economies of scale. Economic efficiencies and higher relative productivity meant that workers could be rewarded with high relative wages. Higher spending power afforded through mass production pushed mass consumerism. The workers with higher wages were able to afford the mass-produced products (and not only motor cars, but electrical goods and food items as well). Mass media and mass advertising developed alongside, in order to showcase the new products available. Commentators talk about the virtuous circle of mass production and mass consumption in terms of the stabilisation of economic and social relations through a form of mass politics and democracy (i.e. political parties representing the masses of people constitute a system within which relations between capital and labour are stabilised through both management and union representation) (Hall and Jacques, 1989). Once they were in work, workers could stay in a job for life, live in a gendered divided family for life, and vote for the same political party for life. Fordism was seen to provide stability, stable hierarchical large-scale organisation and stable industrial or bureaucratic masculinity. Lee sees long-term marriage as Fordist and he sees Parsons as offering a sociological account of its stability in terms of the 'normal family', socialisation and parental authority, fixed social roles and social order, and a gendered division of labour, with women as mothers and housewives. The developmental Fordist state was seen to constitute a stable system for the male labouring subject and the socialisation of children (Lee, 2001: 15). Of course, such a system required specialised forms of labour. There needed to be not only a division of managers and workers, but also the training of labour in order that the men could work as skilled workers making cars, electrical goods and so on. Mass education, then, becomes a prerequisite of the Fordist state. And, as mentioned earlier, it allows for the accumulation of knowledge and technical expertise as one of the engines of growth and technological progress.

Lee points to sociological thought which looks at how the system of Fordism has undergone a decline in the West from the 1970s onwards. Post-Fordism is typified not by mass production and mass consumption, but by flexible specialisation, niche products, the service economy and forms of cultural economy. Where Fordism constituted a form of industrialisation, post-Fordism is seen as dependent on new technologies of computerisation. Following developments in technology in the 1970s and 1980s, firms have been able to build not simply a range of standardised products, but a huge diversity of different products. In car manufacturing, for example, computer technology has enabled cars to be built by robots in such a way that a different car, with a slightly different specification, can be made with only a slight readjustment to the computer program. Instead of massification, flexibility and segmentation typify post-Fordist socioeconomic organisation. For Lee, post-Fordism is significant in terms of how it allows us to understand changes in family forms and the breaking up of the traditional patriarchal family, in particular, a major transformation in intimacy and systems of parenting for children. He argues that 'The flexible "new economy" means that one's geographical location, one's employment status, one's range of skills and, above all, one's self-identity now remain open to change. It might seem that the flexibility of today's intimate relationships is the direct result of flexible working conditions' (Lee, 2001: 17). For Lee, adulthood, in conditions of post-Fordism, is no longer secure, no longer the complete end point for children's development and hence no longer the measure by which we assess and find meaning in children's lives. Both adulthood and childhood are now dictated by uncertainty and ambiguity (19).

Jens Qvortrup has significantly argued that children are locked into the systemic nature of economic production: 'Children's obligatory tasks have and basically always had a correspondence to the prevailing forms of production: they have a *system immanent* nature' (Qvortrup, 2001: 96). He sees children as productive of 'human capital' and 'wealth in society'. Qvortrup considers the growth of children's schooling against the decline of children's manual labour in the factory, and correlates this with a shift in the dominant mode of economic production. His argument is based on changes in Europe and the USA, although this is never stated explicitly. He argues that '*economic development in general* has entailed a movement from manual activities to abstract or symbolic activities corresponding to a movement from producing use values to producing exchange values and from simple to extended production' (96). As such, he argues, it is obvious that under economic conditions which favour abstract reasoning and symbolic labour, children would be obliged to do similar things, namely within compulsory education. Hendricks similarly argues that 'It is not the case that within the classroom labour ceased; rather it was that its nature changed from being essentially physical to being mainly mental' (Hendrick, 1997: 64). Moreover, as children are agentic subjects, education does not just get done to children, as if they were passive recipients, rather (through their mental and sometimes physical effort) children reproduce themselves 'through school labour' (64). Indeed, Qvortrup argues that without the training of children to work in these terms, the 'new economy' would not survive. Children, though, are not properly compensated for such labour. In preindustrial societies, Qvortrup argues, children's obligatory tasks were decided by the *pater familias*, whereas in modern industrial and postindustrial societies this responsibility is now in the hands of the state. Children have no control nor any claim over any revenue earned from that decision. The state decides the obligatory tasks of children (i.e. what constitutes children's labour and education) and it does so in the context of the form of modern economy. In addition, Qvortrup argues, the demands of a modern economy are such that the training of a labour force takes time. He refers to this in terms of there being a 'diachronic division of labour'. Qvortrup provides an argument in which children don't become economically useless once they are no longer employed in the factory and find themselves at school. Rather, the new economic rationale and organisation of the late nineteenth and early twentieth centuries has demanded that children become constructed as a different kind of resource and shaped as a different kind of capacity. Of course, it was the family which bore the brunt of the loss of income from children no longer directly working. But, although Qvortrup doesn't make this point, families might be seen to recover that loss through the temporal delay in the system and the facilitation of national insurance and pensions through the state (Defert, 1991), inasmuch, that is, that schooling and social insurance as mediated and managed by the state are the twin poles of the Fordist state–society settlement and both work toward the growth, circulation and maintenance of human capital as temporally ordered.

David Oldman provides an important backdrop to these discussions. His work on 'childhood as a mode of production' considers children and adults as constituting two distinct classes, namely as social categories of people defined through their economic antagonism to each other and inasmuch as adults benefit as a class from the exploitation of children as a class (Oldman, 1994: 154). Children growing up, he argues, produces human capital for children (not only through the school, but on the street and at home), but also the process of growing up provides adults, through their labour for children (or 'childwork', as Oldman refers to it) with economic benefits. The growth of childwork over the late nineteenth and twentieth centuries constitutes a process, not of welfare, but of exploitation (155). Oldman refers to the class relations between children and adults and the economic exploit-ation of children by adults in terms of a 'generational mode of produc-tion', and he distinguishes this from a capitalist mode of production (i.e. constituted through market relations and relations between capital and labour) and a patriarchal mode of production (i.e. as constituted through gendered relations of power and exploitation in the domestic economy). But each mode of production is articulated with the others and works toward the social reproduction of each (165). Although some of this argument is similar to Qvortrup's, there are significant differences, not least inasmuch as Oldman sees children's growing up as a priori structurally controlled by adults, and it is only by virtue of this initial control that adults are seen to be able to exploit children, namely to extract the surplus value of their labour and to accumulate that capital at the expense of child workers (163).

There is a big question, though, as to whether what Qvortrup and Oldman in their different ways are describing are forms of children's labour, or whether they are contributing to a different discussion about children and childhood as a site of adult productivity and investment and the growth of human capital, but not children's labour as such. Although Qvortrup sees children's domestic labour (e.g. helping in the household, caring for parents, siblings or other relatives, and so on) or helping in a family business or doing paper rounds and so on as a minor factor in our understanding of children's labour, others insist on the significance of that labour (Morrow, 1994). Karen Wells refers to it in terms of an 'economy of care' (Wells, 2009). Children's work is often 'hidden work'; it is low status and often similar to 'women's work'; and it is this kind of work that is distributed globally across north and south. Children are involved in helping elderly parents and smaller children; they tend the animals; they clean the house. This kind of work is often low paid or not paid at all. It is domestic work that is often seen to exist outside the capitalist economy (Wells, 2009: 101).

Before concluding this section, we should consider a slightly differ-ent understanding of modern forms of labour and the role of children therein. Social and political theory, originally emerging from Italy in the context of workerist movements in the 1970s, talked about the crisis of Fordism in the 1970s (due to the oil crisis and the international economic crisis) and its reorganisation as post-Fordism in terms not simply of the transformation of markets (from mass to segmented) or the impact of computer technology or the role of new communications technology in facilitating globalisation, but of the power of labour in bringing about, but also within, these new conditions inasmuch as these new conditions afforded new forms of affective, communicational and collective labour. Antonio Negri and Michael Hardt, for example in *Empire* (2000) and *Multitude* (2004), argue that the world of work now is not that of the manual worker working in the factory, but the immaterial social worker whose labour takes place as much at home as in the office, on the internet as much as face to face, and with colleagues from across the world as much as fellow workers in the same office building. Whereas for Marx, they argue, labour and the extraction of surplus value from labour was understood in terms of a measurable labour understood in relation to measurable labour time, cutting-edge social, economic and cultural developments mean that labour can no longer be understood in such measurable terms. Instead, they argue, the extraction of surplus value needs to be understood in the context of the collective life of productive subjects. In conditions of post-Fordism, it is the whole life of workers – their bodies and their biographies – that is seen as the basis upon which exploitation occurs. But, although this sounds totalising and pessimistic, Hardt and Negri argue that it is precisely because of these conditions that labour is able to resist and to creatively and productively bring about change. Information technology allows workers to collectively mobilise new lines of connection across life and capital and to facilitate new forms of political alignment and articulation. The precarious working patterns and working lives of these new workers ('the precariat', as some call them) constitute 'both an experience of exploitation and a (potential) new political subjectivity' (Gill and Pratt, 2008: 3). The new workforce is understood primarily in terms of its communicative and emotional capacities, what Hardt and Negri refer to as 'immaterial production', and in terms of its immanent global sociality.

Although not without difficulties and problems, the work of Hardt and Negri and others in this field offers an interesting perspective on children's labour. Children's communicational and affective labour – which many (following Zelizer) have understood in terms of a construction of children's uselessness – might be seen as a site of productivity not inasmuch as childhood constitutes a site of human capital investment, but inasmuch as both children's cognitive labour in schools and children's labour in 'the economy of care' might be seen to constitute different aspects of a single form of biopolitical productivity. This would accord with, but extend and develop, Zelizer's suggestions at the end of her book regarding children's emotional and symbolic value and its influence on capital and market value (Zelizer, 1994: 212). But we would need to add to the equation the more general affective labour performed by children in the familial economy, inasmuch as family happiness constitutes a central signifier of the modern economy, and also the labour of children in the presentation of their bodies for the extraction of exchange value (e.g. through the circulation of their photographic, film and other forms of image). If the extraction of surplus value occurs as much in the home and in 'private life' as in the office, the shop floor or the factory, then children through their activities and through their very bodies might be seen to deliver such economic value. Immaterial production, for Hardt and Negri, is defined in terms of its cooperative and social nature. It concerns the production of relationships and of things in common. Moreover, they argue, these social things are not consumed and used up; rather, they increase with use. This is not to say that capitalism does not expropriate that which is common. Of course it does; it tries to put that which is common into the hands of private owners.

Significant issues are raised by these different ways of understanding children's labour in the twentieth and twenty-first centuries. Hardt and Negri's analysis of post-Fordism is provocative inasmuch as it enables us to think about forms of children's productivity, their abstracted labour and their collectivity, but not in a manner that reduces these to a question of social class. For Hardt and Negri, the production of a global common does not derive from a new economic class. Instead, they use the term 'multitude' to signify an attempt to move beyond the logic of class and problems of thinking about class in terms of identity (i.e. in terms of what is to be included or excluded from a particular class; should we define class as 'in itself' or 'for itself', and so on). It is used in terms of a collection of singularities, which, they argue, cannot be reduced to a single identity (i.e. in our case to childhood as a class of persons defined through a unitary relation to either the social, the cultural or the economic). There are questions, though, as to whether it makes sense to refer to all emotional and cognitive activity as work and also, even if it were analytically feasible to do so, whether we can lump together all the different activities which could come under this heading as constitutive of the same kind of political subjectivity.

Admittedly Hardt and Negri argue that these do not define a class identity but rather constitute the resources, as it were, through which people come together in all their differences. This, then, raises another set of issues regarding the extension of the categories of emotional and informational labour: either we are all emotional and informational workers by virtue of all activities being defined as such, or only some people by virtue of the kinds of activities they do (and whether these activities are paid) can be included in this category of emotional and informational labour. If the former, then the category seems analytically facile; if the latter, then the big question is how we understand divisions of people (as classes of people?) in the context of the distribution of those forms of labour and in the context of a global division of labour. So far we've outlined a story of children's labour in terms of a history from preindustrial to industrial to postindustrial. It would be a mistake to read this history as a model for understanding a geographical distribution of types of labour and work organisation, not least because it enframes a long-standing colonial ideology of development and progress.

Children's labour and the global economy

Children's labour is unevenly distributed across class, gender and global geography. Much of the work conducted by children across the globe is agricultural and mostly done in the context of local family households. In Africa, for example, children tend livestock and bring in the crops at harvest time. Some farming is commercial in coastal West Africa and the East African plateau (Canagarajah and Nielson, 2001). Similarly, in Latin America most child labour is agricultural. Mexico has the highest rates globally for agricultural child labour and such labour remains largely within the family (Bey, 2003). Families provide a space for the training of labour and parents and older family members supervise that socialisation. UNICEF's report, *The State of the World's Children* (1997), considered children's labour in the context of their development, and it did so in terms of a profile of children's work across the world, defined, that is, in terms of specific forms of work, some more detrimental to child development than others. It stated that 246 million children were engaged in child labour; 171 million of these children worked in hazardous conditions (for example, working in mines or with chemicals); 300,000 children 'worked' as armed combatants; and 1.2 million children were trafficked every year. Child labour by region was as follows: in Asia and the Pacific, 127.3 million children below 15 years of age (19% of the region's population) worked; in sub-Saharan Africa, 48 million (29%) worked; in Latin America and the Caribbean, 17.4 million (16%) worked; and in the Middle East and North Africa 15% were working. In the 'developed countries' 2.5 million children were working, and in the 'transition economies', 2.4 million. The report was predicated on a definition of children's work as articulated in the United Nations Convention on the Rights of the Child (UNCRC) (1989). Article 32(1) states:

States Parties recognize the right of the child to be protected from economic exploitation and from performing any work that is likely to be hazardous or to interfere with the child's education, or to be harmful to the child's health or physical, mental, spiritual, moral or social development.

William Myers has argued that this wording needs to be seen in the context of a longer history of concerns about children's labour, children's rights and protection, and the globalisation of European models of childhood and understandings of work therein. He contrasts it with the International Labour Organisation's Minimum Age Convention (no. 138) of 1973, which sought to raise the minimum age of persons able to enter employment and which was in keeping with an understanding of children's work as detrimental to their physical and mental development. The International Labour Organisation (ILO) was set up in 1919 as an outcome of the Treaty of Versailles (after the First World War), and one of its main tasks was to work toward the abolition of child labour. Myers argues that the ILO 'drew on accumulated European concepts and experiences to create its international child labor standards and policies' (Myers, 2001: 45), namely that it posed child labour against children's schooling, inasmuch as the latter provided the proper place for children's development. Myers argues that successive ILO conventions on child labour were based on a model of children's work that was framed by European industrialisation, the concentration of industrial work in urban areas, and recourse to the state as a means to alleviate problems of children's labour. Of course, such an argument assumes, for example, the success of child labour legislation in the nineteenth and early twentieth centuries in Europe, and also the force of the law rather than other social and cultural factors (which, as we've seen, historians such as Hendricks and Zelizer argue are more significant). Nevertheless, Myers argues that the focus on industrialisation and legislation

are anachronistic in most of today's developing countries, where child employment is overwhelmingly agricultural, where social welfare laws have relatively little impact on the everyday life of the poor, where labor inspection services tend to be precarious and corrupt, and where national governments have extreme difficulty extending full primary education coverage to the rural and urban periphery areas where most working children live. (Myers, 2001: 45–6)

Moreover, Myers argues that Convention 138 was written partly in the context of protecting adult forms of labour from poaching by children and with little understanding of the role of children's contribution to the familial economy in developing countries. Very few non-western countries signed up to the convention until the end of the twentieth century, when financial and technical assistance was linked to a country's signing.

The UNCRC Article 32, then, Myers agues, is framed in the context of a whole package of articles which 'are more accommodating of diversity', which do not specify a minimum age for employment, and which help to attenuate concerns about children's labour with the demand that children should be able to have a say in the governing of their lives (Myers, 2001: 48). But also, importantly, it does not pose children's work per se against children's education and development; rather, it poses it only in the context of hazardous and exploitative work. And it is in this context that the ILO's Worst Forms of Child Labour Convention 182 is shaped. This convention states that 'worst forms of child labour' include forms of slavery, trafficking, bondage, compulsory labour, use of children in armed conflict, child prostitution, use of children for pornography, use of children in the illicit drugs trade or any 'work which, by its nature or the circumstances in which it is carried out, is likely to harm the health, safety or morals of children' (Convention 182, Article 3). The adoption of Convention 182 in 1999 helped to properly cement a distinction across different forms of children's work as defined by a criterion of harm. Thus, for example, in UNICEF's *State of the World's Children*, 'children's work' is defined as work by children over 12 years that doesn't negatively affect health nor education; 'children's labour', is defined as work harmful to children;

and 'children's bonded or enforced labour, slavery, prostitution' is defined as work clearly illegal and with no justification according to principles of social justice (see also Fyfe, 1993).

The more recent focus on 'worst forms of children's labour' brings into consideration a wide range of bonded activity done to and by children, and notwithstanding this broad definition, Convention 182, Article 3 certainly raises the problem of how children's labour is defined. Bonded labour includes, for example, children in Sierra Leone captured by rebel and government forces and made to carry arms or to provide sexual services for older troops. The definition also includes trafficked children from Eastern Europe who are used in the sex trade industry, as workers in brothels in Western Europe. It might also include children working in poisonous hot conditions in the sulphur mines in Bolivia or children forced off the land to work in the coltan mines in the Democratic Republic of Congo. These very different, although often equally appalling, forms of work cannot be posed as if they constitute the antithesis of development and modern forms of society. On the contrary, what they indicate is the intimate and inter-connected nature of modern social life and appalling forms of child labour. The fight over minerals in Africa (whether diamonds, oil, or metals such as coltan for mobile telephones), the development of the global sex industry (tourism, prostitution, film and internet pay-to-abuse), but also the increasing and unstoppable demand for consumer goods (from refrigerators, cars, plastics, and so on) fuel forms of child labour, which is cheap, non-unionised and expendable in the global south. Although some of this process implies an increasing urbanisa-tion of child labour, evidence also suggests that processes of develop-ment and modernisation lead to the 'intensification and expansion of children's work in the countryside' (Katz, 2004: 143).

There is a concern that a focus on the worst forms of child labour is set against best forms of children's schooling and play in a way that poses the former as antiquated and the latter as modern and enlight-ened; the former as an affront to childhood and the latter as a proper recognition of the value of childhood. In such binaries, children's schooling is valued for its own sake (i.e. as proper to children's development), but also inasmuch as that development matches the development of the nation-state. Children in school constitute a form of capital investment, one which benefits all concerned. But children's activities need to be understood in the context of the broader set of economic relations (multiscalar and at once local, regional and global), such that children's labour cannot simply be defined by the type of activity but also by the articulation of that activity within that broader set of economic relations. What this means is that we don't formulate children's work in the context of a contrast between work and school or work and leisure, such that work, schooled education and leisure are understood with regard to comparative value and human capital investment.

Research by Stuart Aitken, Sylvia Lopez Estrada, Joel Jennings and Lina Maria Aguirre on children working as checkout packers in Tijuana supermarkets (Aitken et al., 2006) helps to set in context the complex economic, social and cultural relations across local and global spaces. The economic growth of Mexico has led to a movement of people from the countryside to the city and to the northern towns bordering the USA, including Tijuana. In the past, many Mexican children would have learned how to labour (a phrase which the authors repeat from Willis' initial formulation (1977)) in the context of their family, but increasingly this now takes place in the context of welfare institutions and schools. Poor children still contribute significantly to their families' economic wellbeing, 'but Mexican families are increasingly less likely to monitor the ways their children learn to labor because children increasingly divide the day among different spaces and away from other family members' (Aitken et al., 2006: 370–1). Aitken and his co-researchers looked specifically at a government programme intended to support the supermarket packers, called the Paidimenta Program. The programme was designed to help train children between the ages of 9 and 14 years in a culture of work, to facilitate academic study, and to assist in the management of their money. The researchers considered the juggling of working at the supermarket, schoolwork, work in the family, and leisure time and they considered the movement of the children through the town, from home to work to school and back again. In their paper they discuss this in the contexts of broader economic and social changes to the town and the processes of globalisation. They argue that 'Tijuana's local geography – its physical and social landscape – is intimately entwined with global processes and children are caught up in, voluntarily participate in, and inform larger transformations'. Moreover, 'as economic changes over the last two decades have transformed grocery consumption in Tijuana, then so too have the lives of child packers at the supermarkets expanded spatially and intensified temporally' (Aitken et al., 2006: 383). Children, by virtue of working, are able to leave the home and family and discover new parts of the city, to travel through the town on the minibus, and to meet new people. And their time becomes intensified through the mixing of different kinds of work at school, in the home and at the supermarket. In doing so, these children make themselves and are made in space, in a dynamic process which Aitken and colleagues talk about (borrowing from Henri Lefebvre's formulation (1991)) as 'trial by space'. In this sense, then, there is not a simple trade-off between school and work, as if one were better than, or substitutable with, the other; rather, it is across different forms of labour that the children negotiate their identities as forms of geographical performance.

Conclusion

In this chapter we have considered children's labour in the context of its relation to different modes of production (agrarian and mercantile, industrial and postindustrial). In doing so, the vestiges of earlier economic and social relations are not easily forgotten, but are instead increasingly entangled in, on one level, an obviously uneven and unequal distribution of labour and accumulated capital, and, on another level, a complex that is not easily unknotted. It would be a mistake to understand children's labour in terms of a moral response either on the basis of an ideal and idealised child, or on an equally simplistic model of historical development. For example, the transition from the image of the industrial working class as figured through forms of masculinity (the dirty overalls, the hard boots, the leathery and tarnished skin, the hard stoical and disciplined aggression, the early death) to the clean, cognitive, fresh-faced work of postindustrial global capital demonstrates a history of children's work as a gendered and ethnocentric global stereotype. What we know is that global capital now distributes and regulates labour (including children's labour) in a complex scaling (across local, national and global) of demand and ideology. The recent campaigns about children working in India in the clothing industry do not stop the constant demand for cheap clothes, nor similarly does the knowledge of children's deaths from cobalt mining in the Democratic Republic of Congo dictate the choice of mobile phones.

12 | *Rights and political participation*

In this chapter I consider the issue of children's rights and political participation. Of course, although we might endow *ceteris paribus* any persons or even things with legal rights, not everyone or thing is deemed to have the capacity for political participation. Initially, we will consider some of the philosophical and cultural history attached to the question of children as rights bearers and as political animals. We then consider how the capacity for modern rights and political participation is distributed unevenly across the globe and discuss this in the context of the universalisation of children's rights, as enshrined, for example, in the United Nations Convention on the Rights of the Child (UNCRC). Finally in this chapter we ground the questions of children's rights and politics in the context of national sovereignty, modern forms of governmentality and forms of political enunciation, or expression. As Hannah Arendt declared after the Second World War, 'only with a completely organized humanity could the loss of home and political status become identical with expulsion from humanity altogether' (Arendt, 1962: 297). The question regarding children, though, is doubly confounded in that ordinarily the constitution of their very being (with regard to their infancy and lack of maturity) places them a priori outside of both the political and global humanity.

The capacities of children: genealogies of the family and the political

Didier Reynaert and colleagues state: 'The academic children's rights discourse since the adoption of the UNCRC has been preoccupied with highlighting the childhood image of the competent child' (Reynaert et al., 2009: 520). Yet, the question of children's competency and incompetency with regard to their rights and their political participation has a much longer history. A key facet of that history has been the relation of children, with regard to their infancy or lack of maturity, to both reason and speech. The ancient Greek philosopher Aristotle makes a distinction in the *Politics* between voice (*phōnē*) and speech (or language) (*logos*) inasmuch as voice is the noise of animals and speech is the articulation of reason by men within an organised political unit, namely the city-state (*polis*). Unlike bees, or other animals such as guinea pigs even, which are able to express signals as to whether they are in pain and perhaps even pleasure, men have speech (and not voice alone) and are able to articulate rights and wrongs, the good and the bad, and the safe and the harmful. The management of the household (*oikos*), which, for Aristotle, is concerned with reproduction, is qualitatively different from the organisation and management of the state (*polis*). Voice is that which resides in the household, but it is speech that is heard on the stage of masculine politics. In such a framing, politics is articulated in the public realm and concerns public affairs; in contrast, the household concerns women and children and matters of reproduction. In such a framing, infants are those pre-adults who are literally without speech and who literally come before adulthood and language; but infancy also defines the state of those outside of politics, political organisation and political expression. To be a citizen then implied being a man, having freedom and governing oneself accordingly; it did not include women, children or slaves. Moreover, the government of the state implied an equality and similarity among free men. Much has changed since the fourth century BCE, but equally there are many continuities regarding how we conceptualise the political as logocentric (or overly rational) and how we do so to the exclusion of children and others and to the exclusion of 'childish', non-'rational', and 'physical', non-logocentric forms of expression and organisation.

John Eekelaar, in a paper from 1986, provides an account of the emergence of children's rights in the context of English law. For Eekelaar, children's rights are framed in relation to, initially, *patria potestas* and then parental rights. In the past children were seen very much as the property of the father and, latterly, both parents. Even in cases, for example in the eighteenth century, where the child's interests were perceived, these were very much in terms of their threatening other people (i.e. inasmuch as the failure of a father to look after his child may then lead to the harming of others). Moreover, in cases where the father was wanting to claim possession of his child and the court refused on the basis that the child may be put into bodily danger (the 'welfare principle'), Eekelaar states that the application of this principle in the nineteenth century was only in cases where the child's wellbeing was seriously threatened (Eekelaar, 1986: 168). And yet he states: 'Immorality, profligacy, impiety and radical social views, all of which might undermine the child's commitment to the dominant social values, were frequently the bases for denying custody to fathers (and sometimes to mothers)' (168). The interests of the child thus emerge in relation to perceived community and societal interests. In this sense, the protection of children was in the first instance the protection of society. It is only once the correlation of these interests can be distinguished, Eekelaar argues, that children's rights can be seen to emerge. He specifies this further by differentiating between 'basic' interests, developmental interests and autonomy interests. The first he understands in terms of 'general physical, emotional and intellectual care within the social capabilities of his or her immediate caregivers' (170). These aspects are considered in the context of the 1969 Children and Young Persons Act, which allows the state to intervene in a child's life if their 'proper development is being *avoidably prevented or neglected* or his health is being *avoidably impaired or neglected* or he is being ill-treated' and he is 'in need of care and control which he is unlikely to receive unless the court makes an order' (quoted 171). As this legislation is directed to minimal protection rather than positive care, Eekelaar considers it in terms of basic interests. In contrast, developmental interests refer to the positive facilitation of a child's life (e.g. with regard to health and education) such that they are not disadvantaged disproportionately. Eekelaar discuss these in the context of the Matrimonial and Family Proceedings Act of 1984, which states that 'first consideration' should be given to the welfare of children interests, and in terms of the House of Lords ruling regarding a divorce case, *Richards* v. *Richards* (1984), in which the wife, 'without offering any substantial justification', withdrew the children from the home into a 'very inferior environment'. The House of Lords held that decisions 'must not be based on the paramountcy of the child's interests'. In doing so, they held that the child's interests were not superior and hence went against the Court of Appeal, which held that 'the father's interests must give way to those of the children' (175). Eekelaar explains this in terms of the broader political climate at the time surrounding the rights of fathers with respect to divorce proceedings. The interests of children were thus seen to provide mothers in divorce cases with an advantage over the fathers. As *The Times* of 7 January 1983 remonstrated: 'Should the children's needs be allowed to override all other considerations? ... The requirements of justice to the family as a whole may not always coincide with what appear to be the children's immediate needs' (quoted 176). Finally, Eekelaar discusses autonomy interests in the context of the legal case of a mother, Victoria Gillick, taking to court her local health authority (*Gillick* v. *Wisbech and Norfolk Area Health Authority*, 1985). Gillick had argued that prescribing contraception to a person under 16 years old was akin to encouraging sex with a minor, and that such medical treatment would be treatment without consent as vested in the parent. The significant outcome of the Law Lords was that which came from the wording of Lord Scarman, who stated: 'As a matter of Law the parental right to determine whether or not their minor child below the age of sixteen will have medical treatment terminates if and when the child achieves sufficient understanding and intelligence to understand fully what is proposed.' Eekelaar argues that this ruling 'with respect to children's autonomy interests cannot be over-rated' (181). In the context of the UK, the Children Act of 1989 has been a significant moment in the history of children's rights. It made the paramountcy principle (i.e. that the welfare of the child is paramount) central in legal and state dealings with children (for example, in divorce cases) and also introduced limits on state intervention into the family with respect to notions of significant harm to the child. In addition to welfare rights, the act also made provision for children's liberty rights in terms of their having a say about, for example, which parent they live with or their refusing medical or psychiatric examination (Roche, 2002). The extent to which these interests dominate discussions of children's rights and the extent to which they are underpinned by broader dynamics of social change have provided the very rich terrain of sociological discussion in this area.

Ulrich Beck, in 'Democratization of the family', has argued that 'the dynamism of political freedom must be considered a core dynamism of modernity' (Beck, 1997: 151) and, as such, is part of the mix that is changing the nature of contemporary society. In the paper he is particularly concerned with how this relates to the process of detraditionalisation in modern societies, namely how traditional forms of authority (e.g. regarding church, factory and family) no longer have the hold they once did. He asks what this might mean for the family and how it can be understood in terms of a process of democratisation. In this sense, Beck's argument is rooted in a history of the family as understood with reference to patriarchal and paternal authority, namely in the context of a notion of the *patria potestas*. As we saw in Chapter 6, many authors from the 1970s onwards have argued that, in conditions of modernity and modernisation, 'the family' is shaped by a contestation of *patria potestas*. Thus, for example, whether we look to Michel Foucault and Jacques Donzelot or to Christopher Lasch and others, it is clear that the 'freedoms' (and I use this term, as does Beck, very broadly here) of children in the home are seen to be a consequence of the realignment of authority across family and state and the distribution of new forms of authority and expertise. Beck, though, wants to add some doubt into some of the more recent claims regarding children's rights, freedoms and political participation. He does so by doubting that 'biographical, inner-directed freedoms' translate simply into 'political, outer-directed freedoms', that the idea of freedom simply becomes an actuality without the provision of state resources, or that freedom as enshrined in legal statute does not always become practised as social action. Moreover, in conditions of late modernity there is no simple recourse to fixed forms of social identity (i.e. natural and ontologically rooted rights and freedoms of particular groups of people with respect to notions of 'race', ethnicity, 'blood ties' and so on). In conditions of late (or 'second', as Beck terms it) modernity, there is no simple recourse to such fixed forms of social identity. The current context, then, is defined, on the one hand, by legal forms of political freedom, referring to a 'juristic/political citizen' which are tied to the statutory laws of the nation-state, but on the other, by social forms of political freedom, which define a 'cultural citizen', and which are open and, as it were, detraditional (Beck, 1997: 160–1).

Beck argues that, in much of the world, despite legal claims to the contrary, 'children are "serfs" by virtue of their birth' (Beck, 1997: 161). But he points to Swedish social democratic family policy as exceptional in that it has provided children with a series of entitlements, not the least of which is the child's claim to a life of their own. It is this, Beck declares, which is 'paramount', and indeed the 'rights of a child to a self-determined life are even enforced against the parents if necessary' (162). In such circumstances, where the state intervenes in order to facilitate the right of the child to a life of their own, the distinction between private and public, between *oikos* and *polis*, is surpassed; this zone of indistinction is discussed by Beck in terms of a 'deprivatization of privacy' (162). What he describes here in the context of Sweden can, though, be seen to be more broadly spread across other national contexts. In the context of 'the family', such biographisation opens up new spaces which often reveal the 'democracy of the family' as a site of mutual ignorance and conflict, as well as negotiation and talk. And in terms of the latter, Beck's analysis is one that frames a more general debate about children's rights and a democratisation of the family that we have seen in Chapter 6, in wide-ranging research from the social theory of Anthony Giddens to the empirically focussed work of Carol Smart on children in situations of divorce and to Sonia Livingstone's work on young people and new media.

The construction of young people in terms of their right to their life implies, Beck argues, that moral authority becomes individualised, not such that individualisation is an external imposing process, but rather such that it is something that young people do to themselves. Moral authority is not something controlled by the church or the state, but by individuals themselves. '"Biographization" of youth means becoming active, struggling and designing one's own life. A life of one's own is becoming an everyday problem for action, staging and self-representation' (163). Moreover, he adds, young people are not socialised, but rather 'self-socialised': 'A life cushioned from the inside against the outside has taken the place of paternal and maternal authority or that of governesses, teachers, police and politicians' (163). For Beck, this implies not the end of the social, but rather peer groups, media, schooling, family and so on are seen as resources and not as enforced functionally defined facets of role modelling. Beck even talks about 'self-normalisation' (164). We might want to be more cautious, though, in our interpretation of these processes. Certainly, what Donzelot and Lasch would add to this is that the process of deprivatisation and the role of the state therein are more significant inasmuch as they have provided the initial supports and infrastructures for these processes of biographisation. The intervention of social workers, medics and many others into the home in the late nineteenth century and the twentieth century has provided an infrastructure which both contests the *patria potestas* and gives the child voice and life. Importantly, the cultural forms of biography have been provided in the context of the state; the prisons, welfare services and other institutions have construed the child in the context of their life history within a case study (Foucault, 1977; Tagg, 1988). And in this sense, the provision of voice, individuality and biography has been closely correlated with the growth of the modern state and its means of discipline, surveillance and government.

The focus on biographisation as a more ambivalent infrastructured process helps to reframe an earlier conceptualisation of children's rights in terms of either liberation or protection. The protectionist thesis (or as Archard refers to it, 'the caretaker thesis'; Archard, 1993) refers to those, ordinarily adults, who act in accordance with overall welfare for the child. Unlike older conceptions of the child as a property of the father, the protectionist thesis is governed by an understanding of those acting in the best interests of the child, such that the act of protection does not imply that the child is the legal property of the adult, nor that the child does not have any individuality or agency. Protectionism is not set against the autonomy or freedom of the child; it simply states that the child does not always know or act in its own best interests and that a higher authority should, and is able to, act on behalf of the child. This welfarist conceptualisation of the child is also linked to the rise of the child as a developmental subject (i.e. by virtue of their relative lack of reason, experience and awareness, the child is unable to act fully on their own behalf). In this thesis authority is distributed unevenly and children, by virtue of their relative lack of maturity, are able to be denied authority (or only granted relative authority) with regard to their own lives. In that respect, although protectionism may be seen positively in terms of, for example, parents providing children with a safe environment in which to grow and learn (i.e. a space free from intruders and dangers), such protectionism can be seen *in extremis* as potentially leading to an absolute control over the child and a complete denial of the child's ability to author its own actions.

In the 1970s there was much criticism of 'the family' as a site not of developmental facilitation but of incarceration and control. This criticism of protectionism *in extremis* was framed from the position of a liberationist discourse. This discourse often sat alongside anti-psychiatry criticisms of the family as a site of schizophrenic production and feminist critiques of the patriarchal family. Thus, Shulamith Firestone in *The Dialectic of Sex*, originally published in 1970, drew on the work of Ariès, not simply to argue for the emergence of a new conception of childhood, but to argue that the institutionalisation of childhood constituted a form of segregation. She argued that those who talked about childhood as an age of innocence, who placed the child on a pedestal, were also those who 'preached the segregation of children from the adult world' (Firestone, 1979: 82). Firestone makes an analogy between women and children: 'In every society to date there has been some form of the *biological* family and thus there has always been oppression of women and children to varying degrees' (73). Firestone claims that there is a 'special tie' that women have with children, such that 'this oppression is intertwined and mutually reinforcing in such complex ways that we will be unable to speak of the liberation of women without also discussing the liberation of children – and vice versa' (73). Moreover, she argues:

if members of the working class and minority groups 'act like children', it is because children of every class *are* lower class, just as women have always been. The rise of the modern nuclear family, with its adjunct 'childhood', tightened the noose around the already economically dependent group by extending and reinforcing what had been only a brief dependence, by the usual means: the development of a special ideology, of a special indigenous life style, language, dress, mannerisms, etc. And with the increase and exaggeration of children's dependence, woman's bondage to motherhood was also extended to its limits. Women and children are now in the same lousy boat. Their oppressions began to reinforce one another. (Firestone, 1979: 89)

The liberation of children, then, was seen alongside other social and political struggles (see Oakley, 1994), and the rights of children seen in terms of the overthrowing of an oppressive and exploitative regime.

Richard Farson and John Holt similarly draw on Ariès to understand modern childhood as a social institution. The institution of 'childhood' is seen as a walled garden, but one that constitutes the segregation and also imprisonment of children. The practices which are seen to make up the institution of childhood are thus critiqued on the basis that they constitute forms of control and dominance. The timetable and scheduling of school classroom activities are seen as controlling, and so too are practices of parental care and love within the family. Central to the liberationist discourse was an understanding of the child as an autonomous and rational agent able to freely make decisions about their own life. As such, divisions between adults and children on the basis of developmental indicators were pushed aside and the rights of children were in large part framed in terms of permitting children to do what they had been denied from doing (i.e. adding them to those spaces from which they had been subtracted). Thus, Holt talks of making available 'the rights, privileges, duties, responsibilities of adult citizens' to 'any young person of any age'. He argues that these rights would include: the right to equal treatment under the law; the right to vote; the right to legal responsibility; the right to work; the right to privacy; the right to financial independence; the right to manage one's education; the right to freedom of movements and habitation; the right to equal receipt of state services; the right to form and enter into relationships; the right to do what an adult can do (Holt, 1975: 15–16). These declarations were associated with various other programmatic statements, such as *The Little Red Schoolbook* (1971), and experimental social forms, many of which found their origins in early twentieth-century idealism about children, such as A. S. Neill's radical school experiment Summerhill, in which children were not told to attend lessons and could follow their own learning path. The late 1960s and early 1970s was also a time in which young people were engaged in school strikes and councils, countercultural protests, public cases such as the Oz trial, which purported to contest ideas about young people and sexuality, and other innovative forms of political engagement. Liberationist discourses relied on an earlier romanticism (found, for example, in Rousseau, but also the eighteenth- and nineteenth-century romantic poets), and as such the simple statement that a liberationist thesis is based on the conceptualisation of children as subjects of rational choices needs to be attenuated with the foregrounding of children as romantic, irrational and natural subjects. More broadly, the discourse of liberation was linked, through writers such as Marcuse and others, with a certain reading of Freud and psychoanalysis regarding sexuality, the unconscious and the repression of the father and society: namely, an idea of the individual as both conscious and unconscious, as a being whose id needs to be released from the tyranny of the ego, and where polymorphous sexuality is seen to be the essential character of their individual being. Although children are constructed in a liberationist discourse as having competency with regard to political and life decisions, they are also, inasmuch as there is a genealogical connection with romanticism, often seen as innocent. It would be a mistake, then, to assume that a liberationist discourse constitutes a single philosophical statement regarding children's rights. On the contrary, it constitutes a mix of often conflicting discourses, which were nonetheless mobilised as a wholesale attempt to recodify children's lives in relation to adults with regard to their authority in authorising their actions and lives. In that sense, what is significant is less the proclamations of autonomy than the detailed attempt to recodify children's conduct as either 'free' or 'not free'. Hence drug taking and sexual activity might be taken as indices of freedom; attending school or doing homework as 'not free'. This process of recodification is not a political platform of children, but largely of adults. Its impact on children is felt across both children's and adults' lives. Moreover, this process of recodification was intended to conceptualise children as having agency and biographies outside of the family and domestic household (but in such a way that is not in a straightforward manner governed by the state). The opposition between liberation and protection is a false opposition inasmuch as both constitute forms of refiguration of children's biographies and their authority (and powers of authorship) with respect to those biographies. Individualisation is not set against a discourse of welfare, but rather both constitute aspects of modern forms of biopolitical governmentality.

If we are to understand the processes of biographisation in the context of the cultural construction of children's voices and agency, then we need to understand how these processes are mediated, but also how those forms of mediation have been significant factors in the emergence of children as authors of their own lives and experiences. It is clear, from what I have argued so far, that children's rights and children's capacity for political rights are caught up in a series of questions about the distribution of authority and the capacity for authorship, namely not simply to see children's rights in terms of what those persons can do, but in terms of how those acts are authored and authorised. In this sense, it is important not only to consider the legal and social construction of children's rights and children's capacities therein, but also their cultural construction and mediation. From the mid to late eighteenth century a medium emerges through which children's experiences can not only be discussed by adults inquiring as to the nature of this type of personhood (something that has happened certainly since the ancients), but rather can become the site in which children themselves can reflect on themselves and give voice to themselves. In 1744, *A Little Pretty Pocket-Book* was published by John Newbery (Darton, 1982). From 1752 to 1800 eleven periodicals were published for the young of England (Drotner, 1988). Across Europe and the US children's novels and fairy tales were published. Although the magazines, novels and fairy tales were often guided by a moral demand for improvement, they offered young people perspectives that were largely absent in the past. Young people were subjects of narrative, rather than the objects of prose. Young people engaged in the pages of these works not simply with adults, but with other young people. The young were given character and voice. Dialogues were held between the young. Whatever the authority of the adult author, a centripetal force had emerged in the context of that authority. A dialogic space for children pulled against an historic adult monologism (Thacker and Webb, 2002). The emergence and development of a domain of literary experience for children was predicated on an ability to move from a stage of illiteracy to literacy, from infancy to childhood. Far from being, as Neil Postman (1994) has argued, a means of differentiating adulthood from childhood, literacy and literary culture for children – and hence the emergence of a cultural medium that makes visible children as a collective experiential subject – is made possible only because children have access to a world of literary signification, to a form of signification that is mobile and translatable, a 'literary culture' that is both literary and visual. This is a cultural form which constitutes a means of communication, a medium through which the collective experiences of children can be made intelligible and, importantly, presents children as having not only voice, but determining agency with respect to events and other people (i.e. to put it crudely, children in children's books and magazines shape what and how things occur and are interpreted). Thus, although Beck is correct in foregrounding the importance of children's relation to and control of their biographies and their correlation with the democratic, it is clear that the focus on the life of the child and on children's determining agency with regard to that life occurs historically much earlier, certainly by the late nineteenth century. Of course, the development of children's media has been such that over the course of the twentieth century children's film, radio, television and latterly the internet importantly contribute to the cultural forms through which children are made visible as agents with the power to live through and determine people and events and extend the range of media through which they are seen not only to have a voice, but to be subjects both with a singular set of experiences and with speech.

In this context, children's experiences and speech are not simply facets of an individual. To construct children as a collectively defined experiential subject and to construct them with speech is to construct them in conditions of dialogue, claim and counter-claim, and authority and counter-authority. Namely, to say that children have speech is not to root them with fixed identities, interests and capacities; rather, it is to open their being to others, but also to allow them to undo the claims that others have had of them in the formation of dialogue; it is precisely to consider children in terms of speech and counter-speech. This is different from assuming that children's rights and the inclusion of children within a democratic political community imply the inscription of children with voice and agency (i.e. as the recognition or endowment of an ontological competency). On the contrary, the significance of presenting children with speech is that they are constructed within dialogic relations which are precisely, to use Jacques Rancière's term, a form of 'dissensus' (Rancière, 2010). Negotiation, as it is sometimes called, is not on the basis of existing and predefined interests and identity. To construe children as subjects of speech is not to constitute them with a prior identity (or community or sense of belonging); rather, their speech raises their identity as a matter of disagreement, a matter which is not simply settled. To pose the question of children's rights in this way is not to provide a model of citizenship, but to look at the resources deployed with respect to rights and the democratic and to position children as a problem therein. Rights are always a form of defence, as Rancière also argues; they are insisted on and performed only inasmuch as they are not purely formal, but draw on the substantive differences now assumed within the domain of the political. In this sense, children (with respect to their infancy or maturity) cannot be seen in terms of the imposition of either an adult-centric or a child-centric model of rights and the democratic (Jans, 2004). To talk about children as rights bearers, then, implies the insistence of children's rights as a problem, or rather as a field of problematisation (in the Foucauldian sense of a field of power, knowledge and subjectivity). In the context of children, this also implies a questioning of the status of speech as the vehicle, medium and *logos* of rights and politics, not least because of children's immaturity with regard to language.

The question of political competency inasmuch as it has been defined in terms of organised speech raises the fundamental problem of those denied membership of a political community on the basis of their incapacity. Priscilla Alderson has notably raised this issue regarding the rights of infants and babies, particularly in the context of their capacity to consent to medical treatment (Alderson, 1993 and 2000). Alderson, for example, although she frames her discussion largely in the context of terms such as 'information', 'discussion' and 'talk', provides a series of examples of the negotiations of babies and small infants. Through this simple format she raises the significant question of how to consider those without speech within a framework of children's rights. She argues, for example: 'A child may be too young or too sick to share verbally in making health-care decisions, yet may influence decisions through expressed feelings and body language' (Alderson, 2000: 123). She gives an example of a child of 6 who after the failure of her first two liver transplants became distressed and resistant. Her parents interpreted this and refused a third transplant attempt. The young girl died. Alderson then argues: 'It is sometimes assumed that words are the only genuine way to communicate, body language is mistrusted as vague and misleading. Yet words too can be misleading or confusing. Bodies can be the source of profound knowledge, when children learn through their illness and disability, and express themselves physically' (123). This case, and Alderson's work in this area, requires us to consider a radical rethinking of what constitutes, for example, the central political categories of 'expression' and 'participation' (Alderson, 2000). In a similar fashion Sirkka Komulainen, in her research on the 'communication difficulties' of young children under 6 years of age, both able and disabled, in educational, medical and health care contexts, considers the fundamental ambiguities at the heart of human communication (Komulainen, 2007). Alderson implicitly assumes the transparency of communication between adult and child and assumes that better understanding vis-à-vis non-verbal communication or childish expression is able to come about through political will, ethical sensibility and greater knowledge. However, Komulainen questions the very basis of such transparency of communication between adults and children in such a manner that the deployment of rational speech models of communication (i.e. assuming that the child's non-verbal expression works on the basis of their rational and reasoned communication akin to verbal speech) complicates the issue. Komulainen cautions 'against too simplistic and/or sensationalized a usage of the term "voice"' (Komulainen, 2007: 22) and argues that 'voice' should be seen as a point of departure and investigation instead of an assumed end point for the individual child with reason, interests and political will.

The sociology of childhood certainly supports but also raises significant problems with a notion of children's rights and political participation as based on their capacities and competencies. Michael Freeman has argued that we should shift our emphasis from considerations of children in terms of the rights of 'having' to the rights of 'being'. If the former is tied up in questions about the capacities and competencies of children, then the latter allows us to consider, he argues, the rights of children 'by virtue of being children' (Freeman, 1998: 442). Rights of being, he suggests, are 'more concerned with dignity and decency, two much neglected concepts' (442). The problem, though, is whether a shift towards the rights of being would simply reconfirm children's rights and participation within a field of intelligibility framed by 'development' and 'family', namely by a logic of welfare and protection; or to pose this in classical terms, there is a question as to the extent to which this would frame children's rights and participation only inasmuch as their being is understood within the context of reproduction rather than the political. What is at stake is precisely the rethinking of both.

Universalism and humanitarian NGOs

On 20 November 1989 the General Assembly of the United Nations adopted the Convention on the Rights of the Child (UNCRC). Framed as a series of 54 articles, the convention constituted a legal document that is now signed by all represented nations of the United Nations and is ratified by all except the USA. The convention comes out of a history of earlier international declarations regarding children's rights, notably the League of Nations Declaration of the Rights of the Child in 1924 and the United Nations Declaration of the Rights of the Child in 1959. Significant also is the foundation, in 1946, of the United Nations International Children's Emergency Fund (UNICEF). The rights of the UNCRC include rights to provision, protection and participation. The convention states that children should be entitled to the resources needed in order to live; to safeguards with respect to abuse, neglect, exploitation and discrimination; and to contribute to the decisions that affect their lives and upbringing. Such rights, then, might include access to education and schooling, to proper family life, to health care, to protection under the law, and to freedom of association and assembly. As already noted, Alderson has argued that the UNCRC should be applicable to all children regardless of perceptions of immaturity or incapacity. She argues that such rights are limited (with regard to reasonable expectations and their enforcement), aspirational (with regard to resources available for their realisation), conditional (upon contingent factors such as national legal structures and capacities of children), and shared (namely, the rights of children are collective with regard to all children and hence not individual) (Alderson, 2000: 23).

Many commentators have argued that the UNCRC continues a long tradition of colonial and imperial discourse regarding European definitions and understanding of childhood; these specific and originally localised definitions and understandings shaped in particular social and historical contexts of power and exploitation and are now deployed globally (i.e. definitions of childhood are always relative to culture, history and social formation). Others have argued, on the contrary, that the definitions of childhood being deployed are ones that accord with the natural body of the child in the context of social structure and are understood through the accumulation of knowledge in the natural and social sciences (i.e. all children everywhere are *ceteris paribus* sufficiently similar to warrant a universal approach). The UNCRC certainly continues with a developmental notion of children and a notion of development which is supported through family, schooling and a protective welfare state. As we have seen earlier, the history of developmentalism has been, and still is to a large extent, the object of much criticism within the sociology of childhood. It would be easy to read the UNCRC as ethnocentric, essentialist and colonial. But Jude Fernando asks whether relativist arguments, which point to the entrenched historic interests encoded in the UNCRC, could be detrimental to the welfare of children as understood in a global context, in the context of a 'transnational political economy' (Fernando, 2001: 19). He asks whether relativist critiques implicitly support neoliberal globalisation in their attack on global standards and measures through which to move aid and resources to those children in conditions of economic and social hardship. He argues that relativist notions of childhood 'effectively result in complicity with the status quo and, moreover, make it difficult to effectively deal with the forces that are working to undermine the quality of children's lives in the South, forces that are themselves transcultural and transnational in nature and effect' (19). In a different vein, Erica Burman has argued that there is a problem with posing our understanding of children's rights in terms of a discursive set of oppositions between western–non-western, local–global and individual–state, and that these oppositions need to be understood in the context of histories of colonialism. She argues, moreover, that

If we commit ourselves to a purely local notion of childhood then we are subject to three kinds of dilemmas. First, we either adopt a moral relativist position or we are positioned as imposing a colonial-tainted code. Second, it appears that we are positioned as having no choice either to collude with paternalism or with fundamentalism. Third, we are in danger of mistaking as authentic those traditional practices which are brought to life through acquiring an anti-imperialistic meaning. (Burman, 1996: 62)

Burman pushes us in the direction of thinking not of binary oppositions but of a more complex relationality.

The UNCRC emerges from, consolidates and further markets and helps construct a proliferation of agencies which operate across the international, the national and the local. Lawyers and legal agencies have been a significant part of this proliferation (Halliday and Osinsky, 2006). And yet although the globalisation of legal languages, intergovernmental agencies and non-governmental agencies (NGOs) certainly constitutes a new dynamic in understanding children's political agency, its impact is uneven and attenuated. It is important to remember that there was widespread agreement on the wording of the convention and, as Burman notes, substantial negotiation behind the scenes regarding what rights got listed as 'rights' within the articles – notably with regard to pressure from the USA for Article 13, on freedom of expression, Article 14, on freedom of thought, Article 15, on freedom of association, and Article 16, on rights to privacy (Burman, 1996). Nevertheless, its wording is sufficiently flexible with regard to its interpretation and implementation.

The articles of the convention only have effect in the context of social practice and infrastructure; national state and governmental agencies clearly shape their take-up, interpretation and the subsequent actions taken. Different national governments have taken on the UNCRC in different ways (Franklin, 2002). Central in this respect is the Committee on the Rights of the Child (CRC), which reports on state parties. Its findings are then picked up in the national press and other media (in a kind of 'name and shame' strategy). Some countries have adopted a children's commissioner or ombudsman (e.g. Sweden, Norway and the UK) to act as both a witness and an advocate for children's rights. But such roles often lack sufficient teeth. These practices and mechanisms are not uniform inasmuch as many countries do not have commissioners. But also, there are difficulties regarding the assessment of the implementation of the UNCRC inasmuch as data is gathered often with only hazily defined standard measures (Ennew and Miljeteig, 1996). Burman typifies this situation in terms of 'the discretionary status of children's rights, available to those countries that can afford to be seen to value them' (Burman, 1996: 50). Equally, there is a problem of codifying children's rights within a technocratic discourse, which some argue simply closes down debate and the actual politics and contingencies underlying those rights (Reynaert et al., 2009: 528). But we should also recognise the agency of children in the mobilisation and interpretation of rights. William Myers, for example, has argued that in the context of children's labour, although the UNCRC is framed within a European understanding of childhood, the articles 'had remarkable resonance with children and grassroots organizations in many developing countries where working children are increasingly undertaking advocacy, mobilization, action projects, and even surprisingly sophisticated research on their own behalf' (Myers, 2001: 50). In that sense, the interpretation and use of the UNCRC is manifold. But this is not to say that there is somehow a dialectic of global and local (as in Giddens' framing of late modernity) or as James and James argue, a 'reflexive and dialectical relationship between the "universalizing tendencies" of law and the relative conservatism of national cultures and politics' (James and James, 2004: 79).

Nick Lee provides an interesting analysis of the UNCRC in terms of its fundamental ambiguity with regard to the construction of childhood (Lee, 2001). He focusses on Article 12, which states that children who are able to express their views should have the right to express those views 'freely in all matters affecting the child', with the proviso that those views are to be weighed 'in accordance with age and maturity'. Moreover, children should be heard in legal and governmental decision-making processes in matters which affect any particular child 'in a manner consistent with the procedural rules of national law' (Article 12, UNCRC, 1989). Lee argues that Article 12 allows children to be viewed outside of a normatively defined developmental discourse and in accord with their status as 'human beings', but he says that the article clearly frames children's expression in the context of their maturity or immaturity and as such their word cannot simply be taken at face value. Its mediation is more problematic. He states: 'The Article, then, is *ambivalent* about children, about their capabilities to have voices of their own, and about the level of attention that should be given to those voices.' Lee understands this in terms of the 'generation' and 'containment' of the 'form of childhood ambiguity' (Lee, 2001: 94). The wording of the UNCRC, and of Article 12 in particular, contains a series of contradictions between an adult framing of children as not yet adult (i.e. in a stage of development, becoming adult) and also an understanding of children as morally equal to adults; between an idea of childhood as a universal and the applicability of the articles to particular children in particular circumstances and conditions; and between the UNCRC's promissory status as an international agreement and its actualisation in particular national jurisdictions. For Lee, these contradictions do not deter from the power of the UNCRC; rather, the fundamental ambiguities about childhood at the heart of the UNCRC constitute its openness and its extension in such a manner that the hope of children's rights rests never solely with either adult or child, nor global or national institution (95).

Notwithstanding the openness of the UNCRC as a legal text and the ambiguities regarding its implicit and explicit claims, it is important to understand the convention in terms of its complex scaling. Namely, the UNCRC cannot simply be understood in terms of universal–particular or global–national scaling, such that a relation of scale between two homogeneous self-enclosed spaces is assumed (i.e. the universal or global in one space and the particular or national in another). In fact, the scaling is more complex. Organisations and agencies construct connections and spaces. Particular places have significance, such as the United Nations headquarters overlooking the East River in Manhattan, New York City, or the offices of Amnesty International in Shoreditch, London, or the refugee camps in Darfur, in the Sudan. And particular forms of connection have different relations of significance across those locations, whether it be funding for campaigns, aid, or the influx of medics equipped with medicines into a war-torn region. Across the variated chains of agency and organisation, children get mobilised as rights' bearers and as political participants and their status and agency vis-à-vis rights and political participation cannot be divorced from these specific chains of agency. It's not clear how much sense it makes to refer, for example, to the United Nations headquarters as global, or the agreements of its members to a convention as universal, or to refer to the malnutrition of a child in Darfur or a teenager on the streets of London as particular.

A particular form of organisation that has mushroomed over the latter part of the twentieth century has been the non-governmental organisation or NGO. NGOs have facilitated connections across international forums and national agencies and local practices. Certainly, their ability to operate effectively is dependent on national governmental organisation (Fernando, 2001). They often operate within nationally defined parameters, channelling support in the context of national legislation and national infrastructures. Much of the mobilisation around the UNCRC has been non-governmental, orchestrating grassroots organisations using the language of children's rights not in a directly legal manner but as a form of mobilisation and action at the level of civil society. In some sense, the rise of global NGOs is closely correlated to the rise of a global discourse of child saving. Non-governmental organisations have been central to the increased visibility of children's rights. As Fernando has argued, 'the continuity of NGOs' efforts is contingent on their ability to raise funds from international donors in developed countries' (Fernando, 2001: 13). He argues that aid allocations have fallen and NGOs have turned to private funding and to areas which are able to garner public sympathy and support. He mentions the example of NGOs turning from education and health care to micro-credit.

These complex spaces of rights, territory and authority are mediated through different forms of cultural mediation (forms of speech, notification, legal discourse, technology, various artefacts and so on). An important aspect of the globalisation of children's human rights has not only been legal and state-governmental discourse, but also mass media discourses and vehicles. Kate Nash's work has developed an analysis of the 'intermestic' (crudely meaning both international and domestic) nature of human rights, which figures such rights in the context of a mixing of both international and national law and culture.

Importantly, for her, the cultural politics of human rights implies serious consideration of the media in its construction of a symbolic space for the struggle over the meaning of rights and for the assembling of a mediated public sphere. The agency and impact of NGOs, but also of the UN and its committees and peripheral organisations, actively create strategy on the basis of such a media space. For Nash, this is a reflexively constructed space in which actors are neither simply dupes nor controllers (Nash, 2009). The regular country reports of the CRC, for example, are not only technocratic and concerned with measurement and implementation, but also focal points for mediated public contestation and struggle.

Sovereignty and humanity

The discourse of children's rights straddles, on the one hand, longstanding discourses and ideas about children in the context of a balancing of powers across family and state in terms of competency, protection and welfare, and, on the other hand, ideas about human rights and humanity that consolidate in the European Enlightenment in the late eighteenth century and which have constituted a fundamental basis upon which national jurisdictions are formed. In the late twentieth and early twenty-first centuries these two genealogies of children's rights come together very forcibly in the figure of what academic and human rights lawyer Jacqueline Bhabha has termed 'Arendt's children' (Bhabha, 2009: 410–51). Bhabha points to the huge number of people who are recognised as 'stateless'. She refers to the United Nations High Commissioner for Refugees (UNHCR) figure of 5.8 million people stateless and also that it is believed that the actual figure is much higher, nearer 15 million (411); but she is interested in the significant number of these stateless people who are children. She refers to them as 'Arendt's children', after Hannah Arendt's writing on the formative role of the stateless in the shaping of the twentieth century. Bhabha indicates that the category 'stateless children' is complex in that it properly includes children who have become refugees and hence have no national government to look over them; but it also includes children who are technically citizens by virtue of birth but who lack legal registered identity. The core definition and features of these children include the following: 'they are minors; they are, or they risk being, separated from their parents or customary guardians; and they do not in fact (regardless of whether they do in law) have a country to call their own because they are either noncitizens or children of nonciti-zens' (413). Arendt's children are seen by Bhabha to be migrant or refugee children who have neither nation nor family to offer guaran-teed protection, education and welfare. They are predominantly poor (and represent a portion of the world's poor); they are unaccompanied by someone who is able to care for them and hence risk neglect, abuse, or exploitation; and they face accumulated risks of economic, social and psychological disadvantage and danger (414).

Hannah Arendt, just after the Second World War and in the context of the Shoah, the huge migratory movement of peoples across Europe, the founding of the State of Israel, and the Universal Declaration of Human Rights, makes a profound and resounding argument about the relationship between human rights and state-lessnes. She writes: 'Much more stubborn in fact and much more far-reaching in consequence has been statelessness, the newest mass phenomenon in contemporary history, and the existence of an ever-growing new people comprised of stateless persons, the most symp-tomatic group in contemporary politics' (Arendt, 1962: 277). The growth of this group of people, Arendt argues, is not due to one single cause; rather, 'every political event since the end of the First World War inevitably added a new category to those who lived outside the pale of the law, while none of the categories, no matter how the original constellation changed, could ever be renormalized' (277). These stateless people, who could not return to their country of origin, nor be fitted in the country of their current habitation, were an exception, outside of the law, without legal protection, 'undeportable', and were heavily policed by police forces that grew as a consequence of this new category of person. Internment camps, refugee camps and concentration camps were set up to house and offer a solution to the 'displaced persons'. For Arendt, it is the sheer number of refugees that is seen to pose the problem, as it had not been before, and to demand the solutions imposed. The Rights of Man in Europe since the French Revolution were shaped within the European nation-state and defined according to formal and substan-tive rights of citizenship. They were defined according to notions of natural man and natural law. Thus the history of European philoso-phy from Rousseau and Hobbes onwards helps to frame this Man. Arendt argues that although the Rights of Man were intended to be 'independent of all governments' and to be inalienable, the rise in the number of refugees after the First World War dispelled that myth (292). She argues: 'The Rights of Man, supposedly inalienable, proved to be unenforceable – even in countries whose constitutions were based upon them – whenever people appeared who were no longer citizens of any state' (293). In the 1920s and 1930s 'the meaning of human rights acquired a new connotation: they became a standard slogan of the protectors of the underprivileged, a kind of additional law, a right of exception necessary for those who had nothing better to fall back upon', and yet at this time it was unclear as to how human rights differed from the rights of national citizens (Arendt, 1962: 293). Arendt argues that whereas the Rights of Man rest upon a notion of human nature and natural law, human rights imply a sense of political community (298). The notion of humanity has replaced that of nature or history, as such, she argues; 'the right to have rights, or the right of every individual to belong to humanity, should be guaranteed by humanity itself'. She continues:

It is by no means certain whether this is possible. For, contrary to the best-intentioned humanitarian attempts to obtain new declarations of human rights from international organizations, it should be understood that this idea transcends the present sphere of international law which still operates in terms of reciprocal agreements and treaties between sovereign states; and, for the time being, a sphere that is above the nations does not exist. (Arendt, 1962: 298)

Thus, those innocent persons, naked in their existence, were not immediately recognised as humans, as part of humanity. Rather those, in their bare humanness, without the protection of the nation-state, were only seen as savages, unclothed beasts. For Arendt, moreover, this bare existence is framed in the context of a classical Greek division between household and state, between the private sphere of the domestic and the public world of politics. She states:

The whole sphere of the merely given, relegated to private life in civilized society, is as consistently based on the law of equality as the private sphere is based on the law of universal difference and differentiation. Equality, in contrast to all that is involved in mere existence, is not given us, but is the result of human organization insofar as it is guided by the principle of justice. We are not born equal; we become equal as members of a group on the strength of our decision to guarantee ourselves mutually equal rights. (Arendt, 1962: 301)

Those forced to live outside political community can only fall back on their humanness, as if like animals in nature.

The political philosopher Giorgio Agamben draws upon Arendt's work (alongside Foucault and Schmitt) as a major framing device in his discussion of modern forms of sovereignty and biopolitical power (Agamben, 1998). For Agamben, the Declaration of the Rights of Man and Citizen of 1789 similarly cements a relationship between rights and citizenship in such a way that resolutely bonds birth to nationhood. It 'names the new status of life as origin and ground of sovereignty and, therefore, literally identifies ... "the members of the sovereign"' (Agamben, 1998: 129). And, moreover, it is precisely because of this correlation that there is, as Arendt also argues, an intimate relationship between totalitarianism and the declaration of rights. Agamben argues that humanitarian organisations 'can only grasp human life in the figure of bare or sacred life' (133). But this needs to be read as precisely the problem. Agamben refers to the appalling genocide in Rwanda and to the imaging of victims in development campaigns. He says:

The 'imploring eyes' of the Rwandan child, whose photograph is shown to obtain money but who 'is now becoming more and more difficult to find alive', may well be the most telling contemporary cipher of the bare life that humanitarian organizations, in perfect symmetry with state power, need. A humanitarianism separated from politics cannot fail to reproduce the isolation of sacred life at the basis of sovereignty and the camp – which is to say, the pure space of exception – is the biopolitical paradigm that it cannot master. (Agamben, 1998: 133–4)

For Agamben, it is this correlation which perhaps more urgently than Arendt, pushes him to figure the refugee as that limit case that surpasses the construction of rights in the context of nation and natality (or birth). The figure of the refugee precisely calls such a paradigm into question.

Bhabha in her writing, although she uses the characterisation of 'Arendt's children', understands the contemporary framing of politics in such a way that allows for international agreements and organisation above and beyond the level of the nation. For example, she gives an example of Tabitha Kaniki Mitunga, a 5-year-old girl from the Democratic Republic of Congo. This little girl, her father killed, was living with family while her mother sought asylum in Canada. On her way to meet her mother, Tabitha was separated from her uncle in

Brussels. She had no passport or legal documents. She was interned in a remand centre and then deported back to the Democratic Republic of Congo. Bhabha uses this example not only to illustrate the tragedy of refugees, but to show how the European Court of Human Rights found the Belgian state responsible for Tabitha's 'inhuman treatment' and hence in breach of her human rights as stated in Article 3 of the European Convention for the Protection of Human Rights and Funda- mental Freedoms (Bhabha, 2009: 433). International law but also NGOs which both support and criticise the deployment of such law constitute a part of the picture which was missing at the time of Arendt's writing of *The Origins of Totalitarianism* in the late 1940s. Bhabha argues that there is still a big deficit between international law and the actualisation of these intentions at a national level. It would be possible to argue that the neglect and exploitation of refugee children is multiplied as a consequence of that deficit. But such an account places too much faith in the law. Rancière has been critical of those models of social justice, which aim to close the gap between law and social practice. He sees this as 'consensual' and hence counter to the funda- mental 'disagreement' that lies at the heart of democracy. As such, he is critical of Arendt (and also Agamben). He states:

It is only if you presuppose that the rights *belong* to definite or permanent subjects that you must state, as Arendt did, that the only real rights are the rights given to citizens of a nation by their belonging to that nation, and guaranteed by the protection of their state. If you do this, of course, you must deny the reality of the struggles led outside of the frame of the national constitutional state and assume that the situation of the 'merely' human person deprived of national rights is the implementation of the abstracted- ness of those rights. The conclusion is in fact a vicious circle. It merely reasserts the division between those who are worthy or not worthy of doing politics that was presupposed at the very beginning. (Rancière, 2004: 306)

For the field of children's rights, this vicious circle rests very squarely not only on the national but also on the familial. For Arendt, the figure of the refugee is typified as having an innocence 'in the sense of complete lack of responsibility' (Arendt, 1962: 295). The bare exist- ence of the refugee is marked as a site of infancy. This trope is similarly repeated in Agamben's discussion of the bare life of the subject in the face of sovereign biopolitical power. For both these writers, there is a sense that the entry into political community involves not only an entry from the private household to the public domain of politics, but also a transition from infancy to maturity, and in Aristotelian terms, from voice to organised speech. For Bhabha, her figure of the Arendt children is such that these children are doubly infantilised, constituted as external to both political community and family. And in this sense, her discussion of children's rights centres on the protection of children as framed within a model of the family, whether provided by parents or state officials acting *in loco parentis*. The issue, then, is not only the formulation of rights in the context of the post-national, but also the imagination of those rights external to the model of the family.

Conclusion

The fundamental problem of children's rights is that we continue to frame them in the context of a substantive model which poses family against state. The case for children's rights is measured in terms of children's competency and capacity to speak and to reason, which has been shaped by their learning and development within a schooled context (inasmuch that school is seen to instil cognitive and symbolic communicational capacity) and is increasingly shaped in the context of globally networked information and communication technology. Moreover, over the course of the twentieth century this form of under-standing gets complexified in the context of the international and a notion of global humanity. The figure of the refugee child is central here inasmuch as it forces us to reframe our 'Keynesian-Westphalian' (to use Nancy Fraser's phrase; Fraser, 2005) model of social justice in conditions of the post-national. There is still a question, though, as to the infrastructuring of children's rights at the post-national level and the interdependences and relations across international and national, but also an issue as to whether the bestowing of rights to refugee children constitutes a form of welfare akin to familial care. At one level, this is clearly not a problem. Children need to be helped. The two genealogies of family–state and humanity–nation are now in practice increasingly intermixed. And yet if the refugee child forces a question-ing of the nation–citizen–nature relation, then Arendt's children should question both that and the familial model of care. To repeat, this is not a call to abnegate responsibility to care for the child; it is, on the contrary, to demand a reframing of children's human rights in the context of *the political* (in Rancière's meaning of the term). This is a huge and difficult question, but a start is to recognise what Rancière says about democracy, namely: 'Democracy is not the power of the poor. It is the power of those who have no qualification for exercising power' (Rancière, 2004: 304). Rights and democracy do not rest on prior definitions and qualifications as to who might or is able to speak. This is not to disavow the issue of competency, but to frame any notion of children's rights in the context of the historical and contingent accumulation of resources and infrastructures concerning what counts as political expression, in what areas, with regard to what topics, with regard to what authority and with what capacity to change people and things.

PART IV

Conclusions

13 | *Conclusions*

In this final chapter I want to summarise my conclusions but also confirm a slightly different orientation for the sociological study of children's agency. In doing so, I want to reduce much of the subtlety of the field into a set of blockages in, or myths of, current thinking, which, although being 'misrepresentative' of the field, nevertheless still provide a sort of default resource. I then want to identify some of the undercurrents of contemporary discussion in the field and particularly with respect to describing and mapping the leading currents and flows of children's agency. This, then, provides the context for thinking further about childhood studies and the contribution of sociology to such an interdisciplinary field, and, finally, suggests a point of urgent discussion.

Five myths of childhood studies

There are currently five long-standing myths which circulate in the discussion of children and childhood. These are the myths of the individual child, of identity and difference, of homogeneous and static space, of unitary scale, and of the ontology of agency. I will discuss each briefly in turn.

The myth of the individual child

The idea that subjects are able to exist, whether as children or adults, independently of others is one that is regularly and repeatedly rejected within sociological thought. Children, from infants to teenagers, are social animals. Over and above any question of dependency, children are, as we all are, connected with others (people and things, relations simple and complex, different forms of materiality, different textures and affects). We should no more believe that children are possessive individuals, than adults. Similarly, children cannot be defined as striving for such personhood as a property (Lee, 2001).

What we have seen over the course of the chapters of this book is that many sociologists of children would explicitly agree with such a position. Many of the sociologists considered in this book would argue that children are thoroughly social beings. Many would also argue that any capacities which are held by children are not held individually, but only by virtue of their relationship with others. For example, the capacities of children are dependent on their locally situated interrelations with other children or with adults. Any capacities are thus seen to be a facet of the situation.

Other sociologists would argue that the solitary individual child is either an ideological and imaginary fiction or an effect of forms of power and knowledge. In the first instance, the individual is a form of security, a mode of identification, which harks back to a primary maternal security. In the second, the individual child is the outcome of discursive mobilisation and institutional weight, which draws on subjects, inscribes their bodies and bestows a soul. In such accounts, the individual is the effect of systemic power.

The myth of the individual child is a myth which does indeed circulate, and yet few explicitly believe in it. It is most often heard in fragments, although it finds its clearest expression in its relation to the myth of the social agent (which I discuss below) as the repository of capacity building.

The myth of identity and difference

There is still a sense that the sociology of childhood works with an understanding of children in terms of their separation from adults, their exclusion from a world of adults and their progression from the one world to the other. In such an interpretation, children are understood in terms of their having an underlying identity and that identity is defined only inasmuch as it is defined against the identity of adults. Children and childhood are defined in terms of their fundamental difference from adults and adulthood. This difference is understood as a consequence of a structural universal (namely that for all history and geography children are and have been understood as different from adults and that irrespective of particular social and cultural formations that fundamental structural universal remains), also as a deep-rooted, sometimes hard-wired, facet of the self-identity of children (namely that inscribed in the bodies and minds of children are self-evident identifiers which hold them to the category 'child' rather than the category 'adult'), and as a generative binary which is only instantiated and actualised in particular empirical settings (namely that, although generational difference is socially specific, it nevertheless is repeated as a constant structure such that the child is not adult and the adult is not child).

Let us consider the example of Ngisti, who, having fled East Africa when she was 16 years old, arrived in the UK, at which point she was detained as attempting illegally to enter the country. She was assessed by professionals working for social services and identified as a 'child', but she was then examined by the Home Office asylum unit in Croydon, south London, was deemed not to be a child and was detained as an 'adult' in a detention centre in Cambridgeshire. Her case, along with those of forty other children, was taken up by Mark Scott of Bhatt Murphy Solicitors, taken to court, and was eventually won with regard to the primacy of the initial assessments of social services. The cases of these children, who were variously fleeing war, civil unrest, torture, rape and sexual assault, were widely reported in the press, and other bodies, such as the UN Refugee Agency, the Royal College of Paediatricians and Her Majesty's Inspectorate of Prisons, raised concerns over the action of the Home Office and Border Agency. For us, the case provides evidence not that the expert judgement of the social services team was essentially correct on the basis that the children were really children (inasmuch as their bodies or minds disclosed a fundamental identity or inasmuch as their decision instantiated a fundamental structural universal regarding the differentiation of childhood from adulthood), but rather that a particular set of people working within particular organisational constraints and professional rules of practice, through their assessment and judgement differentiated these forty children and designated them as children. Moreover, the assemblage regarding the judgement of the social services team was supported and further mobilised with regard to other assemblages regarding paediatric knowledge, human rights legislation and definitions of humanity in the context of the United Nations' definitions of children in the context of migration and detention. There is no sense, then, that we can simply have recourse to a prior definition of the child or childhood (whether as a structural universal or an in-built identity) in the differentiation of adults from children. These divisions are the outcomes of particular performances through particular assemblages and the broader orchestration of assemblages. Outside this nexus of arrangements (and the contestation of judgement and assessment by the Home Office and undoubtedly sections of the right-wing media), Ngisti was not necessarily a child or an adult and her conduct, habits, pleasures and anxieties were not necessarily stamped with that division. Similarly, her construction as a child or an adult or as a child of a particular age with respect to schooling would not be determined by the same forms of judgement, assessment and technologies of observation as those used by the social services team. There is no universal structuring principle (of generationing) which organises and distributes all discourses, practices, bodies, technologies and materialities into 'children' and 'adult'. The distributions are immanent, not external, to the assemblage. That said, there are, of course, overlaps and overdeterminations, and that is pre-cisely why groups of paediatricians might object to the original Home Office judgement. But because there is no clear-cut division, the author-isation of expertise across different assemblages constitutes a form of labour. Any authority that paediatricians in the UK might have with respect to a judgement made by the UK Home Office regarding the detention of child asylum seekers is not an a priori authority; it has to be worked on, it is has to be set up, and there has to be a huge amount of translation work to make it happen – and even then it is not an incon-testable judgement. Any equivalence across assemblages in this sense requires translation work. We cannot assume a generalised series of equivalences in the manoeuvring of children and adults, nor can we assume a principle which divides between the two and locks the mean-ing of each as a binary relation between them.

The myth of divided, separated and homogeneous space

For some reason, as we have seen with Ariès, but also many others, sociologists of childhood find it easier sometimes to think about chil-dren within child-oriented settings, as if peer interactions in playgrounds or school classrooms or elsewhere were not also interactions with other people overlooking or nearby or in the immediate or distant past helping to build, shape and facilitate particular kinds of interactions, and also as if those interactions were not in addition caught up in and necessarily mixed with materials, resources and technologies made and remade through accumulated processes and histories and geog-raphies. Similarly, some sociologists are happy to talk of childhood (or, conversely, of adulthood) as designating a space which is both contained and within which adults (or children) are removed and excluded. When, for example, sociologists talk about the boundaries between adulthood and childhood as blurring or disappearing, they are talking as if these two categories constituted relatively fixed and homogeneous spaces, spaces defined and dominated by those categories. Even if we take the simple example of preschool children's play in a sandpit in a local playground. We may refer to this as a space of childhood. But what do we mean? Do we mean that this is a space within which adults have been excluded? Of course not. This is a space which is built by adults (i.e. those who design the playground and build the sandpit alongside the swings and climbing frames and so on), but it is also built by children (i.e. through their building of sandcastles and roads and other things in the pit itself). The small children, who play in this sandpit, act as attractors and are accompanied by adults (whether parents, guardians, grandparents, siblings or others). Do we mean, then, that it is a childhood space because it is intended for children? Yes, but the 'intention' relies on the work of both adults and children in the making of this. Children's agency is not defined in terms of children or adult spaces, but rather through highly entangled social relations.

The myth of homogeneous divided space relies on a subject position from which one is able to see from a position of vantage, to see the differences between people, and to see their neat spatial distribution. Moreover, this vantage position is such that it is itself untainted by the labour of distributing. What is seen is the clarity of childhood and adulthood and little else. It is from such a position that one can talk of childhood as a becoming inasmuch as one is at a point infinitely receding toward a transcendent point, a point which is both inside and outside the frame. But equally, and contrary to this, such a vantage point allows one to claim the clear position of supporting children, to speak from their standpoint. Such an understanding presumes the fixity of spatial relations prior to their instantiation, such that one is able to take up the position of the child, to speak from their position, only because that position is known (or at least assumed to be known). The distribution of homogeneous space not only forgets the labour of division and the labour of constructing a vantage point (Law and Benschop, 1997), but also the boundary work involved in such demarcation and policing (Star and Griesemer, 1989). In this sense, the labour of division is not only epistemological but also ontological.

The myth of scale

Children's agency is often understood by sociologists in terms of the local, the face to face, and the interpersonal. Sociologists often understand children's agency in terms of social relations within conditions of co-presence. Thus, they like to investigate social interactions in terms of particular interactions within a classroom or in a playground or at home. Children's talk and children's social interaction is understood generally in terms of children's interactions with others nearby in relations of propinquity. However, even when considering, for example, communication at a distance over the internet or by telephone or through some other abstract system, these relations are understood with reference to and by analogy with relations of propinquity. Agency, then, is understood in terms either of the myth of the proprietorial individual or of the resources generated through social relations in conditions of co-presence. Agency is understood as having a kind of 'local feel' to it. And even when we look to actor-network theory or other post-social theories of agency, agency still continues to have that 'local feel'. In contrast, structure is seen as bigger scale, involving actors which are bigger, such as the state, the family, the education system, or which are aggregates of microsociological entities, such as populations. Actor-network theory in some sense offers a corrective to this biscalar world of micro and macro, small and big. But it also tends to reduce the big to the small and hence agents, actors and actants are understood in terms of their highly localised relations of propinquity. Scale in actor-network theory is built up from small to big.

In contrast, what we have seen in the context of the different arrangements considered over the course of this book is that scale is both small and big and more between. Local interactions between two children in a school playground are intersected, for example, with playground designs, teacherly interventions, government policy regarding school formations and the importance of play, the history of developmental psychology and the regulations of class and motherhood. These constitute different elements with different histories and spatial forms and which come together in conditions of complexity. There is no position of vantage, nor prior hierarchy from which to lock the perspective of macro and micro and to normalise its relations. The agency which circulates around children, in this sense, is defined through its multiscalarity and its multidimensionality. Assemblages are rhizomatic and agency needs to be understood in this context. In the context of such multidimensionality and multiscalarity what becomes significant is not the mixing across different scales, but rather the devices and modes of translation which facilitate connection across and in between. Much recent discussion on this question talks of topology as a way of beginning to understand such post-Euclidean and post-Cartesian complex spatiality.

The myth of the social agent

Lastly, we come to the myth of the social agent. It has been said that this is less an ontology and more a point of departure (Prout, 2005). This is certainly correct in some respects, but also wildly wrong in others. Agency, with regard to individual capacity possessed and contained only to be expressed through the intentions (whether conscious or unconscious) of that individual intentional subject, presumes insufficient ground to make the case for an ontology of agency with regard to children, but equally no analytical ground for a point of departure. In this book we considered the arrangements of agency, such that agency neither starts nor finishes with any individual agent. Rather, agency is understood as more akin to agency as discussed within narrative analysis inasmuch as characters might be said to have agency but only inasmuch as that agency is orchestrated within narrative structure and forms of narration and in the context of other characters with agency. We talk about the actions of a character, about their motivations, but not in the sense that we believe that character to be 'real'. But more importantly, this kind of narrative (the narrative of children, as it were) is also one in which there is no single author, but multiple authors. Each contributor is able to change the story and to tell it from their own perspective. Thus any character is encoded within multiple narrations. But even more so, these contributors are themselves narrated within the fictions they write. This is not to say, though, that anything can happen, or that it is all fiction and hence has no substance. On the contrary, it simply means that the stakes are more complex. It does not imply an erasure of differences, unevenness, inequalities and the different forces of different agencies.

It makes little sense to frame children's agency in terms of a simple binary, having or not having agency, capacity and power. Although the presentation of children as active rather than passive had a place in the history of ideas about children and socialisation in the social sciences, it is based on a rather slanted history that ignores as much as it benefits. But more importantly, such a binary, active or passive, constitutes a facile reduction. For example, a story in the *Observer*, a UK-based newspaper, reports on children in Rwanda in 2012, who are malnourished and dying. The problem of the extent of malnourishment among children became acute once the statistical measurements of height and weight were compared to those of European children. The Rwandan health minister and a paediatrician states that 'Those children shown as fine were often malnourished, those as malnourished were acutely malnourished, and so on' (*Observer*, 19 February 2012). But if the statistical comparisons revealed the problem to government, it is the global food markets which create the problem. Rwanda is a country with sufficient food stocks, the story reports, but the cost of maize has increased to such an extent that local people are unable to afford to buy it in sufficient quantity to feed their families. Even if we take into account the framing of the story in a UK national newspaper, in a story written by the paper's food critic, within a genre of images and accounts which positions the child to be looked at, to be the object of empathy, and ultimately to be saved, the disclosure of counternarratives which demonstrate these children's resilience and their making do in the face of such hardship cannot be interpreted within a reduced and limited stage of agency (i.e. as a question of whether the child is active or passive). Such assertions deliver little analytical value. Children's agency is, of course, important, but in the context of the assemblage of elements and with respect to a particular politics of engagement, the question of what is to be done cannot be reduced to the politics of either/or, active or passive.

Descriptive assemblages, social observation and biopower

It is clear from the substance of this book that I am not so much considering children's agency (as it might ordinarily be thought of in the sociology of childhood) as thinking through the *agencement*s or assemblages or arrangements within which children in some form or other find themselves. In this sense, agency is always relational and never a property; it is always in-between and interstitial; and the capacity to do and to make a difference is necessarily dispersed across an arrangement. Moreover, children's agency constitutes a problem space, which is composed of questions, investigations and methods of analysis, but which also invites further questions, investigations and analyses. It is not constituted as a solution. It does not indicate a model that can then be deployed as a form of explanation of different kinds of social conduct. The different spaces of experience, experimentation and power that I consider – concerning the family, schooling, crime, health, play and consumer culture, children's labour and children's rights – constitute particular complexes of arrangements in which 'agency' is a significant factor, but equally it makes little sense to consider these spaces in terms of agency residing within individual children in the context of pre-existent social structures.

The growth of assemblages concerning children's agency can be understood in terms of the growth of biopower, the growth of methods of observation and the growth of descriptive devices. As was noted in Chapter 2 in our discussion of Ariès, the iconographies which develop around forms of family portraiture are significant not because they document the invention of childhood, but because they constitute significant forms of description of children in a manner that codifies them in particular kinds of ways with respect to dress, family status, location in the household and relation to the bucolic. Over the period that Ariès documents, we also see the increasing documentation of children with regard to their bodily conduct and their physiology and increasingly their interior self, defined through physiological, medical, psychological and psychiatric discourses. These discourses make children intelligible through ways of describing them and through methods of observing them. The observations of children, for example by Darwin, provide the basis for expert and scientific deliberation regarding the lives of children. The lives of children are thus defined in terms of their conduct with others and their internal state of growth and development. As we have also noted, this occurs over the course of the eighteenth and nineteenth centuries at a time that Foucault discusses in terms of the emergence and development of modes of governmentality concerned with the life of individuals and populations, namely biopower. It is at this time that we see the changing form of the family and the government of families in terms of their behaviours and psychologies; in terms of their norms and their pathologies. The growth of expertise concerning the lives of children becomes increasingly specialised through the development of paediatric medicine in the twentieth century, the specialisms in psychology and education, and the growth of criminology based on theories of delinquency and crime. We witness across the twentieth century the deployment of forms of government not based solely within the institutions of the school, the clinic, the prison or the family, but more broadly across the population.

It is also across the long period from the eighteenth century to the twentieth century that we see the growth in cultures directly oriented and addressed to children. Magazine and book publishing, radio, television and film, but also consumer cultures more broadly identify 'children' as a discrete and often highly differentiated market. Of course, in the late twentieth and twenty-first centuries the internet and social media add a new dimension to this dynamic. What these cultural forms provide is a series of platforms upon which children's lives can be further described, observed, displayed and circulated. Through different genres and modes of presentation, children's lives become a matter of biography. Across these different media, children's lives are defined in biographical terms. These are lives – whether real or fictional – which are written about and documented. They are recorded and narrativised. They are codified through modes of seriousness, but also melodrama, tragedy, comedy and romance. The affective codification further aligns the lives of children alongside the lives of others, including heroes and villains, horses, rabbits and various other creatures.

Children's agency, then, becomes encoded and distributed inasmuch as it is aligned with the growth in descriptive assemblages and devices and the correlation of these with the extension of biopower. Children's agency is now thoroughly suffused with the question and problem of the writing of children's lives, namely the question of their biography. In this sense, this book has been concerned not with providing a theory of children's agency, nor with providing an empirical study of their interactions, but with the question 'When and where was their agency?' The chapters are not summaries of the field, nor do they review the literature, nor are they surveys of the literature and the field. They are excavations of problem spaces undertaken in order to extract an understanding of children's agency from within those spaces, but also from across those spaces. Leaving the question of agency relatively open and allowing myself the opportunity to read the literature in a way not beholden to the strict intentions of their authors, I have been able to disentangle some striking features of children's agency. In answering the question 'When and where was children's agency?', we can see across the different problem spaces covered in this book some significant (if not necessarily sociologically novel) trends.

First, children over the course of the modern period were initially thought best dealt with within specially designed institutions (schools, families, clinics and so on), but increasingly those institutions were displaced, but not by any means discarded, such that children now roamed the cities, the streets, the shopping centres and the worlds of cyberspace. In doing so, these children were escorted, watched, tagged and cared for, but also some roamed more freely; yet all were entangled with adults. Moreover, it was precisely this entanglement that provided a site of care, but also a site of concern. Children outside of the classroom still needed to learn; children outside the clinic still needed to be healthy; children outside the sandpit still needed to play; children outside of the detention centre still needed to be surveilled; and children outside the family still needed to be parented. Moreover, the other side of this move can be seen in terms of the franchising of services outside the institutions and the mediation of forms of care through various intermediaries, whether particular dedicated persons or forms of technical device. Most obviously, new online discussion services such as Mumsnet provide a means of raising questions about schooling, childcare, problem children, maternity, and so on in a manner that constitutes parenting as intensely mediated by others sharing similar experiences.

Second, there has been a growth in the range of expertise and in the number of experts gathered around children. This has meant an increasing agonism and antagonism concerning the resident authority over a particular child or problem. Thus, the question of who is authorised to speak for children with psychiatric problems no longer simply rests with psychiatrists specially trained in diagnosis and care. Instead, various patient groups, for example, might also lay claim to such authority, not on the basis of psychiatric knowledge, but with respect to intimate knowledge and experience of a community of sufferers. Increasingly, then, the problem spaces of children's agency get further defined as problems inasmuch as there are conflicts of authority and conflicts over the status of knowledge. But also the growth of expertise has meant that synergies have formed across competing expertise and knowledge. Thus, for example, teachers and educationalists that might have been defined in contrast to those employed to market toys to children might now be drawn on by toy companies in the design of toys which may appeal to children and parents with regard to their pedagogic value. Toys may also be designed to facilitate learning within schools. Educational toys are not only those found in the home, which are intended to hothouse children's development, but are also found in the classroom, where they are used as motivational objects and sites of pleasure and pedagogy. They might be intelligent, networked and constitute the platform for a commercialised educational strategy.

Third, there has been a growth in the range and number of observational and descriptive devices such that children are known through a vast array of methods and means. They become intelligible through a vast array of different technologies of observation, aggregation and detail. Children are known rarely as whole persons and more often as aggregates (e.g. through forms of surveying) or as part objects. Thus, for example, infant teeth are identified as a particular set of part objects, which are observed and measured through various dental technologies and which are aligned with commercial organisations selling specifically designed toothbrushes and toothpastes. Moreover, they are increasingly observed, described and known, not by experts on children, sometimes not even by experts, but by humans and increasingly machines trained and designed to gather data and to feed this data on. Their behaviour and attitudes are logged, their transactions are noted, and their agency is, accordingly, increasingly surveilled. Methods of research observation have sought to become more closely aligned to the forms of observation and description of children themselves. In this sense, the growth of large data sets ('big data') and the ease with which such data sets can now be gathered and manipulated are matched by the distribution of data retrieval and generation across a diversity of sources, which may be seen to be closer to the ground rather than those located in the big laboratories or closed-in centres of calculation of old. Of course, the old centralised centres of calculation are still important, but what is increasingly clear is that they are now balanced by 'bottom-up' and 'from-below' data generators, interpreters and analysers. Children, then, are not simply the objects of scientific knowledge, they are increasingly the co-producers of that knowledge, but in ways which are often driven by very different motivations and contexts of use and which, in doing so, radically rearticulate and reorient the domains of certainty and authority.

And fourth, selfhood is increasingly a site of investment for children – through, for example, dress, adornment, writing, the accumulation of music and friendship networks. But, biographies are increasingly being lived inside out. They are no longer contained within individuals. They are thoroughly written and written for publics. They are thoroughly exteriorised. Emotions, friendships, loves, musical tastes, heartaches, anxieties and all are opened up to some and sometimes all. It is also accepted that these biographies will be able to be rewritten, to be commented on and sometimes to be trashed and ridiculed and hated. Biographies are exteriorised, not because there is an individual inter- iorised body outside of which lives are now visible. But rather, biog- raphies are exterior because they are now lived in-between, *in media res*. These lives are interstitial and it is because they are so that they can be taken up, mediated, assembled and infrastructured. In this sense, also, the lives of children are relational. This is the stuff of childhood.

Children's agency, then, is increasingly understood in the context of its circulation outside the institutions of modernity which initially gave it such life, in the context of conflicting authority such that its capacity emerges in the gaps between competing claims and counter-claims, in the context of a huge machinery of observational and descriptive devices which are increasingly aligned with children's everyday lives, and finally in the context of children's increasingly exteriorised biog- raphies such that no longer do children simply define the problem of an interiorised temporal, physiological and psychological complex. Children's agency in the twenty-first century is thus significantly different from that which existed at the beginning of the last century. This is not to say that children's agency is only defined by this leading edge, but rather that this leading edge constitutes potentially momen- tous change.

Post-childhood studies?

One of the big questions within academia concerns the question of whether children are best studied within the remit of an interdisciplin- ary or a transdisciplinary field of childhood studies. Recent focus on children was given a huge push by the framing of what has been called 'the new sociology of childhood'. This paradigm-shifting framing of the field placed the question of children's agency centre stage, and many of its methods and priorities were picked up across a range of disciplines. The intervention, although framed very much within the sociology of childhood, also took stock of other disciplines. Primarily these included social history and anthropology; latterly, media and cultural studies, some parts of social psychology, literary studies, development studies, cultural geography and art history have been added. Many of these disciplines had established parallel intellectual agendas unbeknownst to the sociology of childhood. The success of this interdisciplinary field was largely dependent on a broad consensus regarding three key theoretical tenets: namely regarding children's agency, a common critique of developmentalism, and an emphasis on social constructionist methodologies.

Of course, it is clear that childhood studies, defined as the field of academic disciplines focussed on children, has a much longer history and the range of disciplines is much wider. Across the range of different forms and methods of description and observation from across the academic disciplines, children have been made visible and intelligible to human, social, biological and medical sciences. From height and weight charts to Gessell domes, from ethnographic participant observation to social surveys, and from narrative analysis to aesthetics, children are disclosed as particular kinds of human being. Moreover, across those forms of observation, description and expertise there are many discussions. Paediatricians talk to anthropologists who talk to psychologists who talk to sociologists who in turn talk to literary theorists. There is no shortage of common conversation. But that said, these different disciplines encode often very different forms of causal explanation and often very different modes of professional writing. The weighting within different disciplines of different ideas of causality and of different methods of observing and documenting a relation of cause and effect or the transformation of a body over time means that undoubtedly there are severe epistemological limitations to any common project of childhood studies, over and above broad philosophical debate or problem-based research in which disciplinary anchors are uprooted for the purpose of the project at hand. Yet given this, there are opportunities for dialogue which should not be missed. The commonality of this programme is assisted by, but needs more than, goodwill and conversation.

What lines are to be drawn?

In many ways a broader horizon helps in this dialogue, or rather, in staging the diversity of antagonisms. Nikolas Rose noted, in his 2005 Clifford Barclay Lecture on biomedicine and society, that according to repeated reports from the World Health Organisation, 'the world's biggest killer, the greatest cause of ill health and suffering across the globe, is coded Z59.5 in the International Classification of Diseases. The condition Z59.5 is extreme poverty' (Rose, 2005: 3). He went on to state that despite the reduction of major diseases across the globe, 12.2 million children under 5 died in developing countries from conditions that could have been surmounted for a few US cents per child (see WHO, 2002). The global inequality between rich and poor is huge and growing. Life expectancy in many countries in the global south is such that many of those countries are populated mainly by young people and children. Nearly half the population of Sierra Leone is under 14 years of age. The mix of poverty and large numbers of young people has always been perceived as an explosive synthesis. For example, Giovanna Procacci, in her genealogy of the government of poverty, presents the governmental fears of the eighteenth and nineteenth centuries as follows:

Pauperism is thus poverty intensified to the level of *social danger*: the spectre of the mob; a collective, essentially urban phenomenon. It is a composite (and thereby all the more dangerous) population which 'encircles' the social order from within, from its tenements, its industrial agglomerations. It is a magma in which are fused all the dangers which beset the social order, shifting along unpredictable, untraceable channels of transmission and aggregation. It is insubordinate, hidden from the scrutinizing gaze of any governing instance. (Procacci, 1991: 158)

The pauper was defined in terms of mobility and promiscuity, improvidence and frugality, and ignorance and insubordination.

As I write this conclusion, London and other cities and towns in the UK have seen riots and looting. The 'Arab Spring' has been routinely discussed in terms of the aspirations and enthusiasms of youth. The Occupy Movement in the US and across the globe is often talked about as an expression of the young. Sometimes these arrangements are discussed positively, as hopes for a better future; often they are uneasily dismissed as at root forlorn and wretched. These 'lumpen youths', to use Ibrahim Abdullah and Yusuf Bangura's phrase (Abdullah and Bangura, 1997), have their lumpenness written on their bodies through the adult observers. They have a productivity, a productivity which has not escaped the productivity of others. But Abdullah accounts for lumpen youth in Sierra Leone. He says: 'By lumpens, I refer to the largely unemployed and unemployable youth, mostly male, who live by their wits or who have one foot in what is generally referred to as the informal or underground economy' (Abdullah, 1998: 207). These are largely petty criminals, gangs of young people who begin to form from the mid 1940s in Sierra Leone. They are associated with the rarray boy culture. The composition of this lumpen youth, Abdullah argues, changes in the 1970s when they become mixed with middle-class young people. As such, the solidarities across this formation became more 'replete with the contradictory tendencies inherent in lumpens as a social category' (209). Petty young criminals were now mixed with university and school students and an aggressive anti-establishment popular culture provided a particular type of cultural expression. Throughout much of the late 1970s, 1980s and 1990s the economic situation plus an increasing neoliberal withdrawal of state services provided some of the context for the formation of the Revolutionary United Front in Sierra Leone. In a different context, Senegal in the late 1980s and early 1990s, but with many resonances, Mamadou Diouf talks about how '[e]ach time that the state "unloads" a space, its pretensions to rule are diminished; the liberated space becomes a territory for invention, for dissidence, and for dissonance' and that in their resistance '[t]he young strike a violent blow against the languages of power through the production of synthetic idioms whose elements are borrowed from distant and heterogeneous worlds' (Diouf, 1996: 247–8). What is striking is that across the different contexts the voices, so often called upon to speak for the dispossessed youth, from clergymen to Marxists to philanthropic charities, but also whole swathes of experts from the natural and social sciences, continue to get heard, over and over again, in now globally distributed sermons. But whether these are sufficiently 'organic', in Gramsci's sense and close to the ground, is another matter.

The poor of the world are not only primarily in the global south, but are also increasingly housed or homeless in the increasingly growing global cities. These cities are typified by neoliberal governmental programmes and by a large informal economy, both legal and illegal. These economies are also bulked up by huge numbers of children.

Mike Davis asks the question: 'To what extent does an informal proletariat possess that most potent of Marxist talismans: "historical agency"?' He continues:

Portentous post-Marxist speculations like those of Negri and Hardt, about a new politics of 'multitudes' in the 'rhizomatic spaces' of globalization remain ungrounded in any real political sociology. Even within a single city, slum populations can support a bewildering variety of responses to structural neglect and deprivation, ranging from charismatic churches and prophetic cults to ethnic militias, street gangs, neoliberal NGOs, and revolutionary social movements. But there is no monolithic subject or unilateral trend in the global slum; there are nonetheless myriad acts of resistance. Indeed, the future of human solidarity depends upon the militant refusal of the new urban poor to accept their terminal marginality within global capitalism. (Davis, 2006: 202)

The resistance to poverty, the urgent demand that this presents, is one that is certainly articulated by Marxism and the Left, but for Davis, it is not they who have the ears and hearts of those residents in the planet of slums. That voice, he argues, has been given increasingly to 'Mohamed and the Holy Ghost' (Davis, 2004a: 30). He declares:

What is clear is that the contemporary megaslum poses unique problems of imperial order and social control that conventional geopolitics has barely begun to register. If the point of the war against terrorism is to pursue the enemy into his sociological and cultural labyrinth, then the poor peripheries of developing cities will be the permanent battlefields of the twenty-first century. Some templates are obvious. Night after night, hornetlike helicopter gunships stalk enigmatic enemies in the narrow streets of the slum districts, pouring hellfire into shanties or fleeing cars. Every morning the slums reply with suicide bombers and eloquent explosions. If the empire can deploy Orwellian technologies of repression, its outcasts have the gods of chaos on their side. (Davis, 2004b: 14–15)

It seems that children may be not only outcast, but increasingly have chaos on their side. But if anything, this book has attempted to indicate some of the rich research which lays bare the technological, infrastructural support for these voices and actions from those outcast. For sociologists, it is important, in our mapping of children's lives, in our understanding of their biographies, certainly to be guided by humanity, but we cannot return to a bifurcated ontology which poses technology against agency (Agamben, 2009).

Our intention in investigating research on children's agency has been framed in the context of sociological reflection, not moral argument. A concern with the agency of children and a concern to document the transformation of children's agency are not driven by an ideological agenda to see children's agency everywhere or to see it as a universal, unitary phenomenon. It is the task of a sociology of children to document that capacity when observed, but also to recognise incapacity, abuse, power relationality, torture and exploitation. But the task also relies on a recognition of children's dependency. Dependency implies a notion of hanging from and being reliant upon, such that the one relied upon is weighed down by virtue of that dependency. Over and above the necessary connectedness of materiality, some social relations are defined through the weighing down, but not necessarily a burden, of some in the context of others. In the world we live in now – pretty much everywhere across the globe, irrespective of wealth or poverty, peacefulness or states of warfare – those who care for children (whether parents, grandparents, social workers, doctors, nurses, teachers, aunts, uncles and children themselves) understand that dependency as a relation which is thoroughly mediated by conflicting and increasingly surplus information.

Bibliography

Abbott, Pamela, and Wallace, Claire (1992) *The Family and the New Right.* London: Pluto Press.

Abdullah, Ibrahim (1998) 'Bush path to destruction: the origin and character of the Revolutionary United Front/Sierra Leone'. *Journal of Modern African Studies* 36(2), 203–35.

Abdullah, Ibrahim, and Bangura, Yusuf (1997) 'Lumpen youth culture and political violence: Sierra Leoneans debate the RUF and the civil war'. *Africa Development* 22(3/4), 171–216.

Abernethie, Loraine (1998) 'Child labour in contemporary society: why do we care?' *International Journal of Children's Rights* 6, 81–114.

Agamben, Giorgio (1998) *Homo Sacer: Sovereign Power and Bare Life.* Stanford University Press.

(2006) *Infancy and History: The Destruction of Experience.* London: Verso.

(2009) *What is an Apparatus? and Other Essays.* Stanford University Press.

Aitken, Stuart, Estrada, Sylvia Lopez, Jennings, Joel, and Aguirre, Lina Maria (2006) 'Reproducing life and labor: global processes and working children in Tijuana, Mexico'. *Childhood* 13(3), 365–87.

Alanen, Leena (1994) 'Gender and generation: feminism and the "child question"', in Jens Qvortrup, Marjetta Bardy, Giovanni Sgritta and Helmut Wintersberger (eds.), *Childhood Matters: Social Theory, Practice and Politics.* Aldershot: Ashgate.

(2000) 'From sociologies of childhood to generational analysis'. Paper delivered to the Childhood and Social Theory Colloquium, University of Keele.

Alderson, Patricia (1993) *Children's Consent to Surgery.* Milton Keynes: Open University Press.

(2000) *Young Children's Rights: Exploring Beliefs, Principles and Practice.* London: Jessica Kingsley.

Alexander, Claire (2008) *(Re)thinking Gangs.* London: Runnymede Trust.

Alexandre-Bidon, Danièle, and Lett, Didier (1999) *Children in the Middle Ages: Fifth–Fifteenth Centuries.* Translated by Jody Galdding. University of Notre Dame Press.

Allan, Graham, and Crow, Graham (2001) *Families, Households and Society*. London: Palgrave.

Althusser, Louis (1969) *For Marx*. London: Verso.

(1971) *Lenin and Philosophy and Other Essays*. London: Monthly Review Press.

Applbaum, Kalman (2006) 'Pharmaceutical marketing and the invention of the medical consumer'. *PLoS Medicine* 3(4), e189.

Archard, David (1993) *Children: Rights and Childhood*. London: Routledge.

Archer, Louise (2001) 'Muslim brothers, black lads, traditional Asians: British Muslim young men's constructions of race, religion and masculinity'. *Feminism and Psychology* 11(1), 79–105.

(2003) *Race, Masculinity and Schooling: Muslim Boys and Education*. Milton Keynes: Open University Press.

Arendt, Hannah (1962) *The Origins of Totalitarianism*. New York: Harcourt Brace Jovanovich.

Ariès, Philippe (1962) *Centuries of Childhood*. London: Jonathan Cape.

Armstrong, David (1979) 'Child development and medical ontology'. *Social Science and Medicine* 13, 9–12.

(1983) *Political Anatomy of the Body: Medical Knowledge in Britain in the Twentieth Century*. Cambridge University Press.

(1995) 'The rise of surveillance medicine'. *Sociology of Health and Illness* 17(3), 393–404.

Bal, Mieke (2009) *Narratology: Introduction to the Theory of Narrative*. 3rd edn. University of Toronto Press.

Bandura, A., Ross, D., and Ross, S. A. (1961) 'Transmission of aggression through imitation of aggressive models'. *Journal of Abnormal and Social Psychology* 63, 575–82.

Barrett, Michele, and McIntosh, Mary (1991) *The Anti-Social Family*. 2nd edn. London: Verso.

Barry, Andrew (2001) *Political Machines*. London: Continuum.

Bazalgette, Cary, and Buckingham, David (eds.) (1995) *In Front of the Children: Screen Entertainment and Young Audiences*. London: British Film Institute Publishing.

BBC/ICM (2007) BBC Commissioned Survey on Families in the UK: http://news.bbc.co.uk/1/shared/bsp/hi/pdfs/05_11_07familypoll.pdf

Becchi, Egle, and Dominique, Julia (1998a) *Histoire de l'enfance en Occident de l'antiquité au XVII siècle*. Vol. I. Paris: Éditions du Seuil.

(1998b) *Histoire de l'enfance en Occident du XVII siècle à nos jours*. Vol. II. Paris: Éditions du Seuil.

Beck, Ulrich (1997) 'Democratization of the family'. *Childhood* 4(2), 151–68.

Beck, Ulrich, and Beck-Gernsheim, Elisabeth (2001) *Individualization: Institutionalized Individuals and its Social and Political Consequence*. London: Sage.

Beck-Gernsheim, Elisabeth (2002) *Reinventing the Family: In Search of New Lifestyles*. Cambridge: Polity Press.

Becker, Howard (1966) *Outsiders: Studies in the Sociology of Deviance*. New York: Free Press.

Bennett, Tony (1986) 'Popular culture and "the turn to Gramsci"', in Tony Bennett, Colin Mercer and Janet Woollacott (eds.), *Popular Culture and Social Relations*. Milton Keynes: Open University Press.

Berriman, Liam (2012) 'Design and engagement across young people's virtual spaces'. PhD thesis. Goldsmiths College, University of London.

Bey, Margeurite (2003) 'The Mexican child: from work with the family to paid employment'. *Childhood* 10(3), 287–99.

Bhabha, Homi (1988) 'The commitment to theory'. *New Formations 5*, 5–23.

Bhabha, Jacqueline (2009) 'Arendt's children: do today's migrant children have a right to have rights?' *Human Rights Quarterly* 31(2), 410–51.

Bhaskar, Roy (1979) *The Possibility of Naturalism*. Brighton: Harvester Press.

Billig, Michael (1997) 'From codes to utterances: cultural studies, discourse and psychology', in Marjorie Ferguson and Peter Golding (eds.), *Cultural Studies in Question*. London: Sage.

Bloch, Marc (2006) *The Historian's Craft*. Manchester University Press.

Boswell, John (1988) *The Kindness of Strangers: The Abandonment of Children in Western Europe from Late Antiquity to the Renaissance*. New York: Pantheon.

Boulton, Richard (2012) 'Children with HIV: the consolidation of medicine, science and the social into the clinical practice of paediatric HIV'. PhD thesis. Goldsmiths College, University of London.

Bowlby, John (1965) *Childcare and the Growth of Love*. Harmondsworth: Penguin.

Bowles, Samuel, and Gintis, Herbert (1976) *Schooling in Capitalist America: Educational Reform and the Contradictions of Economic Life*. London: Routledge & Kegan Paul.

Braudel, Fernand (1980) *On History*. University of Chicago Press.

Breggin, Peter (2000) Testimony before the Subcommittee on Oversight and Investigations Committee on Education and the Workforce, US House of Representatives, 29 September. www.breggin.com/index.php?option=com_content&task=view&id=80 (accessed 03/05/2011).

Brooks, Rodney (2002) *Flesh and Machines: How Robots will Change Us*. New York: Vintage.

Brosco, Jeffrey P. (2001) 'Weight charts and well-child care: how the paediatrician became the expert in child health'. *Archives of Pediatrics & Adolescent Medicine* 155(12), 1385–9.

Brown, Kenneth D. (1996) *The British Toy Business: A History Since 1700*. London: Hambledon Continuum.

Brown, Sheila (2005) *Understanding Youth and Crime: Listening to Youth?* Milton Keynes: Open University Press.

Brunsden, Charlotte (2000) *The Feminist, the Housewife and the Soap Opera*. Oxford: Clarendon Press.

Buckingham, David (1993) *Children Talking Television: The Making of Television Literacy*. London: Falmer Press.

(2000) *After the Death of Childhood: Growing Up in the Age of Electronic Media*. Cambridge: Polity Press.

(2009) *The Impact of the Commercial World on Children's Well-Being: Report of an Independent Assessment*. London: DCSF and DCMS.

Buckingham, David, and Sefton-Green, Julian (1994) *Cultural Studies Goes to School: Reading and Teaching Popular Media*. London: Taylor & Francis.

Burman, Erica (1996) 'Local, global or globalized? Child development and international child rights legislation'. *Childhood* 3(1), 45–66.

Burt, Cyril (1925) *The Young Delinquent*. University of London Press.

Bynner, John (2001) 'Childhood risks and protective factors in social exclusion'. *Children & Society* 15(5), 285–301.

Callon, Michel (1986) 'Some elements of a sociology of translation: domestication of scallops and the fishermen of St Brieuc Bay', in John Law (ed.), *Power, Action and Belief: A New Sociology of Knowledge?* London: Routledge & Kegan Paul.

Callon, Michel, and Latour, Bruno (1981) 'Unscrewing the big Leviathan: how actors macro-structure reality and how sociologists help them to do so', in K. Knorr-Cetina and A. V. Cicourel (eds.), *Advances in Social Theory and Methodology: Toward an Integration of Micro- and Macro-Sociologies*. London: Routledge & Kegan Paul.

Canagarajah, Sudharshan, and Nielson, Helena Skyt (2001) 'Child labor in Africa: a comparative study'. *Annals of the American Academy of Political and Social Science* 575(1), 71–91.

Canguilhem, Georges (1994) *The Normal and the Pathological*. New York: Zone Books.

(2000) *A Vital Rationalist: Selected Writings from Georges Canguilhem*. New York: Zone Books.

Castañeda, Claudia (2002) *Figurations: Child, Bodies, Worlds*. Durham, NC: Duke University Press.

Christensen, Pia (1998) 'Difference and similarity: how children's competence is constituted in illness and its treatment', in Ian Hutchby and

Jo Moran-Ellis (eds.), *Children and Social Competence: Arenas of Action*. London: Falmer Press.

(2000) 'Childhood and the cultural constitution of vulnerable bodies', in Alan Prout (ed.), *The Body, Childhood and Society*. London: Macmillan.

Clark, Cindy Dell (2003) *In Sickness and in Play: Children Coping with Chronic Illness*. New Brunswick, NJ: Rutgers University Press.

Cook, Daniel Thomas (2003) 'Spatial biographies of children's consumption: market places and spaces of childhood in the 1930s and beyond'. *Journal of Consumer Culture* 3(2), 147–69.

(2004) *The Commodification of Childhood: The Children's Clothing Industry and the Rise of the Child Consumer*. Durham, NC: Duke University Press.

Corsaro, William (2003) *We're Friends Right?: Inside Kids' Culture*. Washington, DC: Joseph Henry Press.

(2005) *The Sociology of Childhood*. 2nd edn. London: Sage.

Cross, Gary (1997) *Kids Stuff: Toys and the Changing World of American Childhood*. Cambridge, MA: Harvard University Press.

Cunningham, Hugh (2005) *Children and Childhood in Western Society Since 1500*. Harlow: Pearson.

Danby, Susan, and Baker, Carolyn (1998a) 'How to be masculine in the block area'. *Childhood* 5(2), 151–75.

(1998b) '"What's the problem?" Restoring social order in the preschool classroom', in Ian Hutchby and Jo Moran-Ellis (eds.), *Children and Social Competence: Arenas of Action*. London: Falmer Press.

Daniel, Paul, and Ivatts, John (1998) *Children and Social Policy*. London: Macmillan.

Darton, F. J. Harvey (1982) *Children's Books of England*. Cambridge University Press.

Darwin, Charles (1877) 'A biographical sketch of an infant'. *Mind* 2(7). 285–94.

Davis, Mike (2004a) 'Planet of slums: urban involution and the informal proletariat'. *New Left Review* 26, 5–34.

(2004b) 'The urbanization of empire: megacities and the laws of chaos'. *Social Text* 22(4), 9–15.

(2006) *Planet of Slums*. London: Verso.

(2008) 'Reading John Hagedorn', in John Hagedorn, *A World of Gangs: Armed Young Men and Gangsta Culture*. Minneapolis: University of Minnesota Press.

De Certeau, Michel (1984) *The Practice of Everyday Life*. Berkeley: University of California Press.

Defert, Daniel (1991) 'Popular life and insurance technology', in Graham
    Burchell, Colin Gordon, and Peter Miller (eds.), *The Foucault Effect:
    Studies in Governmentality*. London: Harvester Wheatsheaf.
Delanda, Manuel (2002) *Intensive Science and Virtual Philosophy*. London:
    Continuum.
Deleuze, Gilles (1992) 'What is a *dispositif*?', in Timothy J. Armstrong (ed.),
    Michel Foucault: Philosopher. London: Harvester Wheatsheaf.
    (1994) *Difference and Repetition*. London: Athlone Press.
Deleuze, Gilles, and Guattari, Felix (1983) 'Rhizome', in *On the Line*.
    New York: Semiotexte.
    (1988) *A Thousand Plateaus: Capitalism and Schizophrenia*. London:
    Athlone Press.
DeMause, Lloyd (1974) *The History of Childhood*. New York: Psycho-
    History Press.
Dimitriadis, Greg (2001) 'Pedagogy and performance in black popular cul-
    ture'. *Cultural Studies ⇔ Critical Methodologies* 1(1), 5–23.
Dingwall, R., Eekelaar, J., and Murray, T. (1983) *The Protection of Children*.
    Oxford: Basil Blackwell.
Diouf, Mamadou (1996) 'Urban youth and Senegalese politics: Dakar 1988–
    1994'. *Public Culture* 8(2), 225–49.
Dixon, Suzanne (ed.) (2001) *Childhood, Class and Kin in the Roman World*.
    London: Routledge.
Donald, James (1992) *Sentimental Education: Schooling, Popular Culture
    and the Regulation of Liberty*. London: Verso.
Donaldson, Margaret (1978) *Children's Minds*. London: Fontana.
Donzelot, Jacques (1979) *The Policing of Families*. London: Hutchinson.
Douglas, Mary (2010) *Purity and Danger: An Analysis of Concepts of
    Pollution and Taboo*. London: Routledge.
Dreyfus, Hubert, and Rabinow, Paul (1983) *Michel Foucault: Beyond Struc-
    turalism and Hermeneutics*. Brighton: Harvester Press.
Drotner, Kirsten (1988) *English Children and their Magazines, 1751–1945*.
    New Haven, CT: Yale University Press.
Dumit, Joseph (2004) *Picturing Personhood: Brain Scans and Biomedical
    Identity*. Princeton University Press.
Durkheim, Emile (1979) *Essays of Morals and Education*. London:
    Routledge.
    (1982) *The Rules of Sociological Method*. New York: Free Press.
Eekelaar, John (1986) 'The emergence of children's rights'. *Oxford Journal
    of Legal Studies* 6(2), 161–82.
Ennew, Judith, and Miljeteig, Per (1996) 'Indications for children's rights:
    progress report on a project'. *International Journal of Children's Rights*
    4(3), 213–36.

Epstein, Debbie, and Johnson, Richard (1998) *Schooling Sexualities*. Buckingham: Open University Press.

Etheridge, Susan (2004) '"Do you know you have worms on your pearls?" Listening to children's voices in the classroom', in Peter B. Pufall and Richard P. Unsworth (eds.), *Rethinking Childhood*. Newark, NJ: Rutgers University Press.

Etzioni, Amitai (1968) *The Active Society*. New York: Free Press.

Fabian, Johannes (1983) *Time and the Other: How Anthropology makes its Object*. New York: Columbia University Press.

Farson, Richard (1974) *Birthrights: A Bill of Rights for Children*. London: Macmillan.

Ferguson, Harry (2004) *Protecting Children in Time: Child Abuse, Child Protection and the Consequences of Modernity*. Basingstoke: Palgrave Macmillan.

Fernando, Jude (2001) 'Children's rights: beyond the impasse'. *Annals of the American Academy of Political and Social Science* 575(1), 8–24 .

Firestone, Shulamith (1979) *The Dialectic of Sex: The Case for Feminist Revolution*. London: Women's Press.

Fischman, Gustavo, and McLaren, Peter (2005) 'Rethinking critical pedagogy and the Gramscian and Freirean legacies: from organic to committed intellectuals or critical pedagogy, commitment, and praxis'. *Cultural Studies ⟺ Critical Methodologies* 5(4), 425–46.

Fiske, John (1989) *Understanding Popular Culture*. Sydney: Allen & Unwin.

Flandrin, Jean-Louis (1964) 'Enfance et société'. *Annales ESC* 19, 322–9.

Fossier, Robert (1997) *La Petite enfance dans l'Europe médiévale et moderne*. Toulouse: Presses Universitaires du Mirail.

Foucault, Michel (1970) *The Order of Thing: An Archaeology of the Human Sciences*. London: Tavistock Press.

(1973) *The Birth of the Clinic*. London: Tavistock Press.

(1977) *Discipline and Punish: The Birth of the Prison*. Harmondsworth: Penguin.

(1979) *History of Sexuality*. Volume i. Harmondsworth: Allen Lane.

(1980a) 'The confession of the flesh', in Colin Gordon (ed.), *Michel Foucault: Power/Knowledge*. Brighton: Harvester Press.

(1980b) 'The politics of health in the eighteenth century', in Colin Gordon (ed.), *Michel Foucault: Power/Knowledge*. Brighton: Harvester Press.

(1991) 'Governmentality', in Graham Burchell, Colin Gordon and Peter Miller (eds.), *The Foucault Effect: Studies in Governmentality*. London: Harvester Wheatsheaf.

(2003) *Abnormal: Lectures at the Collège de France, 1974–1975*. New York: Picador.

(2004) *Society Must Be Defended*. Harmondsworth: Penguin.

Frankenberg, Ronnie (1990) 'Review article: disease, literature and the body in the era of AIDS – a preliminary exploration'. *Sociology of Health and Illness* 12(3), 351–60.

Franklin, Bob (2002) *The New Handbook of Children's Rights: Comparative Policy and Practice*. London: Routledge.

Franklin, Sarah (2000) 'Life itself: global nature and the genetic imaginary', in Sarah Franklin, Celia Lury and Jackie Stacey (eds.), *Global Nature, Global Culture*. London: Sage.

Fraser, Mariam (2001) 'The nature of Prozac'. *History of the Human Sciences* 14(3), 56–84.

Fraser, Nancy (2005) 'Reframing global justice'. *New Left Review* 36, 69–90.

Freeman, Michael (1998) 'The sociology of childhood and children's rights'. *International Journal of Children's Rights* 6, 433–44.

Freud, Sigmund (1991) *The Interpretation of Dreams*. Harmondsworth: Penguin.

Furudi, Frank (2002) *Paranoid Parenting: Why Ignoring Experts May be Best for your Child*. Chicago: Chicago Review Press.

Fyfe, Alex (1993) *Child Labour: A Guide to Product Design*. Geneva: International Labour Organisation.

Garvey, Catherine (1977) *Play*. London: Fontana.

Gessell, Arnold (1943) *Infant and Child in the Culture of Today*. New York: Harper & Bros.

Giddens, Anthony (1979) *Central Problems in Social Theory: Action, Structure and Contradiction in Social Analysis*. London: Macmillan.

(1984) *The Constitution of Society: Outline of the Theory of Structuration*. Cambridge: Polity Press.

(1991) *Modernity and Self-Identity: Self and Society in the Late Modern Age*. Cambridge: Polity Press.

(1992) *The Transformation of Intimacy: Sexuality, Love and Intimacy in Modern Societies*. Cambridge: Polity Press.

(1998) *The Third Way: The Renewal of Social Democracy*. Cambridge: Polity Press.

Gill, Rosalind, and Pratt, Andy (2008) 'Precarity and cultural work in the social factory? Immaterial labour, precariousness and cultural work'. *Theory, Culture and Society* 25(7–8), 1–30.

Gillespie, Marie (1995) *Television Ethnicity and Cultural Change*. London: Routledge.

Giroux, Henry (2001) 'Cultural studies as performative politics'. *Cultural Studies ⟺ Critical Methodologies* 1(1), 5–23.

Gittins, Diana (1993) *The Family in Question: Changing Households and Familiar Ideologies*. London: Macmillan.

(1998) *The Child in Question*. London: Methuen.

Goodman, Irene (1983) 'Television's role in family interaction: a family systems perspective'. *Journal of Family Issues* 4(2), 405–24.

Goodwin, Marjorie Harness (2002) 'Exclusion in girls' peer groups: ethnographic analysis of language practices on the playground'. *Human Development* 45(6), 392–415.

Gordon, Linda (1989) *Heroes of their own Lives: The Politics and History of Family Violence*. Champaign: University of Illinois Press.

Gramsci, Antonio (1971) *Selections from the Prison Notebooks*. London: Lawrence & Wishart.

Grint, Keith, and Woolgar, Steve (1997) *The Machine at Work: Technology, Work and Organization*. Cambridge: Polity Press.

Hacking, Ian (1991) 'How should we do the history of statistics?', in Graham Burchell, Colin Gordon and Peter Miller (eds.), *The Foucault Effect: Studies in Governmentality*. London: Harvester Wheatsheaf.

Hagedorn, John (2008) *A World of Gangs: Armed Young Men and Gangsta Culture*. Minneapolis: University of Minnesota Press.

Hall, Stuart (1980) 'Cultural studies: two paradigms'. *Media, Culture and Society* 2(1), 57–72.

(1981) 'Notes on deconstructing the popular', in Ralph Samuel (ed.), *People's History and Socialist Theory*. London: Routledge & Kegan Paul.

Hall, Stuart, and Jacques, Martin (1989) *New Times: The Changing Face of Politics in the 1990s*. London: Verso.

Hall, Stuart, and Jefferson, Tony (eds.) (1976) *Resistance Through Rituals: Youth Subcultures in Post-War Britain*. London: HarperCollins.

Hall, Stuart, Critcher, Chas, Jefferson, Tony, Clarke, John, and Roberts, Brian (1978) *Policing the Crisis: Mugging, the State, and Law and Order*. London: Macmillan.

Halliday, Terence, and Osinsky, Pavel (2006) 'Globalization of law'. *Annual Review of Sociology* 32, 447–70.

Hallsworth, Simon, and Silverstone, Daniel (2009) '"That's life innit": a British perspective on guns, crime and social order'. *Criminology and Criminal Justice* 9(3), 359–77.

Halsey, Karen, and White, Richard (2008) *Young People, Crime and Public Perceptions: A Review of the Literature*. Local Government Association Research Report F/SR 264. Slough: National Foundation for Educational Research.

Hanawalt, Barbara (1993) *Growing Up in Medieval London: The Experience of Childhood in History*. Oxford University Press.

Haralovich, Mary Beth (1988) 'Suburban family sit-coms and consumer product design: addressing the social subjectivity of homemakers in the 50s', in Philip Drummond (ed.), *Television and its Audience*. London: British Film Institute.

Haraway, Donna (1991) 'A manifesto for cyborgs', in Donna Haraway, *Simians, Cyborgs and Women*. London: Free Association Press.

(2003) *The Companion Species Manifesto: People, Dogs and Significant Otherness*. Chicago, IL: Prickly Paradigm Press.

Hardt, Michael, and Negri, Antonio (2000) *Empire*. Cambridge, MA: Harvard University Press.

(2004) *Multitude: War and Democracy in the Age of Empire*. Harmonds-worth: Penguin.

Hartley, John (1987) 'Television audiences, paedocracy and pleasure'. *Textual Practice* 1(2), 121–38.

Healy, David (2006a) 'Framing ADHD children: a critical examination of the history, discourse, and everyday experience of attention deficit/hyperactivity disorder'. *Social History of Medicine* 19(1), 177–8.

(2006b) 'The latest mania: selling bipolar disorder'. *PLoS Medicine* 3(4), e185.

Hebdige, Dick (1979) *Subculture: The Meaning of Style*. London: Methuen.

(1988) *Hiding in the Light*. London: Routledge.

Hendrick, Harry (1990) 'Constructions and reconstructions of British childhood: an interpretative survey, 1800 to present', in Allison James and Alan Prout (eds.), *Constructing and Reconstructing Childhood: Contemporary Issues in the Sociological Study of Childhood*. London: Falmer Press.

(1997) *Children, Childhood and English Society, 1880–1990*. Cambridge University Press.

Henriques, J., Hollway, W., Urwin, C., Venn, C., and Walkerdine, V. (1998) *Changing the Subject: Psychology, Social Regulation and Subjectivity*. 2nd edn. London: Routledge.

Herrnstein, Richard J., and Murray, Charles (1994) *The Bell Curve: Intelligence and Class Structure in American Life*. New York: Simon & Schuster.

Heywood, Colin (2001) *A History of Childhood: Children and Childhood in the West from Medieval to Modern Times*. Cambridge: Polity Press.

Hill, Jennifer Ann (2011) 'Endangered childhoods: how consumerism is impacting child and youth identity'. *Media, Culture and Society* 3(3), 347–62.

Hill, M. D. (1855) 'Practical suggestions to the founders of reformatory schools', in J. C. Symons (ed.), *On the Reformation of Young Offenders*. London: Routledge.

Holland, Patricia (1996) '"I've just seen a hole in the reality barrier!" Children, childishness and the media in ruins in the twentieth century', in Jane Pilcher and Stephen Wagg (eds.), *Thatcher's Children? Politics, Childhood and Society in the 1980s and 1990s.* London: Taylor & Francis.

Hollway, W., and Jefferson, T. (2005a) 'But why did Vince get sick? A reply to Spears and Wetherell'. *British Journal of Social Psychology* 44(2), 175–80. A reply to two commentaries on (2005b).

(2005b) 'Panic and perjury: a psycho-social exploration of agency'. *British Journal of Social Psychology* 44(2), 147–63.

Holt, John (1975) *Escape from Childhood: The Needs and Rights of Children.* Harmondsworth: Penguin.

Honwana, Alcinda (2005) 'Innocent and guilty: child-soldiers as interstitial and tactical agents', in Alcinda Honwana and Filip de Boeck (eds.), *Makers and Breakers: Children and Youth in Postcolonial Africa.* Oxford: James Currey.

Honwana, Alcinda, and De Boeck, Filip (2005) 'Introduction: Children and Youth in Africa', in Alcinda Honwana and Filip de Boeck (eds.), *Makers and Breakers: Children and Youth in Postcolonial Africa.* Oxford: James Currey.

Huizinga, Johan (1949) *Homo Ludens: A Study of the Play-Element in Culture.* London: Routledge & Kegan Paul.

Hutchby, Ian, and Moran-Ellis, Jo (eds.) (1998) *Children and Social Competence: Arenas of Action.* London: Falmer Press.

Illich, Ivan (1971) *Deschooling Society.* Harmondsworth: Penguin.

Ismail, Olawale (2009) 'The dialectics of junctions and bases: youth, livelihoods and the crises of order in downtown Lagos'. *Security Dialogue* 40(5), 463–87.

James, Allison (1993) *Childhood Identities: Self and Social Relationships in the Experience of the Child.* Edinburgh University Press.

James, Allison, and James, Adrian (1999) 'Pump up the volume: listening to children in separation and divorce'. *Childhood* 6(2), 189–206.

(2004) *Constructing Childhood: Theory, Policy and Social Practice.* Basingstoke: Palgrave Macmillan.

James, Allison, and Jenks, Christopher (1996) 'Public perceptions of childhood criminality'. *British Journal of Sociology* 47(2), 315–31.

James, Allison, and Prout, Alan (1990) *Constructing and Reconstructing Childhood: Contemporary Issues in the Sociological Study of Childhood.* London: Falmer Press.

James, Allison, Jenks, Christopher, and Prout, Alan (1998) *Theorizing Childhood.* Cambridge: Polity Press.

Jans, Marc (2004) 'Children as citizens: towards a contemporary notion of child participation'. *Childhood* 11(1), 24–44.

Jencks, Christopher (1993) *Rethinking Social Policy: Race, Poverty, and the Underclass.* New York: HarperCollins.

(1996) *Childhood*. London: Routledge.

Jessop, Bob (1995) 'The regulation approach, governance, and post-Fordism: alternative perspectives on economic and political change?'. *Economy and Society* 24(3), 307–33.

Jones, K., and Williamson, J. (1979) 'The birth of the schoolroom'. *Ideology and Consciousness* 6, 59–110.

Jordanova, Ludmilla (1989) 'Children in history: concepts of nature and society', in Geoffrey Scarre (ed.), *Children, Parents and Politics*. Cambridge University Press.

(1999) 'Naturalising the family: literature and the bio-medical sciences in the late eighteenth century', in L. Jordanova (ed.), *Nature Displayed: Gender, Science and Medicine 1760–1820*. Harlow: Longman.

Katz, Cindi (2004) *Growing up Global: Economic Restructuring and Children's Everyday Lives*. Minneapolis: University of Minnesota Press.

Keith, Michael (2005) *After the Cosmopolitan: Multicultural Cities and the Future of Racism*. London: Routledge.

Kellner, Douglas (2001) 'Critical pedagogy, cultural studies and radical democracy at the turn of the millennium: reflections on the work of Henry Giroux'. *Cultural Studies* ⇔ *Critical Methodologies* 1(2), 220–39.

Kember, Sarah (2003) *Cyberfeminism and Artificial Life*. London: Routledge.

Kinder, Marsha (1991) *Playing with Power in Movies, Television and Video Games: From Muppet Babies to Teenage Mutant Ninja Turtles*. Berkeley: University of California Press.

(1995) 'Home alone in the 90s: generational war and transgenerational address in American movies, television and presidential politics', in Cary Bazalgette and David Buckingham (eds.), *In Front of the Children: Screen Entertainment and Young Audiences*. London: British Film Institute.

(ed.) (1999) *Kids Media Culture*. Durham, NC: Duke University Press.

Kline, Stephen (1993) *Out of the Garden: Toys, TV and Children's Culture in the Age of Marketing*. London: Verso.

Knorr-Cetina, Karin (2001) 'Postsocial relations: theorizing sociality in a postsocial environment', in George Ritzer and Barry Smart (eds.), *Handbook of Social Theory*. London: Sage.

Knorr-Cetina, Karin, and Bruegger, Urs (2002) 'Traders' engagement with markets: a postsocial relationship'. *Theory, Culture & Society* 19(5/6), 161–85.

Komulainen, Sirkka (2007) 'The ambiguity of the child's voice in social research'. *Childhood* 14(1), 11–28.

Laclau, Ernesto (1977) *Politics and Ideology in Marxist Theory*. London: Verso.

Laing, R. D., and Esterson, A. (1970) *Sanity, Madness and the Family: An Investigation into the 'Forgotten Illness' – Schizophrenia*. Harmondsworth: Penguin.

Larson, Ann-Claire (1999) 'Governing families with young children through discipline'. *Journal of Sociology* 35(3), 279–96.

Lasch, Christopher (1979) *Haven in a Heartless World: The Family Besieged*. New York: Basic Books.

(1984) *The Minimal Self: Psychic Survival in Troubled Times*. London: Picador.

Latour, Bruno (2000) 'When things strike back: a possible contribution of science studies'. *British Journal of Sociology* 51(1), 107–23.

Latour, Bruno, and Woolgar, Steve (1979) *Laboratory Life: The Social Construction of Scientific Facts*. London: Sage.

Law, John (1999) 'After ANT: complexity, naming and topology', in John Law and John Hassard (eds.), *Actor Network Theory and After*. Oxford: Blackwell.

Law, John, and Benschop, Ruth (1997) 'Resisting pictures: representation, distribution and ontological politics', in Kevin Hetherington and Rolland Munro (eds.), *Ideas of Difference: Social Spaces and the Labour of Division*. Oxford: Blackwell.

Lee, Nick (2001) *Childhood and Society: Growing Up in an Age of Uncertainty*. Milton Keynes: Open University Press.

(2005) *Childhood and Human Value: Development, Separation and Separability*. Milton Keynes: Open University Press.

Lefebvre, Henri (1991) *The Production of Space*. Oxford: Blackwell.

Livingstone, Sonia (2002) *Young People and New Media: Childhood and the Changing Media Environment*. London: Sage.

Locke, John (1996) *Some Thoughts Concerning Education and Of the Conduct of the Understanding*, ed. Ruth W. Grant and Nathan Tarcov. Indianapolis, IND: Hackett.

Mac an Ghaill, Máirtín, (1994) *Making of Men: Masculinities, Sexualities and Schooling*. Milton Keynes: Open University Press.

McRobbie, Angela (1976) 'Girls and subcultures', in Stuart Hall and Tony Jefferson (eds.), *Resistance through Rituals: Youth Subcultures in Post-War Britain*. London: HarperCollins.

(1991) *Feminism and Youth Culture*. London: Macmillan.

Malson, Lucien, and Itard, Jean (1972) *Wolf Children and the Problem of Human Nature*. New York: Monthly Review Press.

Marvick, Elizabeth Wirth (1993) 'Louis XIII and his doctor: on the shifting fortunes of Jean Héroard's Journal'. *French Historical Studies* 18(1), 279–300.

Mayall, Berry (2002) *Towards a Sociology for Childhood: Thinking from Children's Lives*. Milton Keynes: Open University Press.

Medick, Hans (1976) 'The proto-industrial family economy: the structural function of household and family during the transition from peasant society to industrial capitalism'. *Social History* 1(3), 291–315.

Meyrowitz, Joshua (1984) 'The adultlike child and the childlike adult: socialization in an electronic age'. *Daedalus* 113(3), 19–48.

(1987) *No Sense of Place: The Impact of Electronic Media on Social Behaviour*. Oxford University Press.

Miller, Daniel (2011) *Tales from Facebook*. Cambridge: Polity Press.

Miller, Daniel, and Slater, Don (2000) *The Internet: An Ethnographic Approach*. Oxford: Berg.

Miller, Toby, and Leger, Marie Claire (2003) 'A very childish moral panic: Ritalin'. *Journal of Medical Humanities* 24(1/2), 9–33.

Minson, Jeffrey (1985) *Genealogies of Morals: Nietzsche, Foucault, Donzelot and the Eccentricity of Ethics*. London: Methuen.

Mitchell, W. J. T. (1986) *Iconology: Image, Text, Ideology*. Chicago University Press.

Mol, Annamarie (2002) *The Body Multiple: Ontology in Medical Practice*. Durham, NC: Duke University Press.

Morgan, David (1985) *Family, Politics and Social Theory*. London: Routledge.

(1996) *Family Connections: An Introduction to Family Studies*. Cambridge: Polity Press.

Morley, David (1986) *Family Television*. London: Comedia.

(2000) *Home Territories*. London: Routledge.

Morley, David, and Silverstone, Roger (1991) 'Domestic communication'. *Media, Culture and Society* 12(1), 31–55.

Morrow, Virginia (1994) 'Responsible children? Aspects of children's work and employment outside school in contemporary UK', in Berry Mayall (ed.), *Children's Childhoods: Observed and Experienced*. London: Routledge.

Moores, Shaun (1993) 'Television, geography and mobile privatization'. *European Journal of Communication* 8(3), 365–79.

Muncie, John (2004) *Youth and Crime*. London: Sage.

Murray, Charles (1990) *The Emerging Underclass*. London: Institute of Economic Affairs.

Myers, William E. (2001) 'The right rights? Child labor in a globalizing world'. *Annals of the American Academy of Political and Social Science* 575(1), 56–70.

Närvänen, Anna-Liisa, and Näsman, Elisabet (2004) 'Childhood as generation of life phase?'. *Young: Nordic Journal of Youth Research* 12(1), 71–91.

Nash, Kate (2009) *The Cultural Politics of Human Rights: Comparing the US and the UK.* Cambridge University Press.

Neale, Bren (2002) 'Dialogues with children: children, divorce and citizenship'. *Childhood* 9(4), 455–75.

Newton, Hannah (2010) 'Children's physic: medical perceptions and treatment of sick children in early modern England, c. 1580–1720'. *Social History of Medicine* 23(3), 456–74.

Nightingale, Carl (2003) 'A tale of three global ghettoes: how Arnold Hirsch helps us internationalize US urban history'. *Journal of Urban History* 29(3), 257–71.

Oakley, Ann (1994) 'Women and children first and last: parallels and differences between children's and women's studies', in Berry Mayall (ed.), *Children's Childhoods: Observed and Experienced.* London: Routledge.

O'Donnell, Mike, and Sharpe, Sue (2000) *Uncertain Masculinities: Youth, Ethnicity and Class in Contemporary Britain.* London: Routledge.

Office for National Statistics (2009) Marriages – Numbers and Rates (Historic). www.statistics.gov.uk/statbase/Product.asp?vlnk=14275

Oldman, David (1994) 'Adult–child relations as class relations', in Jens Qvortrup, Marjatta Bardy, Giovanni Sgrita and Helmut Wintersberger (eds.), *Childhood Matters: Social Theory, Practice and Politics.* London: Avebury Press.

Ong, Walter J. (1982) *Orality and Literacy.* London: Methuen.

Orme, Nicholas (2001) *Medieval Children.* New Haven, CT: Yale University Press.

Oswell, David (1994) 'This is not a moral panic: children, governmentality and television broadcasting', Citizenship and Cultural Frontiers Conference, Staffordshire University.

(1998) 'Early children's broadcasting in Britain, 1922–1964: programming for a liberal democracy'. *Historical Journal of Film, Radio and Television* 18(3), 375–93.

(2002) *Television, Childhood and the Home: A History of the Making of the Child Television Audience in Britain.* Oxford University Press.

(2006) *Culture and Society: An Introduction to Cultural Studies.* London: Sage.

Parsons, Talcott (1951) *The Social System.* Glencoe, IL: Free Press.

Pasquino, Pasquale (1991) 'Criminology: the birth of a special knowledge', in Graham Burchell, Colin Gordon and Peter Miller (eds.), *The Foucault Effect: Studies in Governmentality.* London: Harvester Wheatsheaf.

Pearson, Geoffrey (1983) *Hooligan: A History of Respectable Fears.* London: Macmillan.

Phillips, Christine B. (2006) 'Medicine goes to school: teachers as sickness brokers for ADHD'. *PLoS Medicine* 3(4), e182.

Pleck, Elizabeth (2004) *Domestic Tyranny: The Making of American Social Policy against Family Violence from Colonial Times to the Present.* Champaign: University of Illinois Press.

Pollock, Linda (1983) *Forgotten Children: Parent–Child Relations from 1500 to 1900.* Cambridge University Press.

Poster, Mark (1978) *Critical Theory of the Family.* London: Pluto Press.

Postman, Neil (1994) *The Disappearance of Childhood.* New York: Vintage.

Procacci, Giovanna (1991) 'Social economy and the government of poverty', in Graham Burchell, Colin Gordon and Peter Miller (eds.), *The Foucault Effect: Studies in Governmentality.* London: Harvester Wheatsheaf.

Prout, Alan (2005) *The Future of Childhood.* London: Routledge and Falmer Press.

(ed.) (2000) *The Body, Childhood and Society.* London: Macmillan.

Pryor, Jan, and Emery, Robert (2004) 'Children of divorce', in Peter Pufall and Richard Unsworth (eds.), *Rethinking Childhood.* New Brunswick, NJ: Rutgers University Press.

Qvortrup, Jens (2001) 'School-work, paid work and the changing obligation of childhood', in P. Mizen, C. Pole and A. Bolton (eds.), *Hidden Hands: International Perspectives on Children's Work and Labour.* London: Routledge and Falmer Press.

Qvortrup, Jens, Bardy, Marjatta, Sgrita, Giovanni, and Wintersberger, Helmut (1994) *Childhood Matters: Social Theory, Practice and Politics.* London: Avebury Press.

Rabinow, Paul (2003) *Anthropos Today: Reflections on Modern Equipment.* Princeton University Press.

Rafalovich, Adam (2004) *Framing ADHD Children: A Critical Examination of the History, Discourse and Experience of Attention Deficit/Hyperactivity Disorder.* Lanham, MD: Lexington Books.

Rancière, Jacques (2004) 'Who is the subject of the rights of man?'. *South Atlantic Quarterly* 103(2/3), 297–310.

(2010) *Dissensus: On Politics and Aesthetics.* London: Continuum.

Reynaert, Didier, Bouverne-de-Bie, Maria, and Vandevelde, Stijn (2009) 'A review of children's rights literature since the adoption of the United Nations Convention on the Rights of the Child'. *Childhood* 16(4), 518–34.

Riché, Pierre, and Alexandre-Bidon, Danièle (1994) *L'Enfance au moyen âge.* Paris: Éditions du Seuil.

Rifkin, Jeremy (1999) *The Biotech Century*. London: Phoenix.

Roche, Jeremy (2002) 'The Children's Act and children's rights: a critical reassessment', in Bob Franklin (ed.), *The New Handbook of Children's Rights: Comparative Policy and Practice*. London: Routledge.

Rose, Jacqueline (1984) *The Case of Peter Pan, or The Impossibility of Children's Fiction*. London: Methuen.

Rose, Nikolas (1985) *The Psychological Complex: Psychology, Politics and Society in England 1869–1939*. London: Routledge & Kegan Paul.

(1989) *Governing the Soul: The Shaping of the Private Self*. London: Routledge.

(2001) 'The politics of life itself'. *Theory, Culture & Society* 18(6), 1–30.

(2005) 'Will biomedicine transform society? The political, economic, social and personal impact of medical advances in the twenty-first century'. Clifford Barclay Lecture. London School of Economics.

(2007) *The Politics of Life Itself: Biomedicine, Power, and Subjectivity in the Twenty-First Century*. Princeton University Press.

Rosengarten, Marsha (2009) *HIV Interventions: Biomedicine and the Traffic Between Information and Flesh*. University of Washington Press.

Sanders, Robert E., and Freeman, Kurt E. (1998) 'Children's ne-rhetorical participation in peer interactions', in Ian Hutchby and Jo Moran-Ellis (eds.), *Children and Social Competence: Arenas of Action*. London: Falmer Press.

Sassen, Saskia (2006) *Territory, Authority. Rights: From Medieval to Global Assemblages*. Princeton University Press.

Savage, Mike (2009) 'Contemporary sociology and the challenge of descriptive assemblage'. *European Journal of Social Theory* 12(1), 155–74.

Savolainen, Jukka, Hurtig, Tuula M., Ebeling, Hanna E., Moilanen, Irma K., Hughes, Lorine A., and Taanila, Anja M. (2010) 'Attention deficit hyperactivity disorder (ADHD) and criminal behaviour: the role of adolescent marginalization'. *European Journal of Criminology* 7(6), 442–59.

Schachar, R., Tannock, R., and Cunningham, C. (1996) 'Treatment', in S. Sandberg (ed.), *Hyperactivity Disorders of Childhood*. Cambridge University Press.

Schaffner, Laurie (2006) *Girls in Trouble with the Law*. New Brunswick, NJ: Rutgers University Press.

Shahar, Shulamith (1990) *Childhood in the Middle Ages*. London: Routledge.

Shorter, Edward (1975) *The Making of the Modern Family*. New York: Basic Books.

Silverman, David, Baker, Carolyn, and Keogh, Jayne (1998) 'The case of the silent child: advice-giving and advice-reception in parent–teacher interviews', in Ian Hutchby and Jo Moran-Ellis (eds.), *Children and Social Competence: Arenas of Action*. London: Falmer Press.

Silverstone, Roger, and Hirsch, Eric (eds.) (1994) *Consuming Technologies: Media and Information in Domestic Spaces*. London: Routledge.

Simon, Brian (1953) *Intelligence Testing and the Comprehensive School*. London: Lawrence & Wishart.

Simone, Abdoumaliq (2004) 'People as infrastructure: intersecting fragments in Johannesburg'. *Public Culture* 16(3), 407–29.

Skeggs, Beverley, and Wood, Helen (2009) 'The transformation of intimacy: classed identities in the moral economy of reality television', in Margaret Wetherell (ed.), *Identity in the 21st Century: New Trends in Changing Times*. Basingstoke: Palgrave/Macmillan.

Smart, Carol, and Neale, Bren (1999) *Family Fragments*. Cambridge: Polity Press.

Smart, Carol, Neale, Bren, and Wade, Amanda (2001) *The Changing Experience of Childhood: Families and Divorce*. Cambridge: Polity Press.

Smith, Dorothy (1981) 'On sociological description: a method from Marx'. *Human Studies* 4(4), 313–37.

Somerville, John (1982) *The Rise and Fall of Childhood*. London: Sage.

Spigel, Lynn (1992) *Make Room for TV: Television and the Family Ideal in Postwar America*. University of Chicago Press.

Stafford, Anne (1981). 'Learning not to labour'. *Capital and Class* 15, 55–77.

Star, Susan Leigh, and Griesemer, James R. (1989) 'Institutional ecology: "translations" and boundary objects: amateurs and professionals in Berkeley's Museum of Vertebrate Zoology, 1907–39'. *Social Studies of Science* 19(3), 387–420.

Steedman, Carolyn (1994) *Strange Dislocations: Childhood and the Idea of Human Interiority, 1780–1930*. Cambridge, MA: Harvard University Press.

Stone, Lawrence (1977) *The Family, Sex, and Marriage in England 1500–1800*. London: Weidenfeld & Nicolson.

Stortz, Martha Ellen (2001) '"Where or when was your servant innocent?": Augustine on childhood', in Marcia J. Bunge (ed.), *The Child in Christian Thought*. Grand Rapids, MI: Eerdmans.

Tagg, John (1988) *The Burden of Representation: Essays on Photographies and Histories*. London: Methuen.

Thacker, Deborah Cogan, and Webb, Jean (2002) *Introducing Children's Literature: From Romanticism to Postmodernism*. London: Routledge.

Thacker, Eugene (2005) *The Global Genome: Biotechnology, Politics, and Culture*. Cambridge, MA: MIT Press.

Thrift, Nigel (2005) *Knowing Capitalism*. London: Sage.

Traina, Cristina L. H. (2001) 'A person in the making: Thomas Aquinas on children and childhood', in Marcia J. Bunge (ed.), *The Child in Christian Thought*. Grand Rapids, MI: Eerdmans.

Transit, Roxanna (2003) 'The ordering of attention: the discourse of developmental theory and ADD'. Paper presented at the conference entitled Vital Politics: Health, Medicine and Bioeconomics in the Twenty-First Century, London: London School of Economics.

Tucker, S. M. (1999) 'Attention deficit hyperactivity disorder'. *Journal of the Royal Society of Medicine* 19(5), 217–19.

Turkle, Sherry (1996) *Life on Screen: Identity in the Age of the Internet*. London: Weidenfeld & Nicolson.

(2011) *Alone Together*. New York: Basic Books.

Tyler, Imogen (2006) 'Chav scum: the filthy politics of social class in contemporary Britain'. *M/C Journal* 9(5). http://journal.media-culture.org.au/0610/09-tyler.php (accessed 01/02/2011).

(2008) '"Chav mum, chav scum": class disgust in contemporary Britain'. *Feminist Media Studies* 8(1), 17–34.

UNICEF (1997) *The State of the World's Children*. Oxford University Press.

Urwin, Cathy (1984) 'Power relations and the emergence of language', in J. Henriques with W. Hollway, C. Urwin, C. Venn and V. Walkerdine (eds.), *Changing the Subject: Psychology, Social Regulation and Subjectivity*. London: Methuen.

US Census Bureau (2008) *America's Families and Living Arrangements*. www.census.gov/population/www/socdemo/hh-fam/cps2008.html

Valentine, Gill (1996) 'Angels and devils: moral landscapes of childhood'. *Environment and Planning B: Society and Space* 14, 581–99.

Venkatesh, Sudhir (1998) 'Gender and outlaw capitalism: a historical account of the Black Sisters United "girl gang"'. *Signs* 23(3), 683–709.

(2009) *Gang Leader for a Day*. Harmondsworth: Penguin.

Voloshinov, Valerian (1973) *Marxism and the Philosophy of Language*. New York: Seminar Press.

Wacquant, Loïc (2002) 'Scrutinizing the street: poverty, morality and the pitfalls of urban ethnography'. *American Journal of Sociology* 107(6), 1468–532.

(2008a) 'Ordering insecurity: social polarization and the punitive upsurge'. *Radical Philosophy Review* 11(1), 9–27.

(2008b) *Urban Outcasts: A Comparative Sociology of Advanced Marginality*. Cambridge: Polity Press.

Walkerdine, Valerie (1984) 'Developmental psychology and the child-centred pedagogy: the insertion of Piaget into early education', in J. Henriques with W. Hollway, C. Urwin, C. Venn and V. Walkerdine (eds.), *Changing the Subject: Psychology, Social Regulation and Sub-jectivity*. London, Methuen.

(1987) 'Femininity as performance'. *Oxford Review of Education* 15(3), 267–79.

(1997) *Daddy's Girl: Young Girls and Popular Culture*. London: Methuen.

Walkerdine, Valerie, and Lucey, Helen (1989) *Democracy in the Kitchen: Regulating Mothers and Socialising Daughters*. London: Virago.

Wells, Karen (2009) *Childhood in a Global Perspective*. Cambridge: Polity Press.

Winnicott, D. W. (1986) *Playing and Reality*. Harmondsworth: Penguin.

Willis, Paul (1977) *Learning to Labour: How Working-Class Kids Get Working-Class Jobs*. London: Gower Press.

Wilson, Adrian (1980) 'The infancy of the history of childhood: an appraisal of Philippe Ariès'. *History and Theory* 19(2), 132–53.

Wilson, Elizabeth (1987) *Women and the Welfare State*. London: Tavistock Press.

Wilson, James Q., and Herrnstein, Richard J. (1985) *Crime and Human Nature*. New York: Simon & Schuster.

Wilson, William Julius (1987) *The Truly Disadvantaged: The Inner City, the Underclass, and Public Policy*. Chicago University Press.

(1996) *When Work Disappears: The World of the New Urban Poor*. New York: Vintage.

Wood, Rebecca (2010) 'UK: the reality behind the "knife crime" debate'. *Race & Class* 52(2), 97–103.

World Health Organisation (WHO) (2001) *The World Health Report 2001. Mental Health: New Understanding, New Hope*. Geneva: WHO.

(2002) *Genomics and World Health*. Geneva: WHO.

(2005) *Mental Health: Facing the Challenges, Building the Solutions. Report from the WHO European Ministerial Conference*. Copenhagen: WHO.

Young, Alison (1996) *Imagining Crime*. London: Sage.

Young, Jock (2007) *The Vertigo of Late Modernity*. London: Sage.

Zelizer, Viviana (1994) *Pricing the Priceless Child: The Changing Social Value of Children*. Princeton University Press.

(2002) 'Kids and commerce'. *Childhood* 9(4), 375–96.

Index

Printed in Poland
by Amazon Fulfillment
Poland Sp. z o.o., Wrocław